AFRICAN TRADITIONS IN THE STUDY OF RELIGION IN AFRICA

The historiography of African religions and religions in Africa presents a remarkable shift from the study of 'Africa as Object' to 'Africa as Subject', thus translating the subject from obscurity into the global community of the academic study of religion. This book presents a unique multidisciplinary exploration of African traditions in the study of religion in Africa and the new African diaspora. The book is structured under three main sections – Emerging Trends in the Teaching of African Religions; Indigenous Thought and Spirituality; and Christianity, Islam and Hinduism. Contributors drawn from diverse African and global contexts situate current scholarly traditions of the study of African religions within the purview of academic encounter and exchanges with non-African scholars and non-African contexts. African scholars enrich the study of religions from their respective academic and methodological orientations. Jacob Kehinde Olupona stands out as a pioneer in the socio-scientific interpretation of African indigenous religion and religions in Africa. This book is to his honour and marks his immense contribution to an emerging field of study and research.

VITALITY OF INDIGENOUS RELIGIONS

Series Editors
Graham Harvey, Open University, UK,
Afeosemime Adogame, The University of Edinburgh, UK
Ines Talamantez University of California, USA

Ashgate's *Vitality of Indigenous Religions* series offers an exciting new cluster of research monographs, drawing together volumes from leading international scholars across a wide range of disciplinary perspectives. Indigenous religions are vital and empowering for many thousands of indigenous peoples globally, and dialogue with, and consideration of, these diverse religious life-ways promises to challenge and refine the methodologies of a number of academic disciplines, whilst greatly enhancing understandings of the world.

This series explores the development of contemporary indigenous religions from traditional, ancestral precursors, but the characteristic contribution of the series is its focus on their living and current manifestations. Devoted to the contemporary expression, experience and understanding of particular indigenous peoples and their religions, books address key issues which include: the sacredness of land, exile from lands, diasporic survival and diversification, the indigenization of Christianity and other missionary religions, sacred language, and re-vitalization movements. Proving of particular value to academics, graduates, postgraduates and higher level undergraduate readers worldwide, this series holds obvious attraction to scholars of Native American studies, Maori studies, African studies and offers invaluable contributions to religious studies, sociology, anthropology, geography and other related subject areas.

OTHER TITLES IN THE SERIES

Mobility, Markets and Indigenous Socialities
Contemporary Migration in the Peruvian Andes
Cecilie Vindal Ødegaard
ISBN 978 1 4094 0454 5

Blackfoot Religion and the Consequences of Cultural Commoditization
Kenneth Hayes Lokensgard
ISBN 978 0 7546 6826 8

Indigenous Symbols and Practices in the Catholic Church
Visual Culture, Missionization and Appropriation
Edited by Kathleen J. Martin
ISBN 978 0 7546 6631 8

African Traditions in the Study of Religion in Africa

Emerging trends, Indigenous Spirituality
and the Interface with other World Religions

Essays in Honour of Jacob Kehinde Olupona

Edited by
AFE ADOGAME
University of Edinburgh, UK

EZRA CHITANDO
University of Zimbabwe, Harare, Zimbabwe

BOLAJI BATEYE
Obafemi Awolowo University, Ile-Ife, Nigeria

ASHGATE

Published by
Ashgate Publishing Limited
Wey Court East
Union Road
Farnham
Surrey, GU9 7PT
England

Ashgate Publishing Company
Suite 420
101 Cherry Street
Burlington
VT 05401–4405
USA

www.ashgate.com

British Library Cataloguing in Publication Data
African traditions in the study of religion in Africa : emerging trends, indigenous
    spirituality and the interface with other world religions. – (Vitality of indigenous
    religions)
    1. Africa – Religion – Study and teaching – Africa. 2. Religious education – Africa.
    I. Series II. Adogame, Afeosemime U. (Afeosemime Unuose), 1964–
    III. Chitando, Ezra. IV. Bateye, Bolaji.
    200.7'106–dc22

Library of Congress Cataloging-in-Publication Data
African traditions in the study of religion in Africa : emerging trends, indigenous
    spirituality and the interface with other world religions / [edited by] Afe Adogame,
    Ezra Chitando and Bolaji Bateye.
        p. cm. – (Vitality of indigenous religions)
    Includes index.
    ISBN 978–1–4094–1970–9 (hardcover : alk. paper) – ISBN 978–1–4094–1971–6
    (ebook) 1. Africa – Religion – Study and teaching – Africa. 2. Religion and
    social problems – Africa. 3. Christianity and other religions – African.
    I. Adogame, Afeosemime U. (Afeosemime Unuose), 1964– II. Chitando, Ezra.
    III. Bateye, Bolaji. IV. Series: Vitality of indigenous religions.
    BL2400.A453 2010
    200.9607–dc23
                                                                    2011025374

ISBN 9781409419709 (hbk)
ISBN 9781409419716 (ebk)

MIX
Paper from
responsible sources
FSC
www.fsc.org   FSC® C018575

Printed and bound in Great Britain by the
MPG Books Group, UK.

Contents

List of Figures

List of Contributors

Afe Adogame teaches Religious Studies and World Christianity at the University of Edinburgh. He is the General Secretary of the African Association for the Study of Religions (AASR). He has published extensively in international journals and books. His most recent book publications are the co-edited (with J. Spickard) *Religion Crossing Boundaries: Transnational Religious and Social Dynamics in Africa and the New African Diaspora* (2010) and the edited *Who is Afraid of the Holy Ghost? Pentecostalism and Globalization in Africa and Beyond* (2011).

Rose Mary Amenga-Etego (Ph.D.) is a lecturer in Indigenous African Religions and Gender Issues in Religion and Culture at the Department for the Study of Religions, University of Ghana. She is currently the Anglophone West African coordinator of the Circle of Concerned African Women Theologians (Circle) and the Ghana representative of the African Association for the Study of Religions. She is the author of *Mending the Broken Pieces: Indigenous Religion and Sustainable Rural Development in Northern Ghana* (2011).

J. Kwabena Asamoah-Gyadu (Ph.D.) teaches Christianity in the Non-Western World, Pentecostal/charismatic Theology, and Christology and New Religious Movements at Trinity Theological Seminary, Legon, Ghana, where he is also the Dean of Graduate Studies. Prof. Asamoah-Gyadu studied at the Trinity Theological Seminary, Legon; the University of Ghana, Legon; and the University of Birmingham, UK, where he gained his Ph.D. in Theology in 2000. He has been Senior Research Fellow at Harvard University (2004); Schiotz Visiting Professor of African Christianity at the Luther Seminary, St. Paul, Minnesota, USA; and Senior Scholar in Residence at the Overseas Ministries Study Center at Yale, New Haven, USA.

Bolaji Bateye lectures in the Department of Religious Studies, Obafemi Awolowo University, Ile-Ife, Nigeria. She is a Resource Person at the OAU Centre for Gender and Social Policy Studies and also co-editor of the *Journal of Gender and Behaviour*. She served as a Leventis Scholar at the School of Oriental and African Studies (SOAS), University of London. Dr Bateye has carried out fieldwork on Health, Healing and African immigrant religiosity in the UK and in the United States of America.

Ulrich Berner is Professor and Chair of the Department for the Study of Religion, University of Bayreuth, Germany. His main interests are European Religious History, African Religions, and method and theory in the study of religion. He is also a principal investigator in the Bayreuth International Graduate School of African Studies (BIGSAS).

Adam K. arap Chepkwony is Professor of African and Comparative Religion in the Department of Philosophy, Religion and Theology at Moi University, Eldoret, Kenya. He is the current chairperson of the Dialogue in Religion and Science Group at Moi University. He is a former chairperson of the Department of Religion, Ecumenical Symposium of Eastern African Theologians, and former East African Representative for the African Association for the Study of Religions.

Ezra Chitando is Associate Professor in History and Phenomenology of Religion in the Department of Religious Studies, Classics and Philosophy at the University of Zimbabwe. His research and publication interests include the mainstreaming of HIV/AIDS in African Religious Studies and Theology, method and theory in the study of religion, and religion and gender. He has published on these themes in various journals and books.

Umar Habila Dadem Danfulani is Professor in the Department of Religious Studies, University of Jos, Nigeria, where he served as Dean of Students, Directorate of Students' Affairs from August 1999 to 2005. He earned his Ph.D. from Uppsala University, Sweden (1994). He is the author of *Pebbles and Deities: Pa Divination among the Ngas, Mupun, and Mwaghavul in Nigeria* (1995). He held the Humboldt Research Fellowship at Bayreuth University, Germany in 1996 and the STINT Fellowship in Uppsala, Sweden in 1999.

Lilian Dube (D.Th., Stellenbosch University, 1999) is an Assistant Professor of Theology at the University of San Francisco where she is the chair of African Studies. She is the AASR Representative for North America and Research Associate for the University of South Africa. Dube received the American Association of University Women Fellowship (2001) and the Dorothy Cadbury Fellowship in the UK (2002). The intersection of HIV/AIDS, gender, and religion informs her teaching, research, and publications which include the co-authored (with: (T. Shoko and S. Hayes), *African Initiatives in Healing Ministry* (2011).

Musa W. Dube is a New Testament scholar, teaching in the University of Botswana. She is the author of numerous articles and editor of several books in the areas of New Testament, postcolonial, gender, translation, and HIV/AIDS studies. Her books include *Postcolonial Feminist Interpretation of the Bible* (2000).

Victor I. Ezigbo holds a Ph.D. from the University of Edinburgh. He is Assistant Professor of Contextual and Systematic Theology at Bethel University in St. Paul, Minnesota, USA. He is the author of *Re-Imagining African Christology* (2010).

Muhammed Haron is Associate Professor in the Department of Theology and Religious Studies at the University of Botswana. He has been a visiting lecturer across South Africa and Malaysia. Haron has received several academic awards, including the Prestigious Scholarship Award in 1992/93 from the Human Science Research Council. In addition to numerous articles, he has also published *First Steps in Arabic Grammar* (with Yasien Mohammed) and *The Dynamics of Christian–Muslim Relations in South Africa (circa 1960–2000)* (2006).

Anthonia C. Kalu is a Professor in the Department of African American and African Studies at Ohio State University, Columbus, Ohio. Among her awards are a Ford Foundation postdoctoral fellowship, a Rockefeller writer-in-residence fellowship and a National Endowment for the Humanities Summer Fellowship for teachers. She is currently the Vice President of the African Literature Association. Her research interests include African and African American literatures and literary theory construction, Women in the African Diaspora, African development issues, and Multiculturalism. She has published three books: *Women, Literature and Development in Africa* (2001), *Broken Lives and Other Stories* (2003), and *The Rienner Anthology of African Literature* (2007).

Philomena N. Mwaura (Ph.D.) is a Senior Lecturer in the Department of Philosophy and Religious Studies and Director, Gender and Affirmative Action Implementation Center at Kenyatta University Nairobi, Kenya. She has published widely on various aspects of African Christianity.

Elijah Obinna is a visiting Assistant Professor at the University of Missouri-Columbia, USA. He recently obtained his Ph.D. from the University of Edinburgh. His recent publications include "Past in the Present: Indigenous Leadership and Contemporary Party Politics in Igboland, Nigeria," in Barbara Denison (ed.), *History, Time, Meaning, and Memory: Ideas for the Sociology of Religion* (2011).

Oyeronke Olademo holds a Ph.D. in Christian Studies. She is a widely published international scholar. She has also served as Course Developer in Comparative Religion for the National Open University, Abuja, Nigeria. She was a Fellow and Visiting Lecturer on International programmes such as CODESRIA (1999), Salzburg Seminar (1999), and Women's Studies Programs, Harvard Divinity School (2000). She was recently awarded her chair as Professor of Comparative Religious Studies, University of Ilorin.

Damaris S. Parsitau is a lecturer on African Christianities at Egerton University, Kenya. Her research interests include African Pentecostalism, Religion and Popular Culture, Religion and Gender, Religion and Politics, and Religion and Health. She is widely published in reputable books and journals. She has held Visiting Research Fellowships at the Universities of Cambridge and Edinburgh.

She is the East African Representative for the African Association for the Study of Religions (AASR).

Tabona Shoko is Professor in African Traditional Religion and Phenomenology of Religion in the Department of Religious Studies, Classics, and Philosophy at the University of Zimbabwe. He has held Research Fellowships at the Universities of Sodertons, Sweden (2008); Utrecht, Netherlands (1988–89, 2002), Botswana (1997, 1998–99), Edinburgh (1994, 2004), and the Africa Study Centre, Leiden (2006). His recent publications include *Shona Traditional Religion and Medical Practices: Methodological Approach to Religious Phenomena* (2011). He has also co-authored (with M. Dube and S. Hayes) *African Initiatives in Healing Ministry* (2011).

Lovemore Togarasei is Associate Professor of Biblical Studies in the Department of Theology and Religious Studies, University of Botswana. He is widely published in the areas of the Bible in African Christianity, Pentecostalism, and HIV/AIDS. His most recent publication is an edited book, *The Faith Sector and HIV and AIDS in Botswana*, (2011)

Dodeye U. Williams (Ph.D.) is a Lecturer in the Department of Political Science, University of Calabar, Nigeria. She was a Commonwealth Scholar at the Centre for African Studies, University of Edinburgh, in 2008. Her research interests include Peace and Conflict Studies in Africa, Religion, and Politics. She has published a number of articles in refereed and scholarly journals.

Albert Kafui Wuaku is Assistant Professor of African and Caribbean Religions at Florida International University, Miami, USA. He holds a doctorate in Religious Studies and Socio-Cultural Anthropology from the University of Toronto. He has researched and published many articles and book chapters on Hindu religious traditions taking root in Ghana. His current field research project is on Haitian Vodou healing discourse and practices in Miami.

Preface

Ulrich Berner

It is a pleasure writing a preface to this collective volume published in honour of Jacob Olupona. Space does not allow me to give a comprehensive overview on his contribution to the study of African religions worldwide, with regard to all his publications. Therefore, I shall limit my focus to his contribution to the emergence and development of the study of African religions in my university.

Professor Olupona joined my department at the University of Bayreuth, Germany, for a period of time, about twenty years ago. Although it was rather a short period, his presence had a lasting impact on the development of this department which had been established just a few years earlier. During his stay at Bayreuth University, he was working on a collective volume on *Religion and Society in Nigeria* (1990), co-edited with his colleague Toyin Falola, a historian. This combined an historical perspective with a broad view of the contemporary religious field in Africa. Also at that time he was preparing the publication of his doctoral thesis: *Kingship, Religion and Rituals in a Nigerian Community* (1991). The subtitle of that book—*A Phenomenological Study of the Ondo Yoruba Festivals*—does not reveal the broad range of his methodological approach. He draws on various disciplines, going much beyond traditional phenomenology, as, for instance, by providing descriptions of the kinship system and of economic life—themes that would have been neglected by phenomenology but emphasized in the anthropology and sociology of religion. It is this combination of historical, phenomenological, anthropological, and sociological approaches that has been a model for the study of African religions at the University of Bayreuth.

Jacob was also instrumental in developing his approach to the study of African religions at Bayreuth University, by recommending and sending Nigerian students and scholars to join my department for Ph.D studies and to teach about African religions. Afe Adogame, one of the editors of this book and a former student of Jacob's at the Obafemi Awolowo University, Ile Ife, was the first Nigerian doctoral student in my department. Afe completed his Ph.D. in 1998 and then taught at Lagos for a couple of years before rejoining my university as a teaching and research fellow in 2000. Afe, in turn, recommended Asonzeh Ukah, who completed his Ph.D. in 2004 and has been teaching at Bayreuth, with an emphasis on "religion and the media," since then. Jacob also recommended the late Professor Ogbu Kalu, his former teacher at Nsukka, who spent half a year at Bayreuth as a visiting professor (1999/2000) on an invitation by the Institute of African Studies. I would also like to mention Umar Danfulani from the University of Jos, Nigeria, and Ezra Chitando, University of Zimbabwe, Zimbabwe, one of the editors of this book, both of whom came to Bayreuth for a period of one year, on Humboldt fellowships. So there is a strong tradition of African scholarship in my department in Germany, resulting from Jacob's activities during his short stay at Bayreuth University, twenty years ago.

ULRICH BERNER
Chair of Religious Studies I (Lehrstuhl Religionswissenschaft I)
Faculty of Cultural Sciences, University of Bayreuth, Germany

Introduction
African Traditions in the
Study of Religion in Africa

Ezra Chitando, Afe Adogame, and Bolaji Bateye

Has the academic study of religion in Africa overcome a failure of nerve and summoned sufficient courage to charter an independent intellectual destiny? Have African scholars of religion been bold enough to shake off the "chains of mental slavery" to proceed to develop "African traditions" in the study of religion in Africa? If African scholars have not yet reached these lofty ideals, have they at least covered appreciable ground in the quest to ensure that the study of religion in Africa is, at least in some important aspects, Africanized? This is critical as the absence of African voices in discourses on Africa is as eloquent as it is regrettable. Mogobe Ramose, a philosopher, protests that there have been too many spokespersons for Africa. According to him, Africans have been reduced to silence, even about themselves. Thus:

> It is still necessary to assert and uphold the right of Africans to define the meaning of experience and truth in their own right. In order to achieve this, one of the requirements is Africans should take the opportunity to speak for and about themselves and in that way construct an authentic and truly African discourse about Africa. (Ramose 2003: 1)

The spirit behind Ramose's assertions above forms the background to this book. The academic study of religion has its roots outside the continent. The very category of religion itself has a European history. According to Timothy Fitzgerald (2000: 4), religion should "be studied as an ideological category, an aspect of modern western ideology, with a specific location in history, including the nineteenth-century period of European colonization." Tomoko Masuzawa (2005) undertakes an analysis of the "world religions" category, exposing its connection to European conceptions of "the Other." Although pioneering scholars in the academic study of religion such as Max Müller and James George Frazer were influenced by African Religions in their formulations (Berner 2004), they largely remained faithful to the idea of Europe as the centre of reality.

Overall, the academic study of religion in Africa is an imported product. African scholars of religion are therefore participating in a project that was conceived elsewhere. They are using borrowed tools. Can they format these tools to meet their own needs? Can African scholars ensure that the study of religion in Africa reflects African issues, concerns and approaches? David Chidester asks some questions that are relevant to the quest to develop African traditions in the study of religion in Africa: "If nineteenth-century comparative religion was fashioned at the intersection of academic discourse and imperial force, has the study of religion subsequently undergone a process of intellectual decolonization? Has it become self-critical of its own interests?" (Chidester 2004: 86).

The process of "intellectual decolonization" is necessarily a difficult one since one of the effects of colonization is to induce self-doubt on the part of the colonial subject (see also wa Thiong'o 1986). An inferiority complex develops in the colonial subject, leading to the desire to mimic the colonial master (see for example, Lakunle in *The Lion and the Jewel* (Soyinka 1963), and Chisaga in Hove (1988). African creative writers have been keen to critique this state of affairs and to challenge Africans to stand up and be counted. Ngugi wa Thiong'o (2003) has written of the need to "move the centre" and challenge Eurocentrism. This is the challenge facing African scholars of religion in postcolonial Africa. Can they assume their own distinctive identity, even as they acknowledge their membership to the global community of scholars of religion? As a few scholars begin to draw attention to the fact that the study of religion is a global enterprise (Alles 2008), how do African scholars want to be represented in this undertaking?

The imprint of European traditions on the study of religion in Africa is obvious (Ludwig and Adogame 2004). The discipline in Africa is heavily indebted to the contributions of various categories of European writers, schools of thought and academic institutions. The study of religion in Africa has been shaped by how individual scholars and institutions in metropolitan centres outside the continent have perceived the discipline. This is an outcome of specific historical processes. However, the post-colonial period requires that African scholars challenge their total dependence on methods and theories developed elsewhere. African scholars of religion must demonstrate innovation and confidence to leave their imprint on the discipline in Africa. Only then will African students readily identify with the study of religion in Africa.

In line with the spirit of decolonization that gripped the continent in the 1960s, most departments of religious studies devoted themselves to the task of addressing African issues. Whereas Christianity had originally enjoyed pride of place in departments/faculties of theology, there was now emphasis on adopting a pluralist approach. In particular, the study of African Traditional Religions (now popularly referred to as African Indigenous Religions) was promoted, as it was felt that these religions offered hope in the project of recovering the lost African identity. African scholars of religion therefore positioned themselves as relevant actors in the struggle for growth and vitality. Decades later, we could ask if they in fact succeeded in generating and upholding "African traditions" in the study of religion in Africa.

Are There "African Traditions" in the Study of Religion in Africa?

Whether or not there are "African traditions" in the study of religion in Africa is a contentious point. The presence of "African traditions" in the study of religion in Africa is a partial reality and, largely, remains an aspiration. It is a partial reality to the extent that there have been appreciable efforts by some African scholars to take African religious realities seriously in their work. Such scholars have sought to give priority to African issues in their research endeavours and to critique the applicability of Western approaches to the study of religion in Africa. However, it remains largely an aspiration because most African scholars have struggled to break free from Euro-American intellectual captivity. In the name of upholding "standards" and "protecting the discipline," many African scholars have tended to wait for European and American scholars to provide the lead. In most cases, African scholars have embraced methods and theories that have become popular elsewhere, without having the courage to contribute new perspectives to the study of religion.

It is the dependence on conceptual schemes developed elsewhere that has led to calls for Africanization. According to Tinyiko Maluleke (2006: 72), "For theological and religious education this means that conscious, deliberate ideological choices of teaching style, teaching content and personnel must be made if Africanisation is even to begin." Maluleke is right to insist that there must be an intellectual investment to the project of Africanization. This argument is taken up by the philosopher Kwasi Wiredu in his reflections on decolonizing African philosophy and religion. For Wiredu, decolonization means "divesting African philosophical thinking of all undue influences emanating from our colonial past" (Wiredu 2006: 291). It is therefore vital to promote and nurture "African traditions" in the study of religion in Africa.

The concept "African traditions" is loaded and may give rise to various interpretations. Our use of the term recognizes the diversity of the term "Africa." As practitioners from various disciplines, including history, political science, philosophy and others have shown, "Africa" is a contested category. It can be deployed to achieve specific objectives. It can be an emotive concept meant to elicit particular responses, as can be witnessed within the political arena. We use it here to refer to the academic study of religion in Anglophone Africa. Other studies are required to do justice to the academic study of religion in other regions within sub-Saharan Africa (specifically, the Francophone and Lusophone regions). By "traditions," we seek to capture the idea of doing things that has been handed down from one generation to another. Consequently, our reference to "African traditions" in the study of religion in Africa speaks to the specifically African approaches to the study of religion that have developed over the years. Furthermore, we have limited our perspective to departments of religious studies in public universities, though we are mindful of the reality that the study of religion takes place in other centres, including African Studies Institutes, private/church-related faculties of theology and others.

To speak of "African traditions" in the study of religion in Africa is to make a bold statement. For some, the only viable way of studying Africa is through European perspectives on Africa. As Africa is an "invention" (Mudimbe 1988), it is not possible to study it apart from the gaze of those who participated in its "invention." Furthermore, since the academic study of religion has its origin in Europe, it appears overly ambitious to speak of "African traditions" in this particular discipline. Since when did the "colonial subjects" have the language to speak back? In such a context, it would appear proper to focus on European traditions in the study of religion in Africa as these have held sway over the years.

The challenge of initiating and upholding "African traditions" in the study of religion in Africa can be attributed to a number of factors. First, as indicated in the foregoing section, the discipline has its origin in Europe. This has given the impression that the study of religion can only be legitimate if it follows the model developed in Europe (as well as North America). Many African scholars of religion have upheld the European model of religious studies. Such a development has compromised the emergence of African traditions in the study of religion in Africa. This has seen African scholars continuing to apply methods and theories developed in foreign metropolitan centres, with a limited interrogation of their value in African contexts.

Second, many African scholars of religion have received their advanced training outside the continent. African students who enroll for higher degrees in Europe and North America operate from a position of relative powerlessness. They are exposed to new methods and theories in the study of religion and they generally end up subscribing to some of these methods and theories. To a very large extent, they are not exposed to African scholars and traditions in the study of religion in these foreign shores. Musa Dube, a New Testament scholar from Botswana, provides useful insights into the struggles of an African scholar undertaking graduate studies in North America. She writes:

> I travelled for education to the countries of those whose his-stories of travel have marked them down as powerful. I have inscribed them as powerful specialists and marketers of their languages and knowledge. Upon arrival, I was a powerless traveller and guest. Unlike travellers and guests that many Southern African people have encountered, I had no power over my hosts/hostesses. In both cases, I was a student with limited power over the contents and requirements of my programmes. The bulk of what I learnt was wonderful, but did not always have direct relevance to my Southern African context, and most of what I learnt in my own home could not be applicable during the period of my study. (Dube 2000: 154)

Third, even when African scholars undertake their graduate studies in African departments of religious studies, these departments have not prioritized intellectual independence from universities in metropolitan centres. The academic study of religion in Africa continues to defer to external voices. For instance, most course outlines remain heavily dependent on formulations by outsiders and the reading lists hardly feature African scholars. While there is some merit in seeking to be/remain, "internationally competitive," in many instances the rigidity stifles creativity and growth.

Fourth, it has been difficult to initiate and nurture "African traditions" in the study of religion in Africa because of the general state of African institutions of higher learning (see, for example, Martin and West 1999). Many departments of religious studies in Africa have lost competent and promising researchers and teachers to institutions in Europe and North America. Although some of these scholars have continued to write on religion in Africa, others have diverted their attention to other themes. Furthermore, institutional decay, lack of visionary leadership within universities, bad governance at national level, commercialization and other factors have militated against the vibrancy of religious studies in Africa.

Fifth, the absence of a clear vision has compromised the emergence of "African traditions" in the study of religion in Africa. Although a pan-African organization such as the African Association for the Study of Religions (AASR), that was formed in Harare, Zimbabwe, in 1992, has the desire to promote "African traditions" in the study of religion in Africa, such an initiative needs to be supported. There is need for African scholars to come to a realization that the current situation is not satisfactory and to come up with effective strategies to promote quality African scholarship in religious studies. Senior African scholars have to invest in mentoring to ensure that more African scholars research and publish on the numerous religions of Africa. While African scholars from various disciplines have been highly critical of the lack of succession planning on the part of politicians, they have not been shining examples either! There may be no "African traditions" in the study of religion in Africa if the practitioners of the discipline do not consciously set out to induct and support younger scholars in the field.

Sixth, the low numbers of women African scholars of religion has had a negative impact on the growth of "African traditions" in the study of religion in Africa. Any discipline that does not accord space to women will not operate at optimum capacity. Departments of Religious Studies in Africa continue to be dominated by men and to make token concessions to women (Chitando and Chirongoma 2008). Given the potential that African women scholars of religion have demonstrated over the last decade, it is crucial that the discipline accords more space to women to ensure its dynamism and growth. African women scholars of religion will challenge the discipline to address existential issues that African women face, thereby contribute significantly to the cause of Africanizing the discipline.

Seventh, Western Christian theological assumptions and perspectives continue to have an upper hand in most departments of religious studies in Africa. Although the renaming of most of these departments upon the attainment of independence was meant to signal a move towards a non-theological approach to the study of religion, the reality is that most of the departments are manned by Christians. Such scholars and administrators continue to accord Christianity a privileged position. This is not to deny that Christians can be passionately African; it is to recognize that many African Christians struggle to uphold their African identities. It is therefore difficult to push a truly Africanist agenda in such settings.

Eighth, to some African scholars of religion, the notion of "African traditions" is ideologically alienating. This is akin to the debate regarding "African writers" in African literature. Some "African writers" refuse to embrace the description as they feel it seeks to limit them to "Africa." To them, a writer is a writer and does not need to be circumscribed geographically. Critics question why it appears fashionable to classify "African writers," when writers from other parts of the world are free from being identified with their continent of origin. In similar fashion, some scholars of religion in Africa would not like to be "limited" by being associated with "African traditions." Although we understand the basis of this argument, we are convinced that African scholars do not need to apologize for their African identities.

The need for African scholars to be aware of their marginal position in the global study of religion is acute. Names of African scholars of religion are not featured amongst those who have practiced and excelled in "the craft of religious studies" (Stone 1998). Does this mean that no African scholar of religion has achieved a notable status within the discipline? Such an assumption overlooks the significant work that has been accomplished in the study of religion in Africa, though, admittedly, more needs to be done (see, for example, Chitando 2008). We believe that an African scholar such as Jacob Kehinde Olupona has demonstrated the capacity of an African to make progress within the discipline. Olupona has paid attention to method and theory in the study of religion (Olupona 1996), change within African Indigenous Religions (Olupona 1991), indigenous religious traditions and modernity (Olupona 2004) as well other themes.

"African Traditions" in the Study of Religion in Africa: Mapping the Contours

Despite the challenges that characterize efforts to develop and strengthen "African traditions" in the study of religion in Africa, there have been some notable gains in this direction. African scholars in various fields have sought to reflect on methodological issues and to provide fresh data on religious phenomena. In fact, this has been a significant difference between religious studies in Africa and religious studies in Europe: whereas the study of religion in Europe has tended to be caught up in recondite methodological debates, the study of religion in Africa has been keen to describe religious vitality on the continent. Indeed, contemporary Africa is the researcher's paradise: the numerous religions and ideologies of the world jostle for attention in a thriving market.

Although more can be achieved, scholars in the study of African Traditional Religions have availed themselves of useful data on these religions in various African contexts. They have described these religions in the pre-colonial setting, their interaction with Christianity and Islam as well as their encounter with modernity. In addition, they have been actively involved in the "insider" and "outsider" debate, although their reflections are generally overlooked in works that focus on this theme (see, for example, McCutcheon 1999). African scholars have argued that as "insiders" they are best placed to understand African indigenous religions. From the writings of John S. Mbiti and E.B. Idowu in the 1960s and 1970s to the contemporary period, one can indeed uphold the verdict that there has been a decisive move towards Africanization within the discipline.

Scholars in the study of African Christianity/Christianity in Africa have also demonstrated a lot of confidence and willingness to initiate "African traditions" within the discipline. Whereas the historiography of African Christianity had been dominated by "outsiders," there has been a growing interest and critique by African church historians. The book *African Christianity: An African Story* (Kalu 2007) is indicative of the trend where African scholars have begun to feel confident to narrate the history of African Christianity. This is also reflected in the study of African Pentecostalism where African researchers have provided valuable information on the phenomenon in Nigeria, Ghana, and other African contexts. The same innovation and commitment is also found in studies on African Islam/ Islam in Africa by African scholars.

As noted above, European and American scholars have invested more in reflecting on method and theory in the study of religion. This is one area where African scholars have been found wanting. Unfortunately, this creates the impression that Africans slavishly follow methods and theories that have been developed elsewhere. Nonetheless, there is need to qualify the statement as some African scholars have sought to test methods and theories developed in Europe within specific African contexts and have recommended alternative perspectives. For example, African scholars such as Olupona have employed the phenomenology of religion to study religion in Africa. Such a process has meant that African perspectives and phenomena have been brought to bear on a European approach.

"African traditions" have certainly been initiated in the study of women's religious experiences. Although African women scholars of religion are still few, they have announced their arrival on the scene in an impressive way. African women scholars have challenged the assumptions of male writers on religion, highlighting the need to pay attention to gender dynamics in the study of religion. They have clarified the experiences of African women in mainly African Indigenous Religions, Christianity and Islam. They have also drawn attention to how religion affects women's health in Africa, particularly in the context of HIV and gender-based violence (for an overview, see, for example, Chitando 2009).

How do "African traditions" in the study of religion in Africa emerge and how can they be sustained? First, there must be an Africanization of the personnel studying religion in Africa. This is a critical factor in the emergence of "African traditions" in the study of religion in Africa. For too long, "outsiders" have arrogated the right to speak on behalf of Africans. In order for the study of religion in Africa to thrive, it is imperative that there be African minds, eyes, ears and voices to communicate the reality of religion in Africa. Although "outsiders" are helpful, they should never be a substitute for the indigenous scholar. It must be African scholars who are at the forefront of research and publication on religion in Africa. Only when it is African scholars driving the study of religion in Africa does the possibility of establishing "African traditions" in the discipline emerge.

The basic requirement of having African personnel in the study of religion in Africa has been partly met. Since the 1960s, many departments of religious studies have been recruiting African scholars who have taken over from European and American scholars. Although the insistence on African personnel might appear ideological, one needs to remember that the colonial project suggested that Africans did not possess the necessary intellectual skills to undertake quality research. It is therefore crucial that Africans be seen to be leading research and teaching activities in relation to religion in Africa.

Second, "African traditions" imply employing specifically African approaches to the study of religion in Africa. This requirement emerges from the observation that it is possible to have an African scholar, working in an African department of religious studies, but he or she may be using exclusively European issues, methods, approaches and even examples. Such an African scholar would not be contributing towards the blossoming of "African traditions" in the study of religion in Africa. If anything, he or she would be perpetuating the hegemony of European traditions in the study of religion in Africa. As we have argued, it is a given historical fact that European traditions have been seminal in the study of religion in Africa. However, the challenge for African scholars in the post-colonial period is to mitigate the impact of these European traditions and to promote "African traditions" in the discipline.

A critical review of the academic study of religion in Africa shows that much more work has to be done in the area of developing specifically African approaches to the study of religion. Some critics would be quick to question whether there can be "specifically African" approaches to the study of religion. They would suggest that as there is, for example, no "specifically African water/fire/mathematics, etc.," so there could be no "specifically African" approaches to the study of religion. Such a stance is based on a false universalism. At any rate, it can be demonstrated that the meaning of, for example, "water, fire, mathematics, etc.," will vary from one cultural context to the other. Given that there are currently European approaches to the study of religion, it follows that it is indeed possible (and urgently desirable) that there be African approaches to the study of religion.

"African approaches to the study of religion," however, need not imply something that is totally unrelated to the current European approaches to the study. As Wiredu (2006: 297) cautions, "it is important to understand that the imperative of decolonization does not enjoin anything like parochialism." For us, interrogating European approaches to the study of religion in the face of African religious phenomena may be regarded as a viable strategy in developing "African traditions" in the study of religion in Africa. For example, do theories and projections of secularization work in Africa? How does the African context challenge the methodologies and approaches developed in Europe and North

America? If the religious scene in Africa invalidates certain methodologies, what are African scholars proposing in place of the problematic/limited theories? Rejecting and adjusting current theories and suggesting new approaches to the study of religion in the light of religious data in Africa is an integral part of forming "African traditions" in the study of religion in Africa.

Third, "African traditions" in the study of religion in Africa emerge from an unrelenting focus on African issues. For too long, the study of religion in Africa has adopted the agenda set by others. It has invested in answering questions posed by others, at the expense of addressing African concerns. Although the concept of academic freedom suggests that scholars are free to pursue those issues that are of interest to them, there is need for departments of religious studies in Africa to tackle the pressing issues of the day. Where religion has been used to destabilize peace, there is need for African scholars to undertake objective studies of the processes at play. Where religion disadvantages women in the context of HIV and gender-based violence, scholars of religion must expose the fault-lines. Ensuring that the study of religion is sufficiently attuned to African issues contributes towards viable "African traditions" in the study of religion in Africa.

Fourth, and finally, there must be a sustained and visible trend across different parts of the region in order to justify the application of the term "African traditions." This suggests that African scholars in religious studies must, across different parts of the region and over time, demonstrate a preoccupation with African issues and methods in the discipline. "Traditions" are not formed overnight from unrelated material. Rather, "traditions" come into being over many years on the basis of themes that have family resemblances. It is therefore crucial for emerging African scholars of religion to familiarize themselves with the major issues and dominant approaches and to find their niche within the broad spectrum of the discipline called religious studies as it has evolved in Africa. This will enable "African traditions" in the study of religion in Africa to expand.[1]

The Chapters in This Book

African Indigenous Religions provide the spiritual background to adherents of these religions as well as converts to other religions. They also provide the most strategic area for developing "African traditions." Consequently, chapters in Part I focus on emerging trends in teaching and researching African religions. In the first chapter, Umar Danfulani provides a useful critique of African religions in African scholarship through a historiographical overview. Adam Chepkwony and Tabona Shoko, in Chapters 2 and 3, focus on the challenges and prospects of teaching African religions in tertiary institutions in East Africa and Zimbabwe respectively.

---

[1]   This suggests that "African traditions" are at an incipient stage, that there are in the process of formation, but that they will blossom "going forward." The chapters in this volume confirm this observation.

In Chapter 4, Oyeronke Olademo interrogates the interface between gender and the teaching of religious studies in Nigeria. Musa W. Dube probes achievements and challenges in the mainstreaming of HIV in African religious and theological studies in Chapter 5. These chapters illustrate the strides that have been made in initiating African traditions in the study of religion in Africa.

Part II focuses on emerging themes and perspectives in the study of indigenous thought, religion and spirituality in Africa. Anthonia Kalu (Chapter 6) focuses on the significance of African narrative traditions in the development and expression of African religious thought. Lilian Dube interrogates the persistence of African spirituality in religious song and dance in Chapter 7. Rose Mary Amenga-Etego examines the role of indigenous systems of governance and sustainable rural development in Ghana in Chapter 8. In Chapter 9, Elijah Obinna analyses the persistence of traditional healers in a particular ethnic community in Nigeria. In Chapter 10, Dodeye Williams explores how Christianity is altering the meanings and ritual performance of two indigenous festivals of the Yakurr people in Nigeria. In all, chapters in this section highlight new perspectives and trends in the emergence of African traditions in the study of religion in Africa.

African Indigenous Religions no longer enjoy a monopoly of the spiritual market in Africa. Part III focuses on Christianity, Islam and Hinduism in Africa. The next two chapters (11 and 12) focus on Pentecostalism and charismatic movements. Kwabena Asamoah-Gyadu analyses trends in the study of African Pentecostalism; while Philomena Mwaura and Damaris Parsitau explore perceptions of women's health and rights in Christian New Religious Movements in Kenya. In Chapter 13, Victor Ezigbo offers insights into the process of doing African Christian theology. The appropriation of African religions in the study of the New Testament in Africa is the focus of Chapter 14 by Lovemore Togarasei. Chapter 15 by Muhammed Haron critiques the study of Islam in Southern Africa; and Albert Wuaku in Chapter 16 focuses on folk beliefs about spiritual power and Hinduism in Ghana. These chapters serve to demonstrate the achievements and challenges in the quest to develop "African traditions" in the study of the various religions found on the continent.

The chapters presented in this book draw attention to the vibrancy of religion in Africa. As the various chapters illustrate, religion remains alive and well in Africa. The onus is therefore upon scholars of religion to examine its dynamism and complexities. The sheer breadth of the material presented herein suggests that the study of religion in Africa cannot be indifferent to the African realities that it encounters. This provides ample scope for the emergence and expansion of "African traditions" in the study of religion in Africa. By interacting with indigenous systems of governance, masculinities, gender issues, and the like, the study of religion in Africa takes on an African outlook.

The chapters also highlight the need to adopt an interdisciplinary approach to the study of religion in Africa. As we have noted above, religion in Africa is experienced as a complex and multifaceted phenomenon. This suggests that there is no room for "methodological imperialism" in the study of religion in Africa. No single method can be adequate to clarify the complex nature of religion in Africa. Consequently, all the various approaches to the study of religion (Connolly 1999) need to be applied. However, as we have insisted throughout, these approaches must be domesticated. African religio-cultural realities must be allowed to challenge and transform these approaches. Only an interdisciplinary approach, one that recognizes the diversity and complexity of religion, can do justice to the study of religion in Africa.

It must be acknowledged that some of the chapters could easily have been classified in different Parts. Furthermore, we were unable to mobilize an adequate number of essays that engage the theme of "African traditions" within specific areas of religious studies in Africa in a more direct way. In addition, the absence of chapters on the Africanization of other religions found in Africa, such as Buddhism, Krishna Consciousness, or the Baha'i Faith and others is not intentional. For us, however, such struggles confirm the need to continue to challenge African scholars of religion to take the project of Africanization far more seriously than has been the case up to now. By developing and nurturing "African traditions" in the study of religion in Africa, African scholars would be taking their unique and rightful place in the global study of religion.

Bibliography

Adogame, Afe, "Practitioners of Indigenous Religions in Africa and the African Diaspora," in Graham Harvey (ed.) *Religions in Focus: New Approaches to Tradition and Contemporary Practices* (London and Oakville, CT: Equinox, 2009), pp. 75–100.

—, "Religion in Sub-Saharan Africa," in Peter Beyer and Lori Beaman (eds.), *Religion, Globalization and Culture* (Leiden: E.J. Brill, 2007), pp. 533–54.

Alles, Gregory D. (ed.), *Religious Studies: A Global View* (New York: Routledge, 2008).

Bateye, Bolaji O., "Proverbs: Issues of Yoruba Femininity from a Feminist Hermeneutical Perspective," in Willem Saayman (ed.), *Embracing the Baobab Tree: The African Proverb in the 21st Century* (Pretoria: University of South Africa Press, 1997), pp. 214–24.

Berner, Ulrich, "Africa and the Origin of the Science of Religion: Max Müller (1823–1900) and James George Frazer (1854–1941) on African Religion," in Frieder Ludwig and Afe Adogame (eds.), *European Traditions in the Study of Religion in Africa* (Wiesbaden: Harrassowitz Verlag, 2004), pp. 141–9.

Chidester, David, "'Classify and Conquer': Friedrich Max Müller, Indigenous Religious Traditions, and Imperial Comparative Religion," in Jacob K. Olupona (ed.), *Beyond Primitivism: Indigenous Religious Traditions and Modernity* (New York: Routledge, 2004), pp. 71–88.

Chitando, Ezra, *Troubled but not Destroyed* (Geneva: World Council of Churches, 2009).

—, "Sub-Saharan Africa," in Gregory D. Alles (ed.), *Religious Studies: A Global View* (New York: Routledge, 2008), pp. 102–25.

— and Sophie Chirongoma, "Challenging Masculinities: Religious Studies, Men and HIV in Africa," *Journal of Constructive Theology*, 14.1 (2008), pp. 55–69.

Connolly, Peter, *Approaches to the Study of Religion* (London: Cassell, 1999).

Dube, Musa W., "*Batswakwa*: Which Traveller Are You (John 1:1–18)?," in Gerald O. West and Musa W. Dube (eds.), *The Bible in Africa: Transactions, Trajectories and Trends* (Leiden: E.J. Brill, 2000), pp. 150–62.

Fitzgerald, Timothy, *The Ideology of Religious Studies* (New York: Oxford University Press, 2000).

Hove, Chenjerai, *Bones* (Harare: Baobab Publishers, 1988).

Kalu, Ogbu (ed.), *African Christianity: An African Story* (Trenton, NJ: Africa World Press, 2007).

Ludwig, Frieder and Afe Adogame (eds.), *European Traditions in the Study of Religion in Africa* (Wiesbaden: Harrassowitz Verlag, 2004).

Maluleke, Tinyiko Sam, "The Africanization of Theological Education: Does Theological Education Equip You to Help Your Sister?," in Edward P. Antonio (ed.), *Inculturation and Postcolonial Discourse in African Theology* (New York: Peter Lang, 2006), pp. 63–76.

Martin, W.G. and Michael O. West (eds.), *Out of One, Many Africas: Reconstructing the Study and Meaning of Africa* (Urbana and Chicago: University of Illinois Press, 1999).

Masuzawa, Tomoko, *The Invention of World Religions, Or How European Universalism Was Preserved in the Language of Pluralism* (Chicago: University of Chicago Press, 2005).

McCutcheon, Russell T. (ed.), *The Insider/Outsider Problem in the Study of Religion: A Reader* (London: Cassell, 1999).

Mudimbe, Valentin, *The Invention of Africa: Gnosis, Philosophy and the Order of Knowledge* (Bloomington: Indiana University Press, 1988).

Olupona, Jacob K. (ed.), *African Traditional Religions in Contemporary Society* (New York: Paragon House, 1991).

—, "The Study of Religions in Nigeria: Past, Present, and Future," in Jan Platvoet, James Cox, and Jacob Olupona (eds.), *The Study of Religions in Africa: Past, Present and Prospects* (Cambridge: Roots and Branches, 1996), pp. 185–210.

— (ed.), *Beyond Primitivism: Indigenous Religious Traditions and Modernity* (New York: Routledge, 2004).

Ramose, Mogobe B., "The Struggle for Reason in Africa," in P.H. Coetzee and A.P.J. Roux (eds.), *The African Philosophy Reader*, 2nd edn (London: Routledge, 2003), pp. 1–8.

Soyinka, Wole, *The Lion and the Jewel* (Ibadan: Oxford University Press).

Stone, J.R. (ed.), *The Craft of Religious Studies* (New York: St. Martin's Press, 1998).

wa Thiong'o, Ngugi, *Decolonising the Mind: The Politics of Language in African Literature* (Nairobi: James Currey and Heinemann, 1986).

—, "Moving the Centre: Towards a Pluralism of Cultures," in P.H. Coetzee and A.P.J. Roux (eds.), *The African Philosophy Reader*, 2nd edn (London: Routledge, 2003), pp. 52–7.

Wiredu, Kwasi, "Toward Decolonizing African Philosophy and Religion," in Edward P. Antonio (ed.), *Inculturation and Postcolonial Discourse in African Theology* (New York: Peter Lang, 2006), pp. 291–331.

PART I

Emerging Trends in the Teaching of African Religions

Chapter 1
African Religions in African Scholarship: A Critique

Umar Habila Dadem Danfulani

Introduction: A Historical Survey of African Religions in African Scholarship

In a separate work I have examined the contributions of Western scholarship to the study of African traditional religion, which is indeed historic and has remained valuable to our understanding of the discipline (Danfulani 2004; cf. Platvoet 1996; Onunwa 1984). In fact, despite their lapses, Western scholars are critical and crucial in training African scholars who in turn produced scholarship on African traditional religions, which is now under review in this book. African religions in African scholarship constitutes the second phase of what Jan Platvoet refers to as "Africa as Subject." This, according to him, occurred "when the religions of Africa had begun to be studied also, and increasingly mainly, by African scholars." The first phase belongs to a category he calls "Africa as Object," a period "when its religions were studied virtually exclusively by scholars and other observers, from outside Africa." These are outsiders or non-Africans who studied "Africa as Object" (Platvoet 1996: 118).

The critical examination and historical survey of literature on African traditional religion is not a new theme. It has been discussed in the past in the works of scholars such as p'Bitek (1971a), Westerlund (1985), Ikenga-Metuh (1985a), Onunwa (1984), and Platvoet (1996) among others. In charting a historical survey of African religion in African scholarship, the present book adds new insights by providing a contemporary picture of the current state of research. This contribution is based on the division of the writings of African scholars concerning African traditional religions as provided by Platvoet. He divided them into the following categories and paradigms: amateur anthropologists, professional anthropologists, Christian theologians and historians.

African Amateur Anthropologists/Ethnographers and Nationalists

African scholars who contributed to the early literature on African traditional religions as insiders were initially few. I refer to them as nationalist writers, but Platvoet gives them the befitting term of "amateur anthropologists." Their studies covered mainly anthropology, religious studies, history, and race relations. This group of scholars has been greatly influenced by the life and works of Marcus Garvey. Within this early group of nationalist scholars are Edward Wilmot Blyden and the Fante lawyers J.E. Casely Hayford and John M. Sarbah, scions of well-to-do coastal merchant families who used the Western education they received to present a defence against what they considered a misrepresentation of African culture, and to defend the cause of the Negroes (Platvoet 1996; Onunwa 1984). Joseph Boakye Danquah, another Ghanaian, was later to follow in the same tradition.

Blyden was a brilliant West-Indian-born Sierra-Leonean Creole and Liberian statesman, educator, writer, diplomat, and politician. He was born on August 3, 1832 in Saint Thomas, U.S. Virgin Islands, from where he emigrated to Liberia at the age of 18. He is one of the best known and most highly respected African intellectuals in the Western world.

His primary concern was to grapple with the fundamental problem of his race and how to dispel the lingering myth of European idea of the inferiority of the Negroes. By the early 1870s it became clear to Blyden that the modern trans-tribal West African nation which he envisaged would not come out through any large-scale New World Black emigration to West Africa. He therefore sought to make black Africa a respected and important participant in the community of nations, devoting his life to full-time enlightenment of the Blacks. An important means by which Blyden sought to create the consciousness of belonging to one West African community on the part of the English-speaking West Africans was by fostering pride in the history and culture of the Negro race.

In 1887, Blyden wrote *Christianity, Islam and the Negro Race* in which he advanced the controversial thesis that Islam had an elevating and unifying influence that did not disrupt the African social fabric. In 1908 he published *African Life and Customs* in which he sought to show that there existed an African social and economic system which in no way could be described as "inferior" to any other system (see Ajayi and Ayandele 1974: 28; Frankel 1974: 277; Lynch 1971: xi; Esedebe 1969: 14ff.; and Holden 1966: 111ff.).

J.E. Caseley Hayford was born in Ghana to a clergyman, Rev. Joseph de Graft Hayford. He attended Fourah Bay College (Sierra Leone) before returning to Cape Coast as a teacher. Later, he went to England and studied law. Like Blyden, Hayford became one of the earliest African journalists. He used his privilege as a member of the Gold Coast Legislative Council in 1916 to project "African personality." In his *Ethiopia Unbound: Studies in Race Emancipation* (first published in 1911, Hayford 1969) Hayford argued that the way to project African personality was through the conservation of traditional institutions. Advocating that African religions should be studied diligently, he described Fante religion as an epitome of African Traditional Religion (ATR).

Danquah (1895–1965), a member of the Akim-Abuakwa "royal family", studied law and philosophy in London from 1921 to 1927. He was born Joseph Kwame Kyeretwi Boakye Danquah on December 6, 1895 and died in February 1965 at Nsawam, in Ghana. As a lawyer, he was called to the Bar in 1926 and obtained a doctorate in 1927. He started publishing academic works in 1928. While Danquah was at University College, London, he came under the influence of the "hyper-diffusionist" explanation of human cultures of the pan-Egyptian or "heliocentric" variety of Elliot Smith and W.J. Perry, together with the "pan-Babylonian" or "selenocentric" theory of Winckelmann that put the origin of all cultures in Mesopotamia (Platvoet 1996: 119; van Baal 1971: 101–2). Danquah (1968: 45–6) thus adopted a polemic and apologetic methodology which made him to come to a conclusion that looked rather artificial, since he deduced that Akan names and concepts of God were akin to those of the Ancient Near East—Mesopotamia, thus giving Akan traditional religion a longer pedigree than Islam and Christianity (cf. Onunwa 1984; Platvoet 1996: 119; Smith 1966a: 3–4, 1966b: 107; Dickson 1968: xff.; Westerlund 1985: 30, 49–50). It seems he was also influenced by Wilhelm Schmidt's evolutionary theory of primeval-monotheism or *urmonotheismus* (Platvoet 1996: 119; Dickson 1968: xi). He regarded Akan ancestors merely as mediators that were not approached as independent agents and the gods as deified or divinised ancestors (Danquah 1968: 28, 53; cf. Dickson 1968: xx).

Danquah (1968: 28, 53) practiced law in the Gold Coast and became the leading nationalist politician up to 1947 when he was displaced by Nkrumah. His *Gold Coast Akan Laws and Custom* adds to our understanding of Akan religious rituals and practices, while he dedicates a chapter in his *Akim Abuakwa Handbook* to religion. In 1944 he published *Akan Doctrine of God*, out of a much bigger work. In this book, Danquah reacted against the European denial of the presence of the Supreme God in African life, whom he regarded as the monotheistic Creator-God and African-Ancestor (1968: 7–8, 19ff., 27ff., 58ff., 166ff., and 183, Platvoet 1996: 119; Lugira 1981: 58).

Following in his footsteps was Olumide Lucas (1996), whom Platvoet describes as the Yoruba Egyptologist, who looked at Egypt as the fountainhead of Yoruba religion (Platvoet 1996: 119). This hyper-diffusionist theory of African traditional religion was to have a great influence on a number of Nigerian scholars, particularly in the unitary theory of Bolaji Idowu and Joseph Omosade Awolalu and even in the so called Hebraism of West Africa that sought Semitic origins of African peoples both culturally and linguistically by promoting a Hamitic theory (see Wambutda 1983, 1991: 28–30; Samb 1981; Westerlund 1985: 38, 49; Hackett 1989: 21, 44; Zuesse 1991: 182, and Olupona 1993: 244).

African Anthropologists

Outside native white anthropologists of South Africa, African anthropologists were few and far in between owing to the stigma associated then with its study among early nationalists because of its close association with the colonial enterprise Platvoet (1996) and Westerlund (1989). Fine examples of this category of African scholars are found in Jomo Kenyatta of Kenya and Kofi A. Busia of Ghana. Like Danquah before him, Busia belonged to the Akan royal *odehye* family, while Kenyatta's father and grandfather were leaders in the Kikuyu rural society of Kenya. These scholars studied anthropology abroad. Kenyatta studied under Bronislaw Malinowski (1884–1942) at the London School of Economics from 1935 to 1937, while the Ghanaian anthropologist Busia was at Oxford, where he studied under Alfred Reginald Radcliffe-Brown (1881–1955) and Daryl Fortes from 1940 to 1942, and under Edward E. Evans-Pritchard from 1946 to 1947. Both of them worked for a while as administrators with the colonial government and became politicians in the latter parts of their lives.

Jomo Kenyatta worked with the Town Council of Nairobi from the early 1920s to 1928 when he became the Secretary-General of the Kikuyu Central Association. He later led Kenya to independence as its first Prime Minister after the exit of the British colonial regime in 1960. His anthropological works that focused on traditional Kikuyu society and religion were also very much a part of his political activism, as was his entire work and life. He was an eloquent politician who changed his Christian name of Johnstone to Jomo in 1938, which means "Burning Spear." This coincided with the time when his book *Facing Mount Kenya* appeared. In this book,

> He made the implied political and religious messages even more explicit by putting on the frontispiece of the book of a photograph of himself in traditional attire and a spear in his right hand, while testing the sharpness of its point with his left. There was certainly a political inspiration in the romantic picture which he presented of traditional Gikuyu society: it was orderly and cohesive even when executing "wizards." (Platvoet 1996: 120; Kenyatta 1961: 199ff.)

Facing Mount Kenya (1938) by Jomo Kenyatta remains an excellent source of Gikuyu religion. In it Kenyatta rejected the colonial enterprise as imposed, destructive and unjust and at the same time he discussed the details of Gikuyu traditional religion including the changes that were then taking place within it as a result of the introduction of Christianity. In it he also examined *Arathi*, a new religious movement of prophets that combined Christian and traditional practices and beliefs (Platvoet 1996: 120; Kenyatta 1961: 267ff.). He developed "his own religious evolution towards a post-Christian, neo-traditional synthesis with elements of parapsychology [that] coloured his interpretation of Gikuyu 'magical and medical practices'" (Platvoet 1996: 120; Kenyatta 1961: 299). Malinowski was to chide him (though only mildly) for this approach (Platvoet 1996: 120–1; Malinowski 1938: xii).

Kofi A. Busia (1913–78) served as the first African Assistant District Commissioner from 1942 to 1944 when he quit the position because he fell out with his superiors. He was later appointed government anthropologist in charge of a survey of the Takoradi district from 1947 to 1949, when he took up a position as lecturer in African Studies in the new University College at Achimota. He became Professor of Sociology in 1954, and in 1956 leader of the opposition to Kwame Nkrumah in Parliament.

Busia examined the changes forced upon African traditional structures of governance by the colonial masters. Writing from a sociological viewpoint, he devoted a good portion of his work to commenting on African religion. Busia's work on Akan religion that was published in 1968 (Busia 1968a, 1968b) remains a classic, providing useful ethnographic historical data and accurate descriptions of their belief system. He concluded that African religious heritage is one of the salient determinants of African consciousness (Platvoet 1996: 121).

The major criticism common to anthropological works by both outsiders and insiders is their failure to capture the dynamic aspects of African society (their works are ahistorical, and static because they were written in the anthropological present). The research works of both Kenyatta and Busia were obviously politically motivated as they appeared in "political anthropology."

Okot P'Bitek (b. 1931, d. July 20, 1982) was a Ugandan anthropologist, artist, novelist, playwright/dramatist, footballer, lawyer, satirist, theologian, and post-Christian scholar, and thus an African culturalist. P'Bitek was born in Gulu, Northern Uganda into a Luo family at a time when Uganda was a protectorate of the British Empire. In addition to being the leader of her clan, his mother was a gifted singer, and composer. As a little boy, P'Bitek grew up learning the tales, proverbs and songs of Acholi (or Luo) folklore from his mother. P'Bitek himself was an accomplished dancer and drummer.

The greater part of his works, especially his novels, reflects themes in African traditional religion because African religion is at the root of African culture (P'Bitek 1971a, cf. Lugira 1981: 60). He was also famous for his literary works, with *Song of Lawino* (1960) being among the best known. His approach to the study of religion in *African Tradtional Religion in Western Scholarship* expresses a strong aversion to metaphysical, ontological and/or idealistic thinking (1971: 85). P'Bitek would rather disassociate himself with anthropology altogether because of the challenge his Oxford professors threw at him (1971: ix). His approach was clearly phenomenological in nature because in order to determine the meaning and social significance of the beliefs and practices of African peoples, he studied their religious universals such as deities, spirits, sacrifices, and rituals among others in a comparative manner (Lugira 1981: 60–1). He took both Western and African anthropologists and theologians to task, tacitly using a critical scientific approach. P'Bitek (1971: 129) points out the connection between colonialism and social anthropology of the day from the standpoint of an Africanist, writing "with the passion of defiant Africanness." He opined that anthropologists justified the colonial enterprise by convoluting "the myth of the primitive" (1971: 1). For this reason, P'Bitek did not reserve a place for social anthropology in African universities, because "Africans have no interests in and cannot indulge in perpetrating the myth of the 'primitive'" (1971: 5). P'Bitek observed correctly that:

> Western scholarship sees the world as divided into two types of human society: one, their own, civilized, great, developed; the other, the non-western peoples, uncivilized, simple, undeveloped. One is modern, the other is tribal ... It will be

shown that this kind of thinking is one of the ways in which Western scholarship justified the colonial system. (1971: 15)

P'Bitek divided the context of African religion in Western scholarship into four epochs: first, the Western classical world and its relationship with Africa, second, the time of the early Christian Church Fathers (such as Lactantius Cyprian, Tertullian, and St. Augustine of Hippo) and the pagans, and the third the epoch of European Western superstitions concerning Africa. The fourth epoch refers to present-day studies of African religions. This is made up of of the time of the Christian apologists mounting a counter attack on the eighteenth and twentieth centuries' non-believers, African nationalists fighting a defensive battle against the onslaught on African culture by Western scholarship and colonialism, and Christian missionaries scheming for what they refer to as "dialogue with animism".

P'Bitek makes critical responses to what he considers to be pitfalls in the study of African religion. In this work he was vehemently critical of what he refers to as the "Judaeo-Christian spectacles" (cf. Horton 1984; 1993: 161ff.) of Western theologians and anthropologists such as Edward E. Evans-Pritchard, John Middleton, Victor Tuner, Marcel Griaule, and Placide Temples for recruiting and forcing African gods to fight as mercenaries in foreign battles (P'Bitek 1971: 49ff., 71, 110–11). In this work he also accused African nationalists like Kenyatta, Busia, Danquah, Abraham, and Senghor of addressing their works mainly to unbelieving Europeans. He criticized African theologians such as Idowu and Mbiti for dressing up African deities in Hellenistic robes/garb and parading them before the Western world (P'Bitek 1971: 41, cf. Lugira 1981: 63). These, for him, are intellectual smugglers that have borrowed technical religious expressions which are used for promoting the cause of Christianity but are applied uncritically and wholescale to ATR. He thus rejected terms like "omnipresent," "omnipotent," "omniscient" and "eternal" because these are vehicles of Greek metaphysical thought, which according to him are absent in ATR (P'Bitek 1971: 88). Since, for him, African writers are absolutely under the influence and control of Western scholarship, he suspected that technical terms concerning religion not only originate from the West, but are used for the promotion of Christianity in Africa. What he considers to be Greek metaphysical terms are meaningless in African thought.

As noted above, P'Bitek accused African theologians such as Mbiti, Idowu, and Danquah for dressing up African gods and ideas in Hellenistic robes and garb. According to him, they did this by "smuggling" metaphysical concepts from Greek and Christian scholasticism, such as "omnipresent," "omniscient," and "omnipotent", among others into African beliefs about their deities (P'Bitek 1971: 41, 46–7, 80, 86ff.). P'Bitek furiously rejected the reference to God in African religion because he held that aside from the concept of Jok, which is akin to magic, the Acholi did not have any "recourse to God as a working hypothesis" (P'Bitek 1971: 100). He thus asserted that "all forms of subjectivity, whether […] from anti-Christian, or from pro-Christian prejudice" should be rejected (P'Bitek 1971: 108). He, however, died early.

African Liberal Christian Theologians

Christian theologians were to dominate the study and even the teaching of ATR in African universities. How should we refer to professors and teachers of African traditional religions and history who were/are men and women of the cloth? Do we call them merely theologian academics or academic theologians? Throughout Sharevskaya's 1973 monograph (cf. Lugira 1981: 43) we come across such terms as "Clergyman Africanists," "Western clericals, priests and theologians," "clerical affiliations," "bishop, clerical and fideistically oriented," "clergyman turned anthropologists," and "pillars of clerical thought" that have been dubiously used, but which convey vague messages.

A good example of such scholars is Harry Sawyerr, a canon of the Anglican Church, a veteran teacher, and university administrator. He was a theologian who had been working for the "indigenization of Christianity" (contextualization) through a deep knowledge of African religion. In one of his numerous works. *God: Ancestor or Creator?* (1970), Canon Sawyerr provides a new approach known as the "thematic" approach to the study of God in three West African societies: the Akan, Mende, and Yoruba, using materials by previous scholars in the field. He made copious use of materials in the language, literature, social life, and institutions of each of the three ethnic groups (Onunwa, 1984).

In *The Springs of Mende Belief and Conduct* (1968) jointly written with W.T. Harris, a one-time Methodist missionary to Sierra Leone, on Mende belief and ethics, Sawyerr gives an in-depth description of the traditional concerns of the Mende with special emphasis on the morality and stability of their society. He explores how Christianity could utilize their traditional institutions of discipline and morality in explaining these Christian concepts, and as means of social control. Canon Sawyerr's contribution in presenting African religion as religion *per se* has been both stimulating and interpretative, but his evangelical zeal, like that of other mission-oriented scholars, seems to overshadow his desire to allow the religion to co-exist with Christianity (Onunwa 1984).

For a very long time the academic study of African traditional religion was dominated by priestly Christian academics. This group is made up of pastors and reverend fathers from Evangelical and Catholic circles teaching in universities in Africa. This category of scholarship has contributed more to the study of African traditional religions in terms of numbers of publications. However, in terms of methodology and theoretical presentation, they are uncritically the weakest. Mbiti and Idowu, who were both trained at Cambridge University in the U.K., are the best examples in this category.

Brought up by religiously inclined parents who possessed a very liberal outlook concerning religious matters, John S. Mbiti was born on November 30, 1931 in Kitui Kenya. He was educated at Makerere College Kampala in Uganda, Barrington College in Rhode Island, and at Cambridge University in the U.K., where he took his doctorate in 1963. He joined the Faculty of Makerere University in 1964. After obtaining his doctorate he served for a while in a parish in England.

Mbiti, a Presbyterian minister by calling and training was in addition Professor at Makerere Kampala, and later went to work for the World Council of Churches in Switzerland. He has published over three hundred articles, essays, and poems in journals and other periodicals, aside from several books in the fields of African Christian Theology, biblical studies, Christianity, traditional religions, philosophy, literature, and poetry. Some of his works have remained classics among scholars of African traditional religion. These include *African Traditional Religions and Philosophy* (1969), *Introduction to African Traditional Religion* (1970a), and *Concepts of God in Africa* (1970b).

Bolaji Idowu was born on September 28, 1913 into a lineage of craftsmen; his father dealt in metal work, while his grandfather was a goldsmith.[1] He began school at the CMS School, Ikorodu, Lagos from 1931 to 1933 at a late age because he was engaged in the family business. He went to the Baptist High School, Abeokuta in 1934, and taught for a year before proceeding to the Wesley Methodist Training College, Ibadan the following year. He served as a sub-pastor in Ogere Methodist Church in Ogun State where he was also the headmaster of the primary school. In 1942, he went back to Wesley College, Ibadan for his ordination course and for the Intermediate Bachelor of Divinity degree of the University of London. In 1945, shortly after the end of World War II, Idowu was sent by the Methodist Church to Wesley House, Cambridge. While in England, he attended both Wesley House, Cambridge and Wesley College, Headingley, Leeds. He was appointed a lecturer at University College, Ibadan from September 1958. Being a prolific writer, he made an immense impact upon both scholars and students through his contributions to the study of ATR and his numerous publications on the subject. He was also a priest and later the primate of the Methodist church in Nigeria in 1972.

Idowu discussed the Supreme Being in his doctoral thesis which he presented to the University of London in 1955. He later published it in 1962 under the title *Olodumare: God in Yoruba Belief.* Idowu, projects the basic Yoruba belief in the Supreme Being as monotheism, even though he referred to it as "a diffused monotheism." He explores the relationship between the Supreme Being Olodumare and other subordinate deities in the Yoruba pantheon. Like Parrinder before him, Idowu wanted to provide a theological description of African traditional religion. In his *African Traditional Religion: A Definition* (1973), he rightly rejected terms like "idol worship," "primitive," "pagan," "savage," "fetishism" and "native religion" as incorrect. He concludes, for instance, that describing the religion of the Yoruba by terms like "fetishism" is a mistake (Idowu 1962: 64; cf. Lugira 1981: 42).

In keeping with Idowu's position, Wambutda (1991) states that the Ngas of Nigeria reject *qum* (idols) as *mbi balu* (play toys) until their faces are ritually washed with *moss* (the three-day beer) and the blood of a goat. Godwin O.M. Tasie (1976, 1977, 1979) underscores the same fact when he observes that in Kalabari

---

[1]   See also the chapter by Ezigbo in this volume.

traditional religion "when a god becomes too furious/angry we will show it the wood/tree out of which he was carved."

Other theologian scholars include Awolalu (1979), Awolalu and Dopamu (1979) and later Abogunrin (1989) in Ibadan, Ikenga-Metuh (1981, 1985a, 1985b, and 1987) and Wambutda (1983, 1991) in Jos, Ejizu (1984, 1986) at Port-Harcourt, Adamo (1998, 2006) of Kogi State University, Agbeti (1986, 1991) from Cape Coast University, Pobee (1976, 1991), Bediako (1984, 1995), and Opoku (1978, 1993). If one may, however, draw on the works of Ikenga-Metuh, for example, it would be true to say that his earlier works on Igbo traditional religion, in which he successfully wove together anthropological, phenomenological-comparative, and historical approaches should indeed be situated within the history of religions. However, towards the end of his life, his works tended toward inculturation theology (Ikenga-Metuh 1996).

The indigenous African writers who were trained Christian theologians also claimed to be working at least from an "insider perspective" or from "within" the traditions they studied. Ideologically, they presumed the superiority of Christianity and Western culture over African traditional religions in spite of their protestations to be "objective." This is a perpetuation of the colonial mentality and influence under which they were brought up. A major criticism of this approach has always been that they study African traditional religion only in order to kill it or that they use it as a stepping stone for the growth of Christianity. Thus in spite of their zeal to show that Africans have a religion, there is an attempt to explain that religion in the light of Christianity. By so doing, most of the pictures of traditional religion painted by them looked strange to the votaries of the faith.

African Historians

The historical study of African traditional religions in Eastern, Central and Southern Africa has been successfully demonstrated in a book by Ranger and Kimambo (1971). The influence of this "Ranger School" is apparently not widespread in Africa, and even less so among West African historians. With the exception of a few scholars who are concerned with historical studies of the Church (such as the significant works of Ajayi 1965 and Ayandele 1975), most historians are concerned with economic history. This results from many years of the influence of the socialist school of thought that radiated from centres such as the Ahmadu Bello University, Zaria from the thoughts of Yusuf Bala Usman (1987). The reply of such scholars to capitalist colonialism, neo-colonialism, and imperialism is socialism/ communism. The net effect is that today there are more economic historians in History Departments in Nigerian universities than social historians of religions, or of oral history/pre-history. It is in the light of this that the seminal works of the German Dierk Lange (2004), Isichei (1982, 1983) of Jos/Adelaide, and Adediran of Obafemi Awolowo University, Ife can be fully appreciated.

The historical content of the works of scholars of ATR in African universities is very often scanty and weak. A good example of how it should be done is, however, found in Christian Gaba's historical-culture area approach in collecting and interpreting data on Anlo traditional religion. He described what he refers to as the Anlo traditional believers' conception and communication with the "Holy," thus showing a considerable understanding of the use of the phenomenological method in the study of primal religions (Gaba 1973, cf. Ikenga-Metuh 1981).

While a confessional study of African traditional religion was partially proceeding in Ile Ife, Ibadan, and Jos by Christian-trained theologians, other scholars such as Kalu in Nsukka, Godwin Tasie (1976, 1977, 1979) in Jos, Ade Dopamu in Ife and later in Ilorin, Michael Nabofa in Ibadan and Friday Mbon (1987a, 1987b, 1992) in Calabar, carried on with more historical studies of African traditional religions. Others include Udobata Onunwa and K. Asare Opoku. The works of Ogbu Kalu stand out clearly as the best examples of historical analysis of African religions coming out of Nigeria, making him one of the leading Religious Studies scholars ever produced by the Nigerian university system. Another fine example of a historian of African traditional religion, of course, is found in the person and work of the Harvard scholar Jacob Kehinde Olupona, who is solid and sound in his methodological and theoretical framework even as he blends this with a sociological flavour.

In discussing and presenting good examples of works carried out to the methodological prescription of Harold Turner, Jan Platvoet praised the work of Olupona thus:

> Fine examples of this poly-methodological approach to the study of African traditional religions are Olupona's recent historical and sociological study of the solidifying function of royal rituals in Ondo, Nigeria, and Danfulani's analysis of the central place of Pa divination system in the traditional religions of three Chadic-speaking ethnic groups on the Eastern Bauchi plateau, also on Nigeria. (1996: 128)

In describing the lucid, monumental, and excellent contributions of Olupona to the study of African traditional religion, Platvoet states further:

> Olupona studied Ondo kingship rituals over the past century as the traditional state's civil religion. He shows that the festivals ritualising Ondo kingship define Ondo identity for all Ondo-Yoruba, whether they be traditional believers, Christians, or Muslims. He documents the dynamic versatility and adaptability of this particular Nigerian traditional religion in the specifics of this particular town and time by its excelling in one of the many functions which a traditional religion may have, that of providing its "adherents" with a cherished group identity through public festivals, that is, as a "civil religion." (Platvoet 1996: 152, 1993: 334–7; Olupona 1991)

Olupona's methodological style is usually a unique "combination of a variety of approaches [which] is well-suited to bring out the dynamic character of African religions, traditional and other, in the past as well as in the present" (Platvoet 1996: 153). His co-edited volume (Platvoet and Falola 1991) is a collection of excellent historical and sociological works on religion in Nigeria by a vast array of both experienced and young scholars. He is not only a prolific and brilliant scholar, but one of the leading authorities of African religion. A leading scholar of African American and African Studies, Olupona edited a volume for the *World Spirituality* series in 2004 with the title *African Spirituality: Forms, Meanings and Expressions*. This monumental work is the product of collaborative efforts with a diverse number of scholars across the globe. It probes into the core spiritual values and cultural complexities of religion on the African continent and the variegated ways in which African tradition has been expressed on other continents. Olupona is an erudite scholar whose life works range from studies on religion and peace in pluralistic and diversified societies such as in Nigeria (1992), to the religiously pluriform nature of African indigenous traditions in Africa and the Diaspora (see for example 1983, 1991a, 1991b, 1993 (with Nyang), 2004 and 2007b) and to a specific religious tradition as exemplified in his works on Yoruba religion (see for example 2005 and 2007a).[2]

Conclusion

The history of the study of African traditional religion in African scholarship has come a long way. It is clear that excellent older scholars are ageing fast and replacements are not forthcoming. Younger up-and-coming historians of religions in Africa with a good theoretical and methodological framework background are few and far between. These include Afe Adogame, Mohammad Sani Umar, Elom Dovlo, Matthews Ojo, Deji Ayegboyin, David Ogungbile, Ezra Chitando, Asonzeh Ukah, Tabona Shoko, Cyril Imo, Musa Gaiya, Dogara Gwamna, and this author. However, collaboration with Western scholars is still needed, in the form of training opportunities and short research stays to help as a challenge towards acquiring sharper methodological skills, particularly in developing an interdisciplinary approach to research. Women scholars of Religious Studies are even fewer and this is a reflection of the huge gender divide to the disadvantage of women within academia in Africa.[3] They include Mercy Amba Oduyoye, Mary Getui, Oyeronke Olademo, Grace Wamue, Bolaji Bateye, Pauline Lere, and Sa'adatu Liman, to mention a few.

What will be the picture of Religious Studies or History of Religions in African universities in the next few decades? There is the urgent need to work towards the proper training of younger scholars, both male and female. Scholars of African

---

[2] Some of Olupona's key works are referred to in the bibliography.

[3] See for example the chapter by Olademo in this volume.

traditional religions, both at home and abroad, should be patient and more creative in seeking for new ways of attracting brilliant young scholars to the study of African religion.[4] No doubt the future enterprise of studying African traditional religion is still as enormous as ever, but the road must be trekked by both African and Western scholars, African scholars residing at home and abroad, males and females—the road is wide enough to carry them all.

There should be a return to teaching the basic theories and approaches of Religious Studies in African universities at the undergraduate and postgraduate (Masters) levels by more senior scholars. There must be an urgent return to conducting field research trips with students, while the seminar tradition of presenting research reports is sustained. This will no doubt sharpen the critical minds of students. Scholars coming from abroad should not merely use Africa as a ground for fieldwork, but they should use every opportunity to organize workshops, seminars, and conferences to coincide with the period of their research stay while in Africa and donate books and other research implements to their host organizations. This will avail them the opportunity to assess first hand the level of Religious Studies in their host institutions and to note room for improvement. Jan Platvoet, Jacob Olupona, Gerrie ter Haar, and Rosalind I.J. Hackett among other scholars have set fine examples in this direction.

There is a marked difference between speaking an African language and actually reading and writing it professionally. There is the need for colleagues in African universities to harness available resources towards teaching students linguistic and philological skills to arm them with the necessary techniques for accurately reading, transliterating, and translating their language and culture so that an excellent and high quality hermeneutics of African traditional religion can be attained. When this has been satisfactorily attained, younger scholars of African traditional religion will find it easier effectively to apply the multi-dimensional method (in the words of Shorter 1975), the poly-methodic approach (in the words of Turner 1981), or the interdisciplinary method of doing research, with great results. The art of working in co-operation with colleagues in other disciplines, departments and disciplines should be continually encouraged by scholars of Religious Studies.

Bibliography

Abogunrin, S.O., "Ethics in Yoruba Religious Tradition," in S.C. Crawford (ed.), *World Religions and Global Ethics* (New York: Paragon House, 1989), pp. 266–96

Adamo, David Tuesday, *Africa and the Africans in the Old Testament* (San Francisco and London: Christian Universities Press, 1998).

---

4 See for example the chapter by arap Chepkwony in this volume.

—, *Africa and Africans in the New Testament* (Lanham, MD: University Press of America, 2006).

Adegbola, E.A. Ade (ed.), *Traditional Religion in West Africa* (Ibadan: Daystar, 1983).

Adogame, Afe, "The Use of European Traditions in the Study of Religion in Africa: West African Perspectives," in Frieder Ludwig and Afe Adogame (eds.), *European Traditions in the Study of Religion in Africa* (Wiesbaden: Harrassowitz, 2004), pp. 376–81.

Agbeti, Jacob Koffi, *West African Church History: Christian Missions and Church Foundations, 1482–1919* (Leiden: E.J. Brill, 1986).

—, *West African Church History, Vol II, Christian Mission and Theological Training, 1842–1970* (Leiden: E.J. Brill, 1991).

Ajayi, J.F. Ade, *Christian Missions in Nigeria: The Making of a New Elite* (London: Longman, 1965).

— and Emmanuel A. Ayandele, "Emerging Themes in Nigerian and West African Religious History," *Journal of African Studies*, 1.1 (1974): 1–39.

Arinze, Francis A., *Sacrifice in Ibo Religion* (Ibadan: Ibadan University Press, 1970).

Awolalu, Joseph O., *Yoruba Beliefs and Sacrificial Rites* (London: Longman, 1979).

— and P.A. Dopamu, *West African Traditional Religion* (Ibadan: Onibonoje Press, 1979).

Ayandele, Emmanuel A., *The Missionary Impact on Modern Nigeria, 1842–1914* (London: Longman, 1975).

Baal, J. Van, *Symbols of Communication: An Introduction to Anthropology of Religion* (Assen: van Gorcum, 1971).

Bediako, Kwame, "Biblical Christologies in the Context of African Traditional Religions," in Vinay Samuel and Chris Sugden (eds.), *Sharing Jesus in the Two Thirds World: Evangelical Christologies from the Contexts of Poverty, Powerlessness, and Religious Pluralism* (Grand Rapids: Eerdmans, 1984), pp. 81–122.

—, "The Significance of Modern African Christianity: A Manifesto," *Studies in World Christianity*, 1.1 (1975): 51–67.

Busia, K.A., "The Ashanti of the Gold Coast," in Daryl Forde (ed.), *African Worlds: Studies in the Cosmological Ideas and Social Values of African Peoples* (London: Oxford University Press, 1954, second edn 1970), pp. 190–209.

—, *The African Consciousness: Continuity and Change in Africa* (New York: American African Affairs Association, 1968a).

— , *The Position of the Chief in the Modern Political System of the Ashanti: A Study of the Influences of the Contemporary Changes on Ashanti Political Institutions* (London: Frank Cass, 1968b).

Danfulani, Umar H.D., *Pebbles and Deities: Pa Divination among the Ngas, Mupun and Mwaghavul in Nigeria*, Uppsala PhD Dissertation (Frankfurt am Main: Peter Lang, 1995).

—, "West African Religion in European Scholarship," in Frieder Ludwig and Afe Adogame (eds.), *European Traditions in the Study of Religion in Africa* (Wiesbaden: Harrassowitz, 2004), pp. 341–63.

Danquah, Joseph K. Boakye, *Akan Doctrine of God* (London: Frank Cass, 1944)

—, *The Akan Doctrine of God: A Fragment of Gold Coast Ethics and Religion* (London: Frank Cass, first pub. 1944, 1968).

Dickson, Kwesi, *Akan Religion and the Christian Faith: A Comparative Study of the Impact of Two Religions* (Accra: Ghana Universities Press, 1965).

—, "Introduction to the second edition," in Joseph B. Danquah, *The Akan Doctrine of God: A Fragment of Gold Coast Ethics and Religion* (London: Frank Cass, 1968, first pub. 1944), pp. vii–xxv.

—, *Aspects of Religion and Life in Africa* (The J.B. Danquah Memorial lectures, Ghana Academy of Arts and Sciences, 1977).

— and Paul Ellingworth (eds.), *Biblical Revelation and African Beliefs* (London: Lutterworth Press, 1969).

Ejizu, Christopher, "Continuity and Discontinuity in African Traditional Religion. The Case of the Igbo of Nigeria," *Cahiers des Religions Africaines*, 18, 36 (1984): 197–214.

—, *Ofo, Igbo Ritual Symbol* (Enugu: Fourth Division Publishing Co., 1986).

Esedebe, Olisanwuche, "Wilmot Blyden 1832–1912 as a Pan-African Theorist," *Sierra Leone Studies*, New Series (July 1969): 25.

Evans-Pritchard, Edward E., *Oracles, Magic and Witchcraft in Azande Religion* (Oxford and New York: Clarendon Press, 1937).

Frankel, M. Yu, "Edward Blyden and the Concept of African Personality," *African Affairs*, 73, 292 (1974): 277–89.

Gaba, Christian, *Scriptures of an African People: The Sacred Utterances of the Anlo* (New York and London: NOK, 1973).

Griaule, Marcel, *Conversations with Ogotomemmeli* (Oxford: Oxford University Press, 1965).

Hackett, Rosalind I.J. (1989), *Religion in Calabar: The Religious Life and History of a Nigerian Town* (Berlin: Mouton de Gruyter, 1989).

Hayford, Joseph Ephraim Casely, *Ethiopia Unbound: Studies in Race Emancipation* (London: Frank Cass, 1969, first pub. 1911).

—, *Gold Coast Native Institutions* (London: Frank Cass, 1970).

Holden, E., *Blyden of Liberia: An Account of the Life and Labour of Edward Wilmot Blyden: As Recorded in Letters and Print* (New York: Vintage, 1966).

Horton, Robin, "Judaeo-Christian Spectacles: Boon or Bane to the Study of African Religions," *Cahiers d'Études Africaines*, 96, 24/4 (1984): 391–436.

—, *Patterns of Thought in Africa and the West: Essays on Magic, Religion and Science* (Cambridge: Cambridge University Press, 1993).

Idowu, E. Bolaji, *Olodumare: God in Yoruba Belief* (London: Longman, 1962).

—, *African Traditional Religion: A Definition* (London: SCM Press, 1973).

Ikenga Metuh, Emefie, *God and Man in Igbo Religion* (London: Geoffrey Chapman, 1981).

—, *African Traditional Religion in Western Conceptual Scheme: The Problem of Interpretation—Studies in Igbo Religion* (Bodija, Ibadan (Nigeria): Pastoral Institute, 1985a).

— (ed.), *The Gods in Retreat: Continuity and Change in African Religions* (Enugu: Fourth Division Publishing Co., 1985b).

—, *Comparative Studies of African Traditional Religions* (Onitsha: Imico, 1987).

— (ed.), *African Inculturation Theology: Africanizing Christianity* (Onitsha: Imico, 1996).

Isichei, Elizabeth (ed.), *Studies in the History of Plateau State* (London: Macmillan, 1982).

—, *A History of Nigeria* (London: Longman, 1983).

Kalu Ogbu, U., "Gods in Retreat: Models of Religious Change in Africa," *Nigerian Journal of Humanities*, 1 (1974): 42–53.

Kenyatta, Jomo, "Kikuyu Religion, Ancestor Worship and Practices", *Africa*, X, 3 (1937): 308–28.

—, *Facing Mount Kenya* (London: Secker and Warburg, 1938, 2nd edn, London: Mercury Books, 1961).

—, *My People of Kikuyu and the Life of Chief Wangombe* (London: United Society for Christian Literature, 1944, first pub. 1942).

—, *Harambee! (speeches)*, (Oxford and New York: Oxford University Press, 1964).

—, *The Challenge of Uhuru: The Progress of Kenya, 1968 to 1970* (Nairobi: East African Publishing House, 1971).

Lange, Dierk, *Ancient Kingdoms in West Africa: Africa-Centred and Canaanite-Israelite Perspectives—A Collection of Published Studies in English and French* (Dettelbach: J.H. Röll Verlag, 2004).

Lucas, J. Olumide, *The Religion of the Yorubas* (Brooklyn, NY: Athelia-Henrietta Press, Inc., 1996, first pub. 1948 in Lagos).

Lugira, Aloysius Muzzanganda, *African Religion: A Prolegomenal Essay on the Emergence and Meaning of African Autochthonous Religions* (Nyangwe, Zaire and Roxbury, Massachusetts: Omenana, 1981).

Lynch, Hollis R., *Black Statesman: Selected Published Writings of E.W. Blyden* (London: Frank Cass, 1971).

Maliknowski, Bronislaw, "Introduction", in Jomo Kenyatta, *Facing Mount Kenya* (London: Secker and Warburg, 1938, 2nd edn, London: Mercury Books, 1961).

Mbiti, John S., *African Traditional Religions and Philosophy* (London: Heinemann, 1969).

—, *Introduction to African Traditional Religion* (London: Heinemann, 1970a).

—, *Concepts of God in Africa* (London: SPCK, 1970b).

—, *Bible and Theology in African Christianity* (Nairobi and London: Oxford University Press, 1986).

Meek, C.K., *The Religions of Nigeria* (London: Frank Cass, 1943).

Mbon, Friday, "Aspects of Annang Religion: A Preliminary Exploration," in Rosalind I. J. Hackett (ed.), *New Religious Movement in Nigeria* (Lewiston: Edwin Mellen Press, 1987a), pp. 5–20.

—, "Public Responses to New Religious Movements in Contemporary Nigeria," in Rosalind I.J. Hackett (ed.), *New Religious Movement in Nigeria* (Lewiston: Edwin Mellen Press, 1987b), pp. 209–35.

—, *Brotherhood of the Cross and Star: A New Religious Movement in Nigeria*, Studien zur Interkulturellen Geschichte des Christentums, band 78 (Frankfurt am Main: Peter Lang, 1992).

Nabofa, Michael Young, "Epha: An Urhobo System of Divination and its Esoteric Language," *Orita: Ibadan Journal of Religious Studies*, 1 (1981): 3–19.

—, "The Use of Dance in Urhobo Belief and Worship," *Orita*, 22 (1990): 12–26.

—, "Saliva Symbolism in African Belief," *Orita*, 28 (1996): 11–35.

Olupona, Jacob Kehinde, *A Phenomenological/Anthropological Analysis of the Religion of Ondo-Yoruba of Nigeria* (Boston University Ph.D. Dissertation, 1983).

—, *Kingship, Religion and Rituals in a Nigerian Community* (Stockholm: Almqvist & Wiksell, 1991).

— (ed.), African Traditional Religions in Contemporary Society (New York: Paragon House, 1991).

—, *Religion and Peace in Multi-faith Nigeria* (Oxford: African Books Collective Ltd, 1992).

—, "The Study of Yoruba Religious Tradition in Historical Perspective," *Numen*, 40.3: (1993): 240–73.

—, "Women's Rituals, Kingship and Power among the Ondo-Yoruba of Nigeria," *Annals of the New York Academy of Sciences*, 810 (1997): 315–36.

—, *African Spirituality: Forms, Meanings and Expressions* (New York: Herder & Herder, 2001).

— (ed.), *Beyond Primitivism: Indigenous Religious Traditions and Modernity* (London: Routledge, 2004)

—, "Osun across the Waters: A Yoruba Goddess in Africa and the Americas," *African Affairs* 104, 416 (2005): 548–50.

— (ed.) *Orisa Devotion as World Religion: The Globalization of Yoruba Religious Culture* (Madsion: University of Wisconsin Press, 2007a).

—, *African Immigrant Religions in America* (New York: New York University Press, 2007b).

— and Toyin Falola (eds.), *Religion and Society in Nigeria: Historical and Sociological Perspectives* (Ibadan: Spectrum Books, 1991)

— and Sulayman S. Nyang (eds.), *Religious Plurality in Africa: Essays in Honour of John S. Mbiti* (Berlin: Mouton de Gruyter, 1993).

Onunwa, Udobata Rufus, *The Study of West African Traditional Religion in Time-Perspective*, Nsukka University Ph.D. Thesis, 1984.

Opoku, Kofi Asare, *Speak to the Winds: Proverbs From Africa* (New York: Lothrop, Lee and Shepard, 1975).

—, *West African Traditional Religion* (Accra: FEP International, 1978).

—, "African Traditional Religion: An Enduring Heritage," in Jacob K. Olupona and S.S. Nyang (eds.), *Religious Plurality in Africa: Essays in Honour of John S. Mbiti* (Berlin: Mouton de Gruyter, 1993), pp. 67–82.

P'Bitek, Okot, *Song of Lawino* (Nairobi: East African Literature Bureau, 1960).

—, *African Traditional Religion in Western Scholarship* (Nairobi: East African Literature Bureau, 1971a).

—, *The Religion of the Central Luo* (Nairobi: East African Literature Bureau, 1971b).

Platvoet, Jan G., "Programmatic Statements from Africa, 1982–1992; A Review Article," *Numen*, 40.3 (1993): 322–42.

—, "From Object to Subject: A History of the Study of Religion in Africa," in *The Study of Religions in Africa: Past, Present and Prospects*, Proceedings of the Regional Conference of the IAHR, Harare, Zimbabwe, 1992 (Cambridge: Roots and Branches, 1996), pp. 105–38.

Pobee, John S. (ed.), *Religion in a Pluralistic Society: Essays Presented to Prof. C.G. Baëta* (Leiden: E.J. Brill, 1976).

—, *Religion and Politics in Ghana* (Accra: Asempa Publications, Christian Council of Ghana, 1991).

Quarcoopome, T.N.O., *West African Traditional Religion* (Ibadan: Africa University Press, 1987).

Ranger, Terence and I. Kimambo, *The Historical Study of African Religion, with Special Reference to East and Central Africa* (London: Heinemann, 1971).

Ray, Benjamin C., "Recent Studies in African Religion," *History of Religions*, 12.1 (1972): 75–89.

—, *African Religions: Ritual, Symbolism and Community* (Englewood Cliffs, NJ: Prentice Hall, 1976).

Samb, A., "Dimensions Socio-culturelles et religieuses," *Presence Africaine*, 117/118 (1981): 130–7.

Sawyerr, Harry, *God: Ancestor or Creator?* (London: Longman, 1970).

— and William T. Harris,. *The Springs of Mende Belief and Conduct* (London: Longman, 1968).

Sharevskaya, Berna Isaakovna, *The Religious Traditions of Tropical Africa in Contemporary Focus* (Budapest: Center for Afro-Asian Research of the Hungarian Academy of Science, 1973).

Shorter, Aylward, *African Christian Theology* (London: Geoffrey Chapman, 1975), pp. 39–58.

Smith, Edwin W., *The Golden Stool: Some Aspects of the Conflict of Cultures in Modern Africa* (London: Edinburgh House Press, 1927).

—, "The Whole Subject in Perspective: An Introductory Survey," (1996a), in Edwin W. Smith (1966b), pp. 1–35.

—, *African Ideas of God: A Symposium* (London: Edinburgh House Press, 1996b).

Tasie, Godwin O.M., "Africans and the Religious Dimensions: An Appraisal," *Africana Marburgensia*, 9 (1976): 34–70.

—, *Kalabari Traditional Religion* (Berlin: Dietrich Verlag, 1977).

—, *Christian Missionary Enterprise in the Niger Delta, 1864–1918* (Leiden: E.J. Brill, 1979).

Turner, Harold W., "The Way Forward in the Study of African Primal Religions," *Journal of Religion in Africa*, 12.1 (1981): 10–16.

Usman, Yusuf Bala, *The Manipulation of Religion in Nigeria* (Kaduna: Vanguard, 1987).

Wambutda, Daniel Nimcir, "Masquerades as Depositories of History: The Angas of Plateau as a Case Study," in Nwanna Nzewunwa (ed.), *The Masquerade in Nigerian History and Culture: Being proceedings of a workshop sponsored by the School of Humanities, University of Port Harcourt, Port Harcourt, Nigeria, September 7–14, 1980* (Port Harcourt: University of Port Harcourt Press, 1983), pp. 99–117.

—, *A Study of Conversion among the Angas of Plateau State of Nigeria, with Emphasis on Christianity* (Frankfurt am Main: Peter Lang, 1991).

Welbourn, F.B., "Review of Okot P'Bitek," *Journal of Religion in Africa*, 4.3 (1972): 228.

Westerlund, David, *African Religion in African Scholarship* (Stockholm: Almqvist and Wiksell, 1985).

—, "A Comparative and Historical Approach to African Disease Etiologies," in Anita Jacobson-Widding and David Westerlund (eds.), *Culture, Experience and Pluralism: Essays on African Ideas of Illness and Healing* (Stockholm: Almqvist and Wiksell, 1989).

Zuesse, E.M., "Perseverance and Transmutation in African Traditional Religions," in Jacob K. Olupona (ed.), *African Religions in Contemporary Society* (New York: Paragon House, 1991), pp. 167–84.

Acknowledgements

An earlier version of this chapter was first presented at the conference *Religion Und Kritik: Das Kritikpotential der Religionen und der Religionswissenchaft* that was held from 25 to 28, September, 2005, being the 27th Jahrestagung der Deutschen Vereinigung für Religionsgeschichte (DVRG). Veranstalter Lehrstühl für Religionswissenschaft der Universität Bayreuth in zusammenarbeit mit der Deutschen Vereinigung für Religionsgeschichte e.V.A; held in Bayreuth, Germany at a panel on Methodology convened by Afe Adogame and Ezra Chitando. I am grateful to Ulrich Berner and the organisers of the conference for sponsoring my trip.

Chapter 2

Challenges and Prospects of Teaching African Religion in Tertiary Institutions in East Africa

Adam K. arap Chepkwony

Introduction

In the last twenty years I have been engaged in teaching and doing research in African Religion at university level. In the last few years I have noted that the responses of my students towards the study of African Religion have changed greatly. In my first years of teaching, twenty years ago, my students were excited and engaged in deep discussions on African Religion. They were able to freely share their experiences and critique both African culture and modern life. The students expressed great desire to maintain the values embedded in African culture and religion. In those days I used African culture to explain new unknown concepts of other faiths, since it was familiar to the students. In other words, my method of teaching was from the known to the unknown.

This scenario has, however, changed. The majority of my students now look blank and surprised at the ideas presented about African Religion. They find it difficult to contribute meaningful ideas on the concepts of African Religion. Indeed only a handful of students can share their experiences that relate to Africa culture. The reason behind this lack of acquaintance with African culture can be attributed to the fact that few people practice it anymore and at the same time, there is a lack of interest among the educated and the youth. This development is worrying and indeed a threat to African Religion and African identity.

It is due to the above observation that I see the need of assessing the teaching of African religion in universities in East Africa in particular. In 1999, the African Association of the Study of Religions (AASR) held a conference in Nairobi where I presented a paper entitled "Teaching African Religion in Tertiary Institutions in East Africa." This paper was published as a chapter of a book edited by J.N. Mugambi and Mary N. Getui, *Religions in East Africa under Globalization* (2004). Since then there have been minimum developments in the teaching of African Religion *per se*. This chapter is therefore a revised version of that chapter with updates, new challenges and prospects in the teaching of African Religion.

The study of African religion[1] in tertiary institutions in East Africa is fairly new for various reasons. First, the universities themselves are fairly young, having been established in the last five decades. Second, the subject, African Religion, has been going through the process of being recognized as a discipline of study. Third, some scholars of religion wonder whether it is even possible to talk about African Religion or African spirituality.

The lack of recognition of African Religion is prompted by its pervasive nature. African Religion is not marked by the presence of buildings, scriptures, distinctive religious functionaries and special days of worship in the manner manifested in Christianity and Islam. These features are always not evident in African Religion. Instead, to describe the daily activities of an African is to describe his or her religion. Scholars who have done serious studies among the African people have acknowledged the pervasive quality of African religion. Among such scholars is Myrtle S. Langley, who observed that there are numerous religious non-verbal communication, signs, movements, and behavior among Africans. Regarding the Nandi community of Kenya she observed that: "To those who observe or participate in Nandi rituals today, religious symbols are by far the most elusive and obscure. It took time before I became aware of their pervasiveness and significance" (Langley 1979: 115).

She has further observed that African rituals carry religious implications hardly noticed by unfamiliar persons and "untrained" minds. On the surface, the crisis rituals in Nandi appear to be "non-religious" or "secular." But this initial impression is not borne out by the facts. The fact of the matter is that religious symbols and appeals to *Asis* (God) in prayer occur frequently throughout these and other Nandi rituals (Langley 1979: 115). Similarly, Ian Orchardson, who lived among the Kipsigis of Kenya for many years, observed that "the belief in God appears in most ceremonies which take place at every stage of their lives" (Orchardson 1970: 22). The lack of apparent outward manifestation of a religion has made it difficult to comprehend African Religion and at the same time complicates efforts to teach it exhaustively.

Today, however, much has been researched and written about African Religion. This has further been buttressed by the fact that some universities both in and outside Africa have introduced the teaching of this subject in their programs. In East Africa, several tertiary institutions offer courses on African Religion. For the purpose of this chapter we shall examine the teaching of African Religion in selected public and private universities. We shall also assess the place of African Religion in the study of comparative religion. Further, we shall investigate the challenges faced in the teaching and studying of African Religion. Finally, some recommendations shall be made as a way forward in an effort to promote the teaching of this discipline in East Africa in particular and the world in general.

---

[1]   The term "African Religion" is now widely accepted by most scholars of Africa Religion who see the phenomenon as one in its essence. For a recent and detailed explanation, see Magesa (1997: 24–7).

Public Universities

The first university to be established in East Africa was the University of East Africa at Makerere Hill in Uganda. It was founded in 1922 as a technical college and was elevated to the status of University College in 1944. It, however, offered the degrees of the University of London until 1963 when it awarded its own degrees as the University of East Africa. In 1970, Makerere became the national University of Uganda. As the University of East Africa, the institution had a strong Department of Religious Studies. N.Q. King founded the department as a joint project of the University of Ibadan and Makerere University. Scholars like John S. Mbiti and E.B. Idowu were responsible for the development of the study of African Religion in its early years.[2]

To qualify for the Bachelor of Arts degree in Religious Studies, a student was required to enrol in three departments within the Faculty of Arts during the first year. In the Department of Religious Studies the first year students had to take introductory courses in the Bible, the Quran, African Religion and Philosophy of Religion. In the second and third years, students were required to either take all their courses from the Religious Studies Department or additionally enrol in another Department. One standard course for those who opted for religious studies was Empirical Study of Contemporary Religions in Tropical Africa. That course had a component of directed fieldwork. Indeed by 1966, the department had collected materials on the religion of the Maasai, the Nandi, the Marakwet, the Kamba, and the Luganda among others (King 1967: 15). Today that Department teaches several new courses and has become the largest department of Religious Studies in East Africa with regard to student enrolment.

At Masters level, the Department offered a Master of Arts degree through coursework and examination in African Studies. In this option the students concentrated on the study of religions in East Africa. During the second year they would write a thesis that dealt mostly with African religious practices. There was also an option for M.A. enrolment by thesis only. The candidate who performed well in this option could be upgraded to Ph.D. work. Only the best applicants for M.A. were offered this option. To date Makerere University teaches several courses in African Religion in all its programs.

Besides courses on African Religion, the department encouraged research in African culture and religious themes. Some earlier periodical publications issued by Makerere staff were *Penpoint* and *Dini na Mila* (Religion and Culture). The Department of Religious Studies at Makerere also issued many volumes of *occasional research papers* whose theme was African Religion. They were mimeographed and bound for distribution in East Africa and abroad. The *Journal of African Religion and Philosophy,* which was started in 1989, became a forum for the exchange of ideas in African Religion and Philosophy. Such initiatives

---

[2]   I acknowledge with appreciation the assistance accorded to me by Prof. G.E.M. Ogutu of the University of Nairobi on this subject.

served as permanent records of African scholarship in culture and religion. It is sad, however, to note that most of the above-mentioned journals have not survived to date. Besides Makerere University, Uganda today takes pride in having more than thirty public and private universities, the majority of which teach courses on African Religion.

When Makerere became the national University of Uganda in 1970, two other national institutions were established in Tanzania and Kenya respectively. These are, namely, the University of Dar-es-Salaam and the University of Nairobi. The former did not establish a Department of Religious Studies at its inception. The reason behind it is that the first President of Tanzania, Mwalimu Julius Nyerere, held the view that such a department would create antagonism in a multi-religious and multi-ethnic nation.[3] However, we note that as early as 1966, plans had been made to establish a Department of Islamic Studies. In his Inaugural Lecture delivered on July 14 1966, N.Q. King had this to say:

> In the original development plan of the University of East Africa it was stated that Islamic studies would be concentrated at Dar-es-Salaam because the coastal area was the one in which Islamic culture had the deepest effect. It is indeed to be hoped that Islamic studies will be developed at Dar-es-Salaam. Already the Ag Khan has promised money for a mosque and the East African Muslim welfare association is negotiating for setting up a chair. (King 1967:. 32).

It was further anticipated that the Churches of Tanzania would help to establish the Department of Religious studies, noting that it was to be hoped that the churches of Tanzania, that had agreed to build a joint Chapel on Dar-es-Salaam campus with the help of international organizations, would also offer to establish a whole department of Religious Studies (King 1967: 33). This, unfortunately, did not take place. At the time of writing (2010), however, I had been informed that the Department of Religious Studies at the University of Dar-es-Salaam is in the process of being established. This indeed is a welcome development in this region and there is every reason to believe that it will add value to the programs at the University of Dar-es-Salaam.

At the University of Nairobi, however, the Department of Religious Studies was established upon the request of certain religious bodies. The religious bodies, which included the National Council of Churches of Kenya, were concerned that there was need for trained teachers of Religious Education at the secondary school level. The department was thus founded under the headship of Bishop Stephen Neill. In its program the study of African Religion was included from its inception.

In some way, Nairobi adapted the Makerere program and has not changed much over the years. Until 1978, when the Faculty of Education was moved to Kenyatta College, the department trained students for the Faculty of Education

---

[3]   I am grateful to Dr. N. Nchimbi, currently teaching at the University of Dar es Salaam for information about the development of this subject in Tanzania.

where Religion was offered for those who opted to teach the subject at secondary school level. Besides that, the department offers courses to B.A. and Anthropology students. The courses on African Religion, however, are few at the undergraduate level. There is a need to revise the program for the purpose of increasing the number of courses in this area of study, which is diverse.

At the Masters level, African Religion is offered besides Christianity and Islam. It is noted with concern, however, that no student has ever specialized in African Religion at this level.[4] In spite of this, most of the theses have African Religion as the background or are used for comparison with other faiths. The doctoral program is by thesis only. Again, here, most theses reflect on various aspects of African Religion and culture. Thus the development of African Religion as an academic discipline in Kenya can be traced to the Department of Religious Studies of the University of Nairobi.

The Institute of African Studies of the University of Nairobi also contributes significantly to the study of African Religion. The Institute was founded in 1966 as a cultural division of Development Studies and became an institute of its own in 1970. Since then, it has given priority to research in the field of African pre-history, ethnography, social anthropology, linguistics, musicology, dance, traditional and modern arts and crafts, religion and other belief systems (see University of Nairobi *Calendar 1986/87*). All these aspects are rich sources of African Religion. The Institute has revived the journal, *Mila* which will promote research in the areas of African Culture and Religion.

Kenyatta University, which occupies a unique place in the development of Kenyan institutions of higher learning, is the third university to consider. In its initial curriculum it functioned as a Constituent College of the University of Nairobi from 1978 until 1985 when it became a university with its own charter. This institution is famous for its Faculty of Education which was transferred from the University of Nairobi in 1978 and for a long time the only one of its kind. Indeed, during the years 1989 to 1992, it was the largest Department of Religious Studies in tropical Africa.[5] Kenyattta University has thus concentrated mainly on producing teachers of various subjects to teach at secondary schools, Primary Teacher Training Colleges, and Diploma Teacher Training Colleges. Since these institutions have Religious Education in their curriculum, religion has been a very popular subject at Kenyatta University and indeed at universities that train teachers. Kenyatta University has one of the richest programs in African Religion. The department of Religious Studies offers courses on African Religion and one

---

[4]   I am grateful to Dr. Nashon Ndungu, the former Head of Department of Religious Studies at the University of Nairobi for answering my questions both orally and by responding to my questionnaire.

[5]   This was the era when universities in Kenya took double intake to cater for the old and the new 8–4–4 system of education.

can specialize in it even at undergraduate level.[6] The courses are also offered through an open learning program. More recently, they have introduced theology as a discipline and students in this discipline are required to take several courses on African Religion.

The Masters program is equally strong, with African Religion as an area of specialization among other disciplines. The doctoral program is by thesis only and like other universities already mentioned, a good number of the candidates opt for research with aspects that examine African ways of life. To encourage research in African cultural and religious practices, Kenyatta University used to publish a journal entitled *Utamaduni wa Kiafrika* (African Belief System). Unfortunately, the journal went out of circulation in the mid 1980s. This indeed was a useful forum for exchange and dissemination of African culture. On the other hand, Kenyatta University has an annual cultural festival and also the culture village established in the mid 1990s. The culture village serves as permanent museum of sorts, to preserve and to demonstrate our rich African heritage. The non-teaching department of creative art also contributes to propagating African Religion through its performance of African ritual dances.[7]

The fourth institution I would like to discuss is Moi University. Moi University was founded as the second public university in Kenya in 1984. It was intended to be a technically oriented institution with its focus on problems of rural development in its training and research programs. To support the goals of the new institution, faculties and schools were established. In 1987 the School of Social, Cultural and Development Studies, now the School of Arts and Social Sciences, was established. It is this school that currently houses the Department of Philosophy and Religious Studies. The Department of Philosophy and Religious Studies set out to prepare its programs which borrowed heavily from the University of Nairobi. From its initial stages, it was the desire of the members of the department to divorce the two departments in order to allow philosophy to develop its own establishment. In 1992 the two departments were separated. The new department was named "Department of Religion," dropping the traditional "Department of Religious Studies," Interestingly, the two departments were merged again in 2005 and reverted to the old name: "Department of Philosophy and Religious Studies." A new component in the new program is the inclusion of theology courses for

---

[6]   These courses include: Introduction to African Religious Heritage; African Mythology; Belief Systems in Africa; Religion and African Customary Law in Kenya; African Religious Philosophy; African Marriage and Family; Rituals, Symbols in African Religion; African Religion in Diaspora; Sources of African Religion; African Ethics and Morality; Religion and Political Movements in Africa; Religion, Witchcraft, Magic and Science; Continuity and Change in African Religion; Rites of Passage within African Communities; Cultural Background of African Tradition Religion.

[7]   I am indebted to Dr. Mary N. Getui and Dr. Micheal Katola for information on Kenyatta University.

those interested in the discipline. The component is rich with African Religion courses. These are relevant for pastors and those interested in the ministry.

The undergraduate program is meant to introduce students to religion in general and therefore there is no specialization at this level. Some of the disciplines in the syllabi from the very beginning included courses on African Religion. The curriculum has been revised constantly and each time more courses on African Religion have been introduced. In the newest program implemented in the academic year 2009/2010, a course "African Traditional worldview" was introduced and is compulsory for all Religion, Theology, and Education students. The Masters program admitted its first two students in 1991. The program has four areas of specialization: that is, African Religion, Christianity, Islam, and Oriental Religions. Several students in this program specialize in African Religion. Most of the Masters of Arts field researchers, even those who take Christianity or Islam as an option, write their theses on different aspects of African culture and religion.[8] The department has graduated several students who have specialized in African Religion at this level to date.

The department also has a Doctor of Philosophy degree program.[9] The program, like the Masters one, has four areas of specialization, among them African Religion. This degree program is by course work and thesis, making it a unique program in East Africa. Several research proposals submitted are on African religious practices. Other programs are the Diploma in Religious Studies and the Post Graduate Diploma in Religion. Both programs have incorporated African Religion courses as the background and substructure of other faiths in Africa.

Private Universities

A good number of private universities in East Africa emerged in the 1990s. The majority of these universities are affiliated to religious groups.[10] The major objective of such institutions is to train men and women who will serve in the ministry. These universities see themselves in the overall context of the church's mission of evangelization. Their educational philosophy involves a holistic

---

[8]   Of these programmes, only that on Oriental Religions is unpopular.

[9]   The late Prof. P. Ade Dopamu, while serving as a visiting scholar from Ilorin University, Nigeria, devoted a great deal of attention to this programme.

[10]   Other private universities in East Africa are: Tanzania: Tumaini University at Makumira and Iringa (Lutheran); St. Augustine University at Mwanza (Catholic); Uganda: Uganda Martyrs University at Nkozi (Catholic); The Anglican Christian University at Mkono, Ndejje University; Bugema University at Lowero (S.D.A.); Nkuba University (Anglican) and Mbale International Muslim University; Kenya: St. Paul's University at Limuru, Nazarene University, Kabarak University, Pan Africa University, Methodist University, and Presbyterian University of East Africa among others.

approach: embracing the heart, the head and the hands. The learners are thus equipped with the necessary skills for service for God and humankind. Some of these universities, however, have recognized that the present global crisis demands non-conventional university programs and different ways of educating and forming professionals. They have thus diversified their curricula to target the market-oriented professions.

A survey of the curricula of some private universities indicates that few courses on African Religion are taught. The University of Eastern Africa, Baraton, for example, provides one course entitled "African Traditional Religion."[11] Nairobi Evangelical Graduate School of Theology, on the other hand, has one course in the Department of Mission and Evangelism on "African Traditional Religions." It is made clear in the description of this course that African Religion is not valued for its own merit but rather as a vehicle better to understand Christianity. The Prospectus description of the course "African Traditional Religions," for example, reads: "A study of some of the traditional African religions in an attempt to understand this cultural facet of various people of Africa to give new insight into effective approaches in presenting the gospel of Jesus Christ." Similarly, a course "Worship in Africa," taught in the Department of Communication of Daystar University (see 1998 Prospectus), selects only the elements in African Worship that make "Christian Worship more meaningful in Africa." This line of thought, in which African Religion is used as a stepping stone to Christianity, is clearly portrayed by Burnnette Fish and Gerald Fish in their book *The Kalenjin Heritage* (1955). While discussing the objectives of their book, they wrote:

> It is to be understood that this study has not been made to encourage anyone to return to traditional religious practices. Rather, this may help everyone to understand that not everything in the traditional religion and culture was evil. We have come across cultural practices, as we have with religious practices which we and other can make use of as Redemptive analogies or parallels in Christian ministry. In fact, we as Christians can learn from values of the past. (Fish and Fish 1995: xix)

Such presentations indicate some prejudicial sentiments towards African Religion. Indeed, in the majority of private religious institutions African Religion is taught as if it was a fossil. It needs be appreciated, however, that such evangelical institutions have taken a huge step in shedding their total condemnation of African Religion to the point of seeing some redemptive analogies in it. This indeed is a big step in the right direction.

The above sentiments are equally applicable to the Catholic University of Eastern Africa (CUEA), which was officially inaugurated on November 3, 1992. Having been granted a civil charter, the Institute was established as a private

---

[11]   I recognize and appreciate the assistance I received from Dr. Nehemiah Nyaundi about the teaching program at the University of Eastern Africa, Baraton.

Catholic University of Eastern Africa to cater for the eight AMECEA countries.[12] The University plays a unique role in training both men and women for pastoral as well as for secular professions. The Faculty of Arts and Social Science under which the Department of Religious Studies is housed enjoys the largest popularity of this faculty is associated with African values. According to the Vice Chancellor, Rev. Dr. Ceasar Lukudu, "This faculty has been particularly popular due to its approach to studies; the lecturers do not just transmit information to the students but have a unique way of passing on rich African values to form ethical professionals."[13]

In almost similar words, one of the objectives of the Faculty of Theology is to "Promote authentic African values, way of life, thought and the African identity which will enrich the human and Christian Heritage."[14] From 1993 the Department of Religious Studies, Department of Ethics, and Department of Philosophy and Religious Studies operated as separate departments. In 1999, however, the departments were merged as the Department of Philosophy and Religious Studies. The Department trains teachers for the eight AMECEA countries and beyond. Two of the core courses for Bachelor of Education students interested in religious studies are "Introduction to African Culture and Religion" and "Belief Systems in Africa." Beside these, there are seven more courses on African Religion that can be taken as electives. From the above consideration, there is no doubt that CUEA takes African Religion more seriously than the other private universities. Other institutions that seek to develop the African peoples should emulate this approach.

Having acknowledged the commitment at CUEA, I note that, being a Christian institution, it has fixed its priority on Christian evangelization. This focus is implemented through its constituent Colleges, including the Tangaza College, Hekima College, the Marist International Centre and, more recently, the Gaba College at Eldoret. One of the Institutes at the Tangaza College hosts the Maryknoll Institute of African Studies of St. Mary's University, MN (MIASMU). The objective of its program, according to its 2000 *Prospectus*, is: "To teach systematically, major themes of contemporary cultures and religions of East Africa in such a manner that students appropriate and articulate an African viewpoint on these themes in a professional manner." The program, which has 11 courses specifically on African Religion out of a total of 22 courses, is designed for (1) African and missionary, pastoral and development agents, (2) African and missionary students, and (3) neophytes: students, teachers, NGO personnel from overseas. From the above, it is evident that even the Catholic University does not teach African Religion for its own intrinsic values but as a stepping stone better to understand Christianity in the African context. However, it is important to note that the Institute of African Studies is the best in East Africa in my opinion. It has a rich collection of books and research work that no other university library has.

---

[12]   The AMECEA countries are Kenya, Uganda, Tanzania, Malawi, Zambia, Ethiopia, Sudan, Eritrea; Somalia and the Seychelles are affiliate members.

[13]   The Catholic University of Eastern Africa, 13th Graduation Magazine (n.d.), 1.

[14]   Ibid., p. 2.

African Religion in the Comparative Study of Religions

In all the above-mentioned universities, a course on Comparative Religion or History of Religions is commonly taught. The course is intended to expose students to all religions of the world. My experience and observation is that comparative religionists do not present the study of African Religion favourably in their works. In other words, the study of African Religion to date is not considered at par with other world faiths. As a result, scholars who use such works for teaching the course are naturally biased against African Religion. This has greatly affected the attitude towards the subject, and more so, in institutions which do not offer other courses on African Religion.

In fact, it has been suggested that scholars of world religions have taken little interest in the study of African Religion. Harold W. Turner, for example, has lamented that notable scholars of religion have hardly made any connection with the study of African Religion. According to him, scholars of world religions have absented themselves from the works of African Religion and also from most courses on this subject at university level (Turner 1981: 6). More recently, James Cox has continued to advocate that indigenous religions of the world should be considered at par with other religions of the world.

The fact that African Religion has been ignored is evident in several ways. First, there are works, especially in Comparative Religion, that have completely ignored African Religion (see, for example, Bach 1959; Bouquent 1962; Anderson 1965; Hopfe 1976; Zaehner 1988, among others).Second, there are other works which describe African Religion as "Animistic," "Primitive religions," "primal religions," "prehistoric religions," or "pre-literate religions" (see, for example, James 1961; Wach 1963; Smart 1969; Sherrath and Hawkin 1972; Noss and Noss 1974; Sutherland et al. 1988; Noss and Noss 1990, among others).Ninian Smart, for example, in his *Religious Experience of Mankind* (1969), briefly discussed African Religion in Chapter 2 entitled "Prehistoric and Primitive religions," In this chapter, Smart discussed the so-called "primitive" peoples, that is, the Australian Aborigines, Africans, American Indians, Eskimos, the Ainus of Japan, the people of Tierra de Fuego, Melanesians, and people holding pre-historic beliefs.

When African Religion is lumped together with other religions, we are not being true to the study of Comparative Religion. Such an approach does not allow for full examination of a religion and therefore fails to expose all of its features. The problem of treating African Religion thus, is that only a small aspect of the religion is briefly mentioned. To study one or two characteristics—say animism, magic, ancestors, or polytheism—usually gives the impression that the characteristic covers all aspects of African Religion. It also implies that African Religion lacks other essential features present in other religions. It is no wonder that the majority of scholars and readers in general, think of and even call African Religion animism, magic, polytheism, fetishism, ancestor worship or other such terms propagated by scholars of the origin of religions.

Although Newell S. Booth, Jr. argues that historians of religion have not neglected African Religion, he rightly observes that the approach adopted by historians is faulty. He writes:

> In their writings we frequently find supreme gods, initiation rites, and spirit possession cults from Africa rubbing shoulders with similar phenomena from Siberia, Central America, and Polynesia. This is undoubtedly useful for comparative purposes, but precisely because the phenomena are separated from the context there is danger of losing sight of that which is most distinctively "African." (Booth 1977: 2)

He has further suggested that this is not the "appropriate way to proceed, partly because it tends to obscure the 'pervasive' quality of African Religion" (1977: 6). It is not fair, therefore, to apply different methods to different religions in a book which seeks to show fair comparisons of the faiths as evident in the majority of such works. The style of examining African Religion briefly as prologue, epilogue, or postscripts common in the majority of works of Comparative Religion does not do justice to the religion and should be discouraged. For indeed, this approach has contributed immensely in relegating African Religion to oblivion.

Having said that, it is to be noted that there are new developments in the way works of Comparative Religion are written and the general attitude towards African Religion. *A Comparative Study of Religions* (1990) edited by J.N.K. Mugambi has, for example, placed African Religion at par with other religions of the world. It is further noted that Ninian Smart, in his more recent book, *The World's Religions* (1989), treated African Religion more favourably than he did in his earlier works. It is also encouraging to observe that a good number of universities in America and Europe teach African Religion as course on its own or as one of the religions in the study of comparative religion.

Challenges Facing the Study of African Religion

Studying African Religion as an academic discipline suggests presenting it in a scientific, well planned and directed manner in any institution of learning. This objective has not been accomplished successfully in East Africa due to some problems. In this section, I shall outline some of such hindrances and challenges to the study of African Religion. Apart from the fact that the subject lacks sufficient staff, the majority of lecturers who teach African Religion have little background in the study. The majority of such lecturers studied two or so courses on African Religion at the undergraduate level. At the Masters and Doctoral levels, few took in-depth courses in the discipline. Instead, most take their degree by thesis only. A good number, however, write theses that engage them in field research in African Religion or culture. The rest of the training is a result of classroom experience and personal reading when one finds oneself having to teach the course.

Due to the above observation, some lecturers tend to accept what other scholars have written uncritically. In that way, they follow their pattern, interpretations and examples wholesale. Some, for example, continue to teach authoritatively on concepts that have been proved to be erroneous. On the other hand, in discussing topics like the rites of passage, normally no attempt is made to show the religious nature of such rites, thus giving the impression that the rites are simply cultural practices with no religious significance. The majority of lecturers also present African Religion in general terms, and thus fail to identify the sources of African Religion, like myths, sayings, songs and teachings. In the absence of sacred texts in African Religion, the importance of such sources and relevant interpretations should not be underestimated.

The resources and materials relevant for African Religion in East Africa are still scanty in spite of the fact that there is a lot to be known about African Religion. There are only a few common books widely used in East Africa; mainly those by J.S. Mbiti and a few other scholars. For three decades now, there has not been any significant work on African Religion in East Africa except *African Religion: The Moral Traditions of Abundant Life (*1997) by Laurenti Magesa. More importantly, there have been very few studies done on the religion of specific ethnic groups. Indeed, this shortfall has forced lecturers of African Religion to constantly refer to books on West African Religion, but these books are not easily available.

Due to lack of adequate research and documentation of African religious activities in East Africa, unprofessional and misleading views on African Religion and on-the-spot reports by journalists are commonly seen in daily papers and magazines. These erroneous ideas and misconceptions are normally used by governments and other concerned organizations to condemn African Religion and culture. The lack of relevant material is associated with the difficulties of publishing by African scholars on African religion or culture. Publishers are often interested in non-academic books that sell more easily. Seen from this angle, the study of Africa Religion will take a long time to reach the levels comparable to other major religions such as Christianity, Islam, Judaism, Hinduism, and Buddhism. Similarly, there are few scholars who are interested in writing on this subject. Again, as mentioned earlier, this is compounded by the fact that many of those who teach this course are not experts in this field of study.

There are hardly any African scholars in East Africa who are practitioners of African Religion. We do recognize, however, that all Africans, regardless of their religious faith, practice some aspect of African Religion. Although one does not need to be an adherent of African Religion to teach or write about it, nor does one have to be an African, there is definitely some merit in being one. There is a big difference in terms of approach and commitment when one is a practitioner of a faith. East Africa has a lot to learn from West African scholars in this case, and as long as Eastern African scholars of African Religion remain at the level of teachers, sympathizers and admirers of the faith, African Religion will always remain incomplete.

Unfortunately, until now a disdainful attitude to African Religion has been held by various groups. There are those Africans who have been influenced by Western lifestyle and philosophy who see African Religion as outdated. Some Christians see African Religion as a stepping stone to Christianity. Since Christianity is here, it is argued, African Religion no longer serves any useful purpose except, perhaps, to help one illustrate the Christian faith. Some scientists, on the other hand, see African Religion as a retrogressive subject in the present scientific and technological world. They see no useful contribution in a world that has become a global village. African Religion, according to this view, is taking Africans backwards to their tribal cocoons. This attitude has prejudiced students who would otherwise select African Religion in their university studies.

Finally, there is a general unpleasant attitude to religious studies in Kenya in particular. This is in contrast to science and technology that are believed to be tough, useful and market oriented. Religion on the other hand is perceived to be of little value and is not considered an academic discipline, but associated more with training for the ministry in the church. All these have given the impression that religion, and more so African Religion, is no longer valuable.

Prospects for the Study of African Religion

1. Although we noted earlier that most lecturers on African Religion lack a strong background in studies of the subject, this should not be a source of discouragement. Instead, African scholars should use all available opportunities to engage in research and writing in the area of African Religion. Such scholars should also take great interest in discussing and sharing ideas with elderly members of the community. For indeed this is a rich source of African Religion to date. The experience and the mass of the information acquired from such encounters can never be found in books or in scholarly circles. What is gathered should be preserved and disseminated.

2. Only when the above recommendation has been adhered to, will the serious problem of lack of material be solved. In East Africa, unlike West Africa, for example, very few books on African Religion are in circulation. Most lecturers on African Religion are forced to rely on J.S Mbiti's books, *Introduction to African Religion* (1975) and *African Religions and Philosophy* (1969). What are most needed now are careful studies of specific ethnic groups. It is time now that we moved from Mbiti's general approach to the study of African Religion among specific groups.

3. It is also noted that there are substantial works on the African Religion that are not available in East Africa. The AASR newsletter, for example, carries new titles on this subject regularly, but the books are not available in the local market and when available the prices are prohibitive. There is therefore a need to have local publishers who can produce such books. It is

time, I believe, that universities in East Africa establish publishing houses that venture into publications to cater for the needs of Africa and African scholars. For how much longer will Africa have to depend on America and Europe for books about Africans, by Africans, and for Africans? Professor Jacob Olupona, currently a Professor at Harvard University, must be given credit for advancing this cause. He is at the forefront of publishing and indeed encouraging and even financing works on African Religion.

4. Publishing academic material on African Religion is not easy. It is time now that scholars of African Religion in East Africa made concerted efforts to find ways and means of publishing books of this nature. African scholars need to even consider financing their own publication until such a time when such books will attract the required readership for publishers. In other words, a group of scholars can support financially the publication of a book and go further to market it among their colleagues and students. After a while, such efforts will attract the interest of publishers. Most literate Africans would really like to learn and read about their African traditional faith and more so now that Africans are seeking their own identity.

5. An association that identifies and preserves sacred sites and sacred objects, collects religious artefacts and probably even comes up with a museum of African Religion and culture should be envisioned. The association should also sensitize people on the values embedded in African cultures and give proper interpretations of such values, showing their relevance to contemporary African society. In this way, a negative attitude towards African Religion can be minimized. I must note that in the last few years museums of specific traditions have been established in Kenya. I note in particular the Museum of Koitalel arap Samoe in the Nandi Hills, Kenya. This museum has collections of the traditions of the Nandi communities that help one to understand the history, philosophy, and religion of the Nandi people. Similarly, in 2008, a lecturer at Moi University, Mr. Paul Tum, developed a Historical Museum of Kipsigis culture at Kapkatet, Kenya to depict the Kipsigis indigenous way of life. Of particular interest in this museum are the exhibits of the lost language, herbs, and religious practices.

6. There are no journals at present that deal with African Religion in East Africa. In spite of the many financial problems public universities are facing, Departments of Religious Studies in various universities should jointly venture in publishing a journal. Actually, with a little effort and determination, each department is capable of running a journal, as is done in West Africa and Southern Africa.

7. There is need to eradicate the negative attitude towards African culture and Religion. The only way to solve this problem is to fight against ignorance about this subject and to prove its value and relevance to Africans. The more books and articles written on the subject, the more the truth will be

exposed and made plain to Christians, the elite, governments, and those individuals who see no useful value in African Religion.

8. To sensitize and to improve African Religion as an academic discipline, there is need for regular seminars and conferences on this subject. It is only through such fora that scholars will be encouraged to research in this generally untapped area of study. The fora will serve as useful tools to enrich and to share new insights and even problems facing study. The fora should encourage the participation of lecturers from Departments of Religions and theological institutions who are biased towards African Religion. It is here that such individuals can discuss the subject objectively. On the other hand, the fora should be used clearly to articulate the place of African Religion and development. For indeed, more often than not, African Religion is erroneously portrayed as being anti-development. To this end, there is a need to promote religious understanding among citizens and to co-operate with governments in development and service to humankind.

9. African Religion should be given its prime place as one of the world religions in the study of comparative religion. This will only be possible if the African scholars of comparative religion take the lead by writing books in the subject that represent African Religion comprehensively. These scholars likewise need to constantly and persistently correct wrong notions about African religion.

10. Finally, many people describe Africa Religion in the past, making it look as if the practices and the ideas no longer exist. Many books describe African religious practices in the past, that is, 'was' even when the practices are alive and openly practiced in the community. It is erroneous to think that only the things that were done in the past constitute African Religion. Indeed, since African culture is not static, African people have adopted new ideas and ways of life which should be seen and understood in their new form as African culture and religion.

Conclusion

The importance of African Religion, now more than ever before, is a crucial matter. The majority of the African people are ignorant of the value of their religion because of the influence of other religions and modernity. Many younger people hardly understand what their grandparents believe. This same generation is getting disillusioned by Western culture that has failed to solve their present crises in life. Most youth ask questions in an attempt to understand and cope with emerging global problems, especially those that concern moral issues, family life, responsibility, and commitment. In the absence of satisfactory answers, many turn to traditional options for solutions. Today, many speeches by politicians, the clergy, teachers, laypersons, and even the youth themselves, point to the traditional ways of thinking and life as possible way out.

As the youth of African struggle with the issues in life, one basic question they ask is about their identity. Who are they in this era of globalization as compared to Americans, Europeans, and the Japanese? They also know precisely what they need and what they do not need. Do we in Africa know who we are before we are drowned in this global village? For these reasons, and for the beauty and the pragmatic nature of their religion and culture, African Religion must take prominence in our education system, including tertiary institutions, in the twenty-first century.

References

Anderson, J.N.D. (ed.), *The World's Religions* (London: Inter-Varsity Fellowship Press, 1965).

Bach, Marcus, *Major Religions of the World* (Nashville: Graded Press, 1959).

Booth Jr., Newell S. (ed.), *African Religion: A Symposium* (New York: NOK, 1977).

Catholic University of Eastern Africa, *13th Graduation Magazine* (n.d.).

Fish, Burnett C. and Gerald W. Fish, *The Kalenjin Heritage* (Kericho, Kenya: African Gospel Church, 1995).

Hopfe, Lewis M., *Religions of the World* (Beverly Hills, CA: Glencoe Press, 1976).

James, E.O., *Comparative Religion* (London: Methuen, 1961).

King, N.Q., *The Queen of the Sciences as Modern African Professional Woman* (Nairobi: Oxford University Press, 1967). Inaugural lecture delivered at Makerere University College (University of East Africa), Kampala, Uganda, July 14, 1966.

Langley, Myrtle S., *The Nandi of Kenya* (London: Hurst, 1979).

Magesa, Laurenti, *African Religion: The Moral Traditions of Abundant Life* (Nairobi: Paulines Publications Africa, 1997).

Maryknoll Institute of African Studies of Saint Mary's University College, *Prospectus* (2000).

Mbiti, J.S., *African Religions and Philosophy* (London: Heinemann, 1969).

—, *Introduction to African Religion* (London: Heinemann Educational, 1975).

Mugambi, J.N.K. (ed.), *A Comparative Study of Religions* (Nairobi: Nairobi University Press, 1990).

Nairobi Evangelical Graduate School of Theology, *Prospectus* (1998).

Noss, David and John Noss, *A History of the World's Religions* (New York: Macmillan, 1990).

Noss, John, *Man's Religions* (New York: Macmillan, 1974).

Orchardson, Ian Q., *The Kipsigis* (Nairobi: East Africa Literature Bureau, 1970).

Sherrath, B.W. and D.J. Hawkin, *Gods and Men* (London: Blackie, 1972).

Smart, Ninian, *The Religious Experience of Mankind* (Glasgow: Collins, 1969).

—, *The World's Religions* (Cambridge: Cambridge University Press, 1989).

Sutherland, Stewart et al., *The World's Religions* (London: Routledge, 1988).

Turner, H.W. "The Way Forward in the Religious Study of African Primal Religions," *Journal of Religion in Africa*, 12.1 (1981): 1–15.

Wach, Joachim, *The Comparative Study of Religion* (London: Columbia University Press, 1963).

Zaehner, R.C., *The Hutchinson Encyclopaedia of Living Faiths* (London: George Rainbird, 1988).

Chapter 3

Teaching African Traditional Religion at the University of Zimbabwe

Tabona Shoko

Introduction

This chapter explores the style and approach of teaching African Traditional Religions (ATRs) course at the University of Zimbabwe (UZ). The course has been taught since 1984, mostly to Bachelor (B.A.) students in undergraduate classes of average size 250 and to Masters (M.A.) students. Aspects of the course have also been researched upon by students writing dissertations and theses and by lecturers working on publications on ATRs. The ATRs course makes a survey of methodological and theoretical approaches to the study of the subject and then treats in depth a selection of major themes in ATR by making special reference to the Shona and with a view to achieving knowledge and understanding of the significance of African traditional religious systems.

In teaching ATRs at UZ, the objectives are set out as follows: to acquaint the students with a variety of methods used in the study of African traditional religion; to provide an overview of the African traditional religious world; to cultivate an appreciation of traditional religion in Africa; to try to develop a sense of African identity; and to promote an understanding of the significance of African religious conviction in a pluralistic context.

History, Methods and Theories

The first part of the course is meant to equip students with the history, methods, and theories for the study of ATR. This comprises the following content.

What is African Traditional Religion?

This part defines ATR in its singular form. But it also weighs the usage of the term in its plural forms. Whilst the singular ATR as used by E. Bolaji Idowu (1973) means unity of religions more or less in the way in which Christianity is perceived, the argument is influenced by similarities in African religions. But the other school of thought that highlights ATRs in its plural form notes more the differences between the religions of Africa. Overall the debate between singular and plural formatives tilts towards the plural that argues for different ethnic and dialectical groups in Africa. The issue of Africans living in Diaspora further complicates the debate and the usage of the term ATR. Several scholars in African religion tend to place weight on the use of 'indigenous religions' which means a heritage of the past rather than the use of the term 'traditional' which has connotations of backwardness, primitive and static religions. Rather, ATRs are seen as dynamic religions that are prone to change, and that have been and continue to be transmitted across generations.

Methods and Theories in the Study of African Traditional Religion

The emphasis in this section of the course has been placed on the different methodologies that have been used by scholars in the study of ATRs. These include records of traveller-missionary-explorers' accounts such as those of D. Livingstone, ethnographical data collection and anthropological approaches such as by E.E. Evans-Pritchard (1965), M. Douglas (1966), and M. Gelfand (see below), sociological approaches such as by G. Chavunduka (1978), theological approaches such as by G. Parrinder, J. Mbiti (1975), and E.B. Idowu (1973), comparative approaches by Fr Placide Tempels (1959), historical approaches by T. Ranger (1967), and phenomenological approaches such as by J.L. Cox (1972), E. Chitando (1997), and T. Shoko (2007).

History and Method in the Study of Shona Traditional Religion

In this section we evaluate the history and method in the study of Shona Traditional Religion by discussing books and periodicals on illness and healing. In Zimbabwe, studies by Michael Gelfand, Michael Bourdillon, Hubert Bucher, Herbert Aschwanden, Gordon Chavunduka, and Martinus Daneel have demonstrated, using different approaches, that health and illness behaviour and health and medical care systems are not isolated but are integrated into a network of beliefs and values that comprise Shona society. As a result, we have a reasonable number of high quality studies that cover the more important aspects of Shona medico-religious beliefs and practices. In this respect certain basic facts from previous research may bear significantly on findings about the Shona views of healing and the curative system.

Studies by the late Michael Gelfand, an empathetic medical doctor and lay anthropologist in Zimbabwe dealing primarily with religion, medicine, and culture in the Shona context, feature as the earliest contribution in this field (see Gelfand 1947; 1956; 1962; 1964; 1965; 1985). The bulk of his material appeared at the peak of colonialism when little had been done in medical anthropology. In discussing the Shona mode of living, especially that which pertains to the Shona medical system in Zimbabwe, Gelfand pays attention to the theme of Shona "hygiene," which includes food and dietary habits in the traditional context (Gelfand 1964: 90–122). Of special interest is material about Shona "hygiene" which shows knowledge of how these people generated their own ideas of cleanliness in order to promote health in a Shona tropical environment which is rife with numerous diseases. Having lived for a considerably long time among the Shona and possessing the advantage of his medical background, Gelfand seems to demonstrate ample knowledge about Shona problems of disease causation and health restoration mechanisms.

Michael Bourdillon, an anthropologist who has conducted extensive research among the Shona, has also written material on their medical beliefs. In *The Shona Peoples* (1987), Bourdillon basically distinguishes between two kinds of illness conceived of by the Shona, the "natural" and "serious" illnesses. Bourdillon asserts that he is not an expert on Shona culture but says the Shona themselves have provided him with observations. He then applies his training in social analysis to interpret Shona social life and behaviour. On the whole, Bourdillon has covered a wide range of Shona activities and beliefs.

Hubert Bucher, a Roman Catholic Bishop in Southern Africa, adopts a sociological approach in assessing Shona cosmology. In his book, *Spirits and Power* (1980), Bucher argues that the whole traditional cosmology has been seen to be a "philosophy of power." He contends that the Shona believe that spirits live, act, and share their feelings toward life, well-being, and sorrow. As such, spirits are "symbolic representations or conceptualisations of those manifestations of power which are looming large in their daily lives" (Bucher 1980: 13). Shona chiefs, spirit mediums, ancestral spirits, and stranger spirits, witches and diviner-healers as well as Independent Churches are, according to Bucher, subject to one basic notion of "power."

Another influential source of information relevant to this study is Herbert Aschwanden's *Symbols of Death* (1987), in which he looks at the causes of death and the nature of disease among the Karanga people who are part of the Shona. He brings it under the cosmological perspectives of the Shona people: "For the Karanga, God is the *fons et origo* (source) of everything, and that includes disease and death" (Aschwanden 1987: 13). However, since evil is an impossible attribute of God, disease is normally attributed to humans and spirits who are regarded as active carriers of disease.

An important contribution to this subject has been made by Gordon Chavunduka. In one of his influential works, *Traditional Healers and the Shona Patient* (1978), his major preoccupation was "to discover some of the important sociological determinants of behaviour in illness" (Chavunduka 1978: 1). The believed social causes of "abnormal" illness, Chavunduka maintains, are displeased ancestors, an aggrieved spirit, and the *shave* (alien spirit). Witchcraft is also perceived as another cause of ailments. Chavunduka's subdivision of traditional healers into four main types is very informative and pertinent to this study. He enumerates the types of traditional healers thus; diviners, diviner-therapeutists, therapeutists, and midwives (1978: 21). He says the diviner is only concerned with the cause of illness although other diviners may treat patients. The therapeutists are mainly oriented towards the treatment of physical symptoms and not the cause of the illness. Chavunduka's research is full of informative case studies and statistics. His overriding conviction in undertaking such research is brought out clearly: "The object of this book has been to call attention to the barriers to communication between scientific and traditional healers, and between scientific healers and their Shona patients" (1978: 97). His tabulation of the data is quite helpful in the analysis of the options taken by the patients.

Research on Independent Churches in Zimbabwe is inspired by the missiologist Marthinus Daneel, who treats the Shona medical beliefs and conceptions in the context of these indigenous religious trends. His assertion that Independent Churches are an attempt to link traditional practices and Christianity is crucial. The following has been said of them: "They represent on the whole a positive effort to interpret Christianity according to African insights, especially at the point where indigenous customs and world views are challenged by the new world of the Bible" (Daneel 1977: 184). Daneel says the greatest contributory factor to the growth of these churches is the healing treatment by African prophets. He maintains that this healing is modelled on traditional patterns. He compares the diagnosis and therapy in healing treatment of the *n'anga* and of the prophet and notes striking parallels.

From the above assessment, all the anthropological and sociological scholars on Shona medical views and practices seem to be in factual agreement. However, what characterizes the bulk of anthropological and sociological studies are general descriptions without discerning essential meanings from the descriptions.

Characteristics of African Traditional Religion

In this section we discuss key characteristics of ATRs. The religions are based on oral tradition, meaning they are not written down; there is no missionary zeal to evangelize the religions as compared to Western religions; the religions are secretive, implying the information is discreet and kept in secret by elders; the religions are "this worldly" as opposed to the "other worldly.". Here the emphasis on ATRs is life here and now (Platvoet 1988).

Selected Themes in African Traditional Religions

The ATRs course also examines selected themes in African traditional religion such as the Religious Worldview; the Spirit World; Religious Practitioners; Sacred Places and Objects; Belief Structures, Myths, Rituals, Omens, Dreams, Taboos; Traditional Religion and Christianity; and Traditional Religion and Politics.

The Religious Worldview

The Shona believe in a tripartite view of the universe. This entails belief in the sacred world, which is the abode of God and all spirits. In this part of the world are aspects of the firmament that include the moon, stars, and clouds, which are representations of the sacred entities. The second part is the human world in which humanity is dominant. Here lies the anthropocentric view of the universe. Humans exist in their categories as men and women, chiefs, practitioners, and children. Animals also form a part of this world. Nature is also a component of this human world. And this includes rivers, mountains, trees, grass, and all forms of vegetation. Certain types of animals and species of trees are symbolic representations of some spirits, especially guardian spirits. The last category is the underworld, which is land below the earth. This is the abode of water creatures like the mermaid which are sacred creatures. Human beings who die on earth are also buried underneath the earth. So this underworld is also associated with spirits. Overall, the universe may appear as separate compartments that comprise the sacred, the human, and the underworld. All are interlinked through ritual activity. And human beings are central, thereby portraying the Shona religious world as anthropocentric.

The Spirit World

This spirit world of the Shona include the numerous spirits that populate the universe such as the concept of God or the Supreme Being (*Mwari*); spirits such as the tribal spirits (*mhondoro*), ancestral and family spirits (*midzimu*), alien spirits (*mashavi*), and angry or vengeful spirits (*ngozi*). It also explains the activities of spirits associated with witchcraft, (*zvidhoma*) (*zvitupwani*) or goblins (*zvikwambo*) and nature spirits, ghosts (*magoritoto*), spooks (*zvipoko*), and *tokolotches*.

Supreme Being (Mwari)

Mwari is the personal name for God. The term refers to a God of fertility who is associated with rain. But the Shona also use other names as descriptive or praise names. He is called *Dzivaguru* (big pool), *Musiki* (creator), and *Musikavanhu* (creator of people). *Kusika* is a process of making fire by rubbing two sticks which has connotations of creation (Merwe 1957). Other Shona names for God (see Moyo 1987: 59–60; Bourdillon 1987: 320–1; Daneel 1970a: 15–21; Dahlin 2002: 73–4) include *Muvumbi* (moulder), *Mutangakugara/ Muwanikwa* (first to exist), *Samasimba/Chipindikure* (powerful), *Chirozvamavi namauya* (give and take), *Chikara* (one inspiring awe), *Dedza* (lord of the sky), *Nyadenga/Wedenga* (owner of the sky) and *Wokumusoro* (one of the above). God is also referred to as *Mbuya* (grandmother), and *Zendere* (young woman) who originated from *Mwari* and portray God as female. He is also called *Sororezhou* (head of elephant) which means Father. He is both male and female (Daneel 1970a: 15–21). God is not a remote God but active one. The Shona approach him at the *Mwari* cult at Matonjeni. He is a powerful supreme being. He is concerned with issues at national level and not individuals. His authority is most felt in times of drought and national crisis. He is also involved in moral and political issues. Black and white commercial farmers whose agriculture heavily relies on rain consult the cult for rain. Also some Zionist and Apostolic Independent churches visit the cult for rituals.

Although omnipotent, *Mwari* is not worshipped directly. Rather, *Mwari* is approached only rarely and then through great spirits like Chaminuka or Nehoreka, for example. The Shona do not pray directly to *Mwari* as the Christians do (Gelfand 1962: 142). They turn to tribal spirits (*mhondoro*) for help in tribal matters like famine or war. Hence the deep involvement of the spirits of Nehanda, Nehoreka, Chaminuka and others in the 1962–79 second war of liberation, the Chimurenga war of Zimbabwe.

Ancestor Spirits (Midzimu)

The basis of the Shona religion is the ancestor cult. They believe their lives are controlled by *midzimu* (*mudzimu* s., alt. *vadzimu* pl.) (ancestor spirits). *Midzimu* are spirits of people who died but exist in a spiritual form. The dead include family elders like fathers, mothers, grandfathers, grandmothers, uncles, cousins, and aunts. These are family spirit elders who deal with family affairs. *Midzimu* also include important spirits of chiefs called *mhondoro* (lion spirits). These are important ancestors symbolized by a lion which is powerful and inspires fear but is guardian of the people. They originate from spirits, chiefly of the founder of the dynasty and his sister. They deal with matters at the territorial level. But generally *midzimu* are spirits of patrilineal and matrilineal ancestors. They are referred to as *varipasi* (those below) and dwell in a spirit world called *nyikadzimu*. They are guardian spirits who are influential in people's lives (Bourdillon 1987: 263).

There are qualifications which must be met in order to become a *mudzimu*. First, the deceased must be elderly people who are mature. Second, the dead must leave children behind who will remember the spirit. They honour the ancestors through millet beer and ritual. Third, the deceased must also be morally upright in the Shona culture. This requirement excludes people like witches who destroy the lineage. The most important ritual is *kurova guva* (bringing back home ceremony) (Shoko 2007: 34).

Midzimu provide health and wealth. But ironically *midzimu* can bring illness and disease or misfortunes like drought, plague, pestilence, floods, and bad luck. In the Shona's own statements, they 'open the door' and allow evil. But the Shona are convinced that ancestors are good and benevolent. Another function performed by *midzimu* is to act as intermediaries between the living and God. They channel people's prayers and petitions to God and rain and all resources from God to the people. In the Shona social structure, people approach elders through mediators. A person intending to marry approaches the in-laws through a *munyai*. A chief is approached through a sub-chief (Moyo 1987: 61).

Alien Spirits (Mashavi)

The Shona believe in other spirits which influence their lives. Some of the spirits are positive while others are negative. *Shavi* (alien spirits) are a good example. These are spirits of people who died far away from home and rituals for bringing back the spirits are not held for them. So the spirits find hosts to possess. *Shavi* are also spirits of relatives, neighbours, white people, animals, and objects. They possess people and provide skills in hunting, healing, dancing, and divination (Bourdillon 1987: 283).

There are several types of *shavi* spirits (for types and functions see Gelfand 1962: 84–108). *Shavi dzviti* originates from the Ndebele. *Shavi regudo* is the spirit of a baboon involved in dancing. The host behaves like a baboon. *Shavi rechizungu* is a white person's spirit. Some white people died in Rhodesia years ago and their spirits appear as *mashavi*. The host imitates a European way of life like speaking in English even though the host is illiterate. Other foreign *shavi* are *shavi rechisena* from Mozambique and *shavi romumwenye* from the Remba and Arabic culture. The *shavi* are associated with healing and business. *Chipunha* is the spirit of a child which is playful. Various *shavi* confer benefits. *Shavi roudzimba* specializes in hunting. It is the original spirit of hunters. But certain *shavi* spirits have negative qualities. *Shavi rouroyi* is involved in witchcraft. *Shavi rechihure* is involved in prostitution. *Shavi* also explain extraordinary behaviour in eating *sadza*, drinking tea or beer, smoking *mbanje*, and in athletics. *Jukwa* spirits are responsible for rain. The Shona refer to them as *manyusa*. They are sent by chiefs as messengers to the *Mwari* cult at Matonjeni to ask for rain. They also carry special gifts to present to the oracle. They are involved in rain rituals at the cult (Dahlin 2002: 75). *Njuzu* (mermaid) spirits are associated with water. *Njuzu* spirit can capture someone and he lives underneath water but becomes a skilled *n'anga* called *godobori* (Dahlin 2002: 75).

Avenging Spirits (Ngozi)

Some spirits are malignant. *Ngozi* are spirits of people who died in anger and are often referred to as angry spirits. They are greatly feared by the Shona. The spirits include victims of murder. *Ngozi* may reveal its intention through a spirit medium. The medium can recover the bones of the deceased from where the murder took place. The family consult a *n'anga* who mediates between the angry spirit and the family. The *ngozi* is appeased through compensation. A girl child from the family of the murderer is used as compensation. She is dedicated to the *ngozi* spirit as a symbolic wife. She can marry within the family of the spirit only with the approval of the spirit. Another means of payment is cattle. Some people believe they can stop the angry spirit by cutting off and eating the murdered person's little finger. Others try to stop or neutralize the devastating power of the spirit by protective medicines through the help of a *nánga*. But the exercise is dangerous and *nángas* are not willing to cooperate. The Shona say *Mushonga wengozi kuripa* (medicine for *ngozi* is payment) (Shoko 2007: 42). *Ngozi* spirits can arise for a number of reasons. They may be the spirit of an aggrieved person who is wronged, an ill-treated spouse, someone indebted, or from failure to comply with the deceased's expectations and from witchcraft (Bourdillon 1987: 271). In all cases the attack of *ngozi* is very dangerous.

Witchcraft Spirits

The Shona people share beliefs in witchcraft spirits called *uroyi*. The witches are men and women who are prompted by jealousy to inflict harm on their enemies. There are some spirits associated with witchcraft. *Zvidhoma* are the most dreaded. Some call them *zvitupwani*. They are spirits of dead people manipulated by witchcraft. They are used by witches to kill and harm other people. *Chidhoma* is a stout dwarf in human form. It has an ugly face with a long beard and hairy skin, and a large [bulbous] eye on the forehead. A single clap from the forehead can paralyse the victim. The mouth goes on the side and the voice may be lost. Witches also use them to suck blood from victims, which leads to death. *Zvidhoma* can appear in the form of animals (*zvivanda*) like a cat or bird (*zvishiri*). They can enter a kitchen, eat too much *sadza*, defecate, and break pots and plates (Shoko 2007: 42).

Zvikwambo are spirits of people raised by magic. An alternative term is *zvitokorochi* (tokolotches). The spirits have an appetite for money, sex, and blood. They originate from South Africa, brought by labour migrants in search of economic survival. The owner sources *zvikwambo* from a *nánga*. A contract is made for the spirits to provide wealth and the owner to supply regular sex and blood. So they steal money and give to the owner. He dedicates a woman to the spirits for sexual purposes. They appear as frogs which suck women's breasts for milk. They draw blood from people's bodies and cause death. The owner is expected to fulfil the obligations of the spirits. If he fails to comply *zvikwambo* will demand sex and kill within his own family.

Nature Spirits

Magoritoto (ghosts) are spirits of people who appear in human form as they were in life. The spirits are non-violent but cause fear. They greet a person and pass through on the way. But they can be angry if the person misbehaves. They grow very tall and produce fire. *Zvipoko* (spooks) are spirits of people who wander near the homesteads at the grave site. But they also appear in forests and urbanized centres. These are spirits of people who return to haunt the scenes of their lives and certain places known to them. They can emit fire, which frightens people. They may appear as human beings and cause accidents on the road. Some turn into prostitutes but disappear when the lights are switched on in bed. Others pretend to accompany men to their homes and in the morning the man and his clothes are found on a grave.

Spirits manifest in different ways. They produce fire at night, light in houses, and can appear as burning trees. But they also manifest as objects like a moving bus. People take a ride but find themselves sitting on the ground when the bus moves. In some cases they appear as human figures or voices and whistles. The Shona avoid making visits and journies at night. But some believe they can withstand spirits by protective charms and medicines. Others use *mbanje* or gunpowder as repellent against spirits (Shoko 2007: 43). Generally, the Shona have benevolent spirits in the traditional sense. Some spirits are guardians and protect the living. Other spirits confer skills and benefits to the living. But others are malignant, harmful spirits associated with witchcraft. Christians regard all spirits as *mweya yesvina* (evil spirits). People affected by evil spirits have *mamhepo* (winds) which must be exorcised.

Religious Practitioners

The Shona believe in host of elders, including the chief as the custodian of tradition. He deals with judicial and cultural issues. The medium is a host of a particular spirit who mediates between the living and the dead. The *n'anga* is another practitioner who serves a triple role as diviner, herbalist, and/or diviner-herbalist. The role of leaderships is not only a male monopoly. Women also play a crucial role in Shona traditional religion. There are female *n'angas* in Shona religion and culture. A midwife is a female practitioner whose function is to help women deliver babies. A *mbonga* is a female ritual attendant who brews beer for spirits at national or regional functions. She also supplies medicine for both mother and child. Shona practitioners play a multiple role as councilors, advisers, legal practitioners, and medical specialists (Chavunduka 1978: 24).

Sacred Places and Objects

The Shona hold certain beliefs about places and objects. In their understanding, there are certain places that are imbued with religious significance. The places can accommodate spirits and are sacred. Examples of such places in Zimbabwe are Nyanga mountain, and Buchwa mountain in Mberengwa. Here the mountains are believed to be the abode of spirits. Visitors are cautioned to respect the "owners of the land" who are the spirits or autochthons that once lived in the area. They are also warned not to utter obscene words lest they risk disappearing in the mountains. There are cases of people who violated these norms and ended up entangled in all sorts of misfortune. Some have disappeared forever for failure to honour the dictates of the spirit world. Great Zimbabwe, now the national monument in Masvingo, has ancient ruins and is of traditional significance. The Zimbabwe bird, and stone structures which are traditional symbols on Zimbabwe coins and paper money, are traditionally connected to Great Zimbabwe. There are important caves in Zimbabwe that include Chinhoyi caves and the Matopo hills. The Matopos are believed to be the abode of the Shona Supreme Spirit, *Mwari*, whose cult is consulted in rain oracles by the Shona across the country. There are also large rivers such as the Zambezi that are associated with a big snake called Nyaminyami. Such places are of great significance since they have a traditional spiritual attachment accorded them.

The Shona also believe in sacred objects. These include ritual objects such as *hakata* (divination sticks used by diviners). Other ritual items are beer pots, millet, rapoko, and sorghum that are used in brewing beer for the ancestors. The items are kept in special enclosures that should be kept secret and only accessible by ritual elders. There are other ritual items that include ritual dress. Colour symbolism matters for the Shona people. Whilst black is associated with ancestral spirits, red is connected with *shavi* spirits (Shoko 2007: 45).

Belief Structures: Myths, Rituals, Omens, Dreams, Taboos

The Shona have strong beliefs in myths. These are sacred stories that are told from one generation to another. Examples are cosmogonic myths that describe the Shona as having originated from underground in a marshy place called Guruuswa. In this myth the Shona are said to have originated underground then pulled out onto the dry land. They were men and women who emerged from a marshy place with tall reeds hence *Guru* (big) and *Uswa* (reeds). This has become synonymous with a place of tall grass. Thereafter they received divine instructions to move from their place of birth to their present location in Zimbabwe. However, the place cannot be located geographically, although historians tend to link it with Bantu migration. But symbolically the myth is interpreted to refer to the human process of birth. Whilst tall grass refers to pubic hair, the watery place may indicate the vagina (Lan 1985: 16). All this underlies the fact that myths are metaphors with a hidden meaning. The Mwedzi myth is another example that carries both anthropocentric and nature centric symbolisms. In the Shona cultural conviction matters about sex are secret and sacred.

The Shona express belief in a system of omens interpreted by a specialist. The underlying belief is that spiritual beings can manifest themselves in numerous forms and signs with the aim of revealing to the Shona recipient his impending fate of either illness and disease or misfortune and death. For instance, an owl hooting at rooftop at night signals the presence of a witch. A *ndara* (file snake) arriving at home indicates impending illness and death (Shoko 2007: 77). But there are also good omens. Dreams are sometimes viewed as instrumental in the Shona belief system. They impart messages from the spiritual world. For instance, a dream about fire symbolizes illness, *ngozi*, or death. A person stuck in mud is indicative of impending illness or trouble (Shoko 2007: 76). However, there are also good dreams experienced by the Shona.

The Shona also share belief in taboos. These are rules of behaviour that govern their existence. The underlying belief is that there are certain rules that must be observed by the living and violation of these can meet with punishment from the spirit world. Examples of such taboos are prohibitions against sitting on a log lest the wife dies or licking a cooking stick lest the man develops breasts like a woman. Taboos also include venturing into prohibited forests, rivers, pools, and mountains without clearance by elders (Shoko 2007: 68).

Traditional Religion and Christianity

African Traditional religions are not static but dynamic. The onset of colonization has brought with it new elements that include Christianity. Grappling with the problem of conversion in Zimbabwe, the Shona people have found themselves torn between traditional religion and cultural beliefs on the one hand and Christian faith on the other. The resultant pattern has been that the Shona partially assimilated Christianity, dealing with their traditional chores six days a week and attending Christian church services on Sunday. Or as someone puts it, sticking to the Bible during the day but resorting to tradition at night (Bhebe 1979: 20). The ultimate result has seen the formation of African Independent Churches epitomized by the Zionist and Apostolic Churches. The product has been a Christianized version of tradition or a traditionalized version of Christianity.

Traditional Religion and Politics

On the political front, Zimbabwe inherited a religion that has been predominantly Christian from the colonial powers. The colonizers and missionaries suppressed ATR and relegated the religion as "superstition," "savagery," "barbarism," and "native religion." ATR was not given space in public and religious life. But with the attainment of Zimbabwe independence in 1980, the government adopted a generous religious policy. This meant that the Shona people are at liberty to practice any religion of their choice, such as ATR, Christianity, Islam, Hinduism, the Baha'i Faith, and others. In the study of African traditional religion, it is important to highlight the fact that African traditional religion is equal to other world religions in that it has myths, rituals, sacred practitioners and beliefs. The religion must be accorded its due place and be studied *sui generis*, as a religion amongst the religions of humankind.

Conclusion

Teaching ATR in Zimbabwe has marked the proliferation of traditional religion in a multi-religious context. In this respect, it is imperative to study traditional religion as an equal amongst other religions. Therefore the course on ATR has been designed to integrate issues of history, methodology and theory of the study of the subject. It includes the works of European and African scholars on the discipline. It shows the contribution of African scholars to the growth of the discipline. This has been capped by selection of key themes in the subject such as traditional cosmology and the spiritual worldview. Since teaching and research are integrated, materials have been integrated into dissertations, theses and scholarly publications in the field. It is hoped that with the passage of time, a truly African perspective on the study of ATR in Zimbabwe will evolve.

Bibliography

Aschwanden, H., *Symbols of Death: An Analysis of the Consciousness of the Karanga* (Gweru: Mambo Press 1987).

Bhebe, N., *Christianity and Traditional Religion in Western Zimbabwe 1859–1923* (London: Longman, 1979).

Bourdillon, M.F.C., *The Shona Peoples* (Gweru: Mambo Press, 1987, first pub. 1976).

Bucher, H., *Spirits and Power: An Analysis of Shona Cosmology* (Cape Town: Oxford University Press, 1980).

Chavunduka, G., *Traditional Healers and the Shona Patient* (Gweru: Mambo Press, 1978).

Chitando, E., "Phenomenological Approach to Study of Religion in Africa: A Critical Appraisal," *Journal of Black Theology in South Africa*, 11 (1997): 6–24.

Cox, J.L., *Expressing the Sacred: An Introduction to the Phenomenology of Religion* (Harare: University of Zimbabwe Publications, 1992).

Dahlin, O., *Zvinorwadza: Being a Patient in the Religious and Medical Plurality of the Mberengwa District* (Frankfurt am Main: Peter Lang, 2002).

Daneel, M., "The Growth and Significance of Shona Independent Churches," in M.F.C. Bourdillon (ed.), *Christianity South of the Zambezi*, Vol. 2 (Gweru: Mambo Press, 1977), pp. 177–92.

Douglas, M., *Purity and Danger* (London: Routledge and Kegan Paul, 1966).

Evans-Pritchard, E.E., *Theories of Primitive Religion* (Oxford University Press, 1965).

Gelfand, M., *African Medical Handbook* (Cape Town: African Bookman, 1947).

—, *Medicine and Magic of the MaShona* (Cape Town: Juta, 1956).

—, *Shona Religion with Special Reference to the Makorekore* (Cape Town: Juta, 1962).

—, *Medicine and Custom in Africa* (Edinburgh: E.& S. Livingstone, 1964).

—, *The Witch Doctor* (London: Harvill Press, 1965).

—, *The Traditional Medical Practitioner in Zimbabwe* (Gweru: Mambo Press, 1985).

Idowu, E.B., *African Traditional Religion: A Definition* (London: SCM Press, 1973).

Lan, D., *Guns and Rain: Guerillas and Spirit-Mediums in Zimbabwe* (Harare: Zimbabwe Publishing House, 1985).

Mbiti, J., *Introduction to African Traditional Religion* (New York: Praeger, 1975).

Merwe, W.J. van der, "The Shona Idea of God," *NADA*, no. 34 (1957): 39–63.

Moyo, A., "Religion and Politics in Zimbabwe," in K.H. Peterson (ed.), *Religion, Development and African Identity* (Uppsala: Nordiska Afrikainstitutet, 1987), pp. 59–72.

Platvoet, J.G., *Essays on Akan Traditional Religion* (Harare: University of Zimbabwe, 1988).

Ranger, T.O., *Revolt in Southern Rhodesia: A Study of African Resistance: 1986–1897* (London: Heinemann, 1967).

Shoko, T., *Karanga Indigenous Religion in Zimbabwe: Health and Well-being* (Aldershot: Ashgate, 2007).

Tempels, P., *Bantu Philosophy* (Paris: Présence Africaine, 1959).

Chapter 4

Gender and the Teaching of Religious Studies in Nigeria: A Primary Overview

Oyeronke Olademo

Introduction

The composition and implementation of religious studies (Islamic, Christian and Comparative religious studies) curriculum at tertiary institutions in Nigeria do not prioritize gender and women's issues. The implications of these for religious studies as a discipline and for women who teach the subject are profound. A major proceed of this observation is the latent patriarchal coloring of religious studies teaching in Nigerian universities and other institutions of higher learning. In language, composition, and implementation, religion is presented in the classrooms as being predominantly a male concern, at least at the decision-making level. I recall a meeting on the curriculum for a Masters degree program in my department recently where I could not convince the other members (all male) of the necessity to include feminist writings in our recommendations. Every female scholar I recommended was either rejected because "she has not written enough books" or "too young in age to be studied in a university."

Another, but related, issue worth mentioning is the "straitjacket" approach to the teaching of religious studies in the Nigerian higher education system. The inter-disciplinary approach in teaching and research in the study of religions is only beginning to find acceptance in some departments of religious studies in Nigerian universities. In the Nigerian context of the study of religions, the crucial components gained for professional development from contact with other professionals is often ignored or at best trivialized. It is worth noting, however, that some developments since 1997 suggest a realization of the need to review courses in religious studies in some universities to make academia in tune with realities in the society generally. The department of religions, University of Ilorin, for instance now has courses such as "Christianity and Social Justice," "Christianity and Financial Activities", "The Gospel in Industrial Society", "Feminism and the Bible", "New Age Movements," "Women in African Religion," "Religion and Communication," "Youth and Religion," and "Religion and Science," among others.

Again, there is a dearth of role models for women who teach religious studies in Nigerian higher educational institutions. Mentoring is near impossible between women, hence female teachers of religious studies have to brave working with senior male colleagues as role models. Unless the concerned female teacher is determined to ignore all insinuations about her integrity and level of morality, it becomes difficult to enjoy mentoring from a male colleague. This is because the growth of religious studies in Nigeria was led and is still largely dominated by men. The efforts of the Circle of Concerned African Women Theologians is worthy of mention in providing female scholars of religion with voices and avenues to express themselves. The Circle was founded by Prof. Mercy Amba Oduyoye in 1989 to provide space for African women from Africa to do communal theology based on their religious, cultural, and social experiences. The Circle is involved in research about HIV and AIDS and incorporating this in the training of theologians. It has a mission to undertake research, writing, and publishing on African issues from a woman's perspective. It has about five hundred members with a spread to over 25 countries. Consequently, the situation is changing, but there is room for improvement concerning integrating gender into structures for the study of religions.

This chapter aims at presenting a brief but comprehensive survey of the challenges pertaining to gender and women's issues in the teaching of religious studies in some Nigerian universities. Suggestions on how these challenges may be managed will also be offered. Methodology for the work includes the conduct of interviews with participants and keen observers of the Nigerian higher education system. Relevant literature will be consulted to facilitate a theoretical appreciation of current developments in the Nigerian higher educational system. In addition, books and articles by female teachers of religious studies in Nigerian higher institutions will be examined.

Setting the Context

The issue of gender is basic to nearly all human concerns in society. Gender may be understood to refer to defined capacities and attributes assigned to persons based on their alleged sexual characteristics. It is imbued with complexities that exert profound concerns at various levels and in different sectors of human endeavor. Both at the conceptual and practical levels, gender and its effects on humanity have engaged scholars over the years. What then is gender? Gender is "a concept imbued with notions of differences-hierarchy, opposition and inevitably, power relations." Also, gender is "informed by assumed capabilities for individuals based primarily on their sexual anatomy" (Olademo 2009: 9). There have been debates on the definition of gender, the effect of gender, the composition of gender, and the interrelationship of gender with other socio-analytical tools in scholarship and at the practical level. Thus gender has been at the center of debates and continues to be solely because its purview affects and is affected by power constructions, utilizations, and relations. Consequently, the relevance and imperativeness of gender and its discourse in the teaching of religions in academia emanates from its compelling role as a socio-analytical tool for social practice.

The teaching of religious studies in Nigerian Universities can partly be traced to the interest of religious groups, mainly Christian and Islamic groups/communities.

These groups perceived the study of religions in the university as a possible way to entrench and exert influence on the polity. Although the curriculum and methodology of teaching religions in the universities differ from what obtains in the seminaries or Quranic schools, yet in certain ways there are common features, especially as concerns affiliations.

Nigeria is arguably the most populous African nation with over one hundred universities comprising federal (27), state (36) and privately owned (41) institutions (see www.nuc.edu.ng). All three categories of universities present examples of departments of religious studies with variations in curricula. My aim in this chapter is to review how gender fares in the teaching of religions in Nigerian universities. In this regard, I intend to examine the place of gender in the curriculum, and the methodology for teaching religions. I will also attempt to assess the place of female scholars of religion in Nigerian Universities in terms of teaching and research. In sum, this chapter provides an analysis of the import of gender for the teaching of religions in Nigerian universities.

The Teaching of Religions in Nigerian Universities

Curriculum

I acknowledge a published essay by Jacob Olupona (1996), which focuses on some issues concerning the teaching of religions in institutions of higher learning in Nigeria. Some of his observations may be reiterated in this chapter. Of the over one hundred universities in Nigeria in 2010 (see the list at www.nuc.edu.ng), 40 per cent award degrees in one, two or three religions: Christian, Islamic and/or African religions, at the undergraduate, graduate, and doctoral levels. Generally, these departments of religions or religious studies employ a critical approach to the study of religions as opposed to a theological appraisal as obtains in seminary. In addition to these three major religions, courses are offered on Asian religions from a comparative perspective. Such religions include Hinduism, Buddhism, Taoism, and Confucianism. To a large extent, the content, methodology, and style of teaching these Asian religions depend on the versatility, knowledge, and literature that are available to the lecturer in charge. Moreover, there is no uniformity in the content of courses taught on religions in Nigerian universities save for the 2004 commendable innovation of the National University Commission (NUC) in coming up with a benchmark, which is meant to serve as the minimum requirements for all departments of religions/religious studies in Nigerian universities.

Again, the prevailing religion of the immediate host community often influences where the emphasis of teaching a particular religion rests. This is especially true of Northern Nigeria, which is predominantly Muslim and, as a result, Christian Studies are rarely found in the universities there. The predominantly Christian Southern Nigeria however offers Islamic, Christian and African religious studies in the universities to which they serve as hosts. As opposed to what obtained before 1984, able and qualified personnel are available to teach the three major religious traditions in Nigerian universities. In addition, courses are offered on the sociology of religion in some of these departments of religions.[1] Courses on methods and theory of religion also feature in the curricula of some departments of religions in Nigerian universities. Worthy of note is the shift at policy level concerning the study of African religions in Nigerian universities. Whereas it could be asserted in the past that the study of African religions was perceived as *praeparatis evangelica*, this is no longer true. Some Nigerian universities now offer first degrees and Masters degrees in African religions. The examples of the Department of Religious Studies, University of Ibadan, and the University of Ilorin come readily to mind in this regard. The teaching of African religions can now be said to be at par with the teaching of Christian and Islamic Studies in Nigerian universities as first, Masters, and Doctoral degrees in the three religions are now possible. However, there is disparity on the personal level of the affiliation of teachers of African religions to the religion. A good number of scholars of African religions are non-practitioners and though the argument over whether this is a good or bad thing could go either way, there is something to be gained by considering it. It is heart-warming to note that scholars of religions in Nigerian universities now utilize categories in the discipline's methodology and theoretical schema to describe their work. Indeed, in addition to this, scholars of religion now employ interdisciplinary methods and research tools in their work.

Personnel

As has been noted, it is quite common for scholars to pursue research on their own religious traditions and communities. Consequently, scholars of religion often operate with two if not more identities in the departments of religions. These scholars represent, subscribe to, and criticize their religious traditions at the same time. It is fairly common in departments of religious studies to retain the services of a former brilliant student as a lecturer. As a result of this, some scholars of religions have become lecturers in the very departments which nurtured them and this has serious implications for the system as well as for the individuals concerned.[2] Such implications include the sustenance of an old status quo which may impede innovative initiatives in curriculum review. However, another implication is for innovative reviews suggested by such lecturers to be discounted because they are viewed as upsetting known methodologies in the study of religions. Also, recruitment could be done through advertising positions, holding interviews, and verifying credentials as well as proficiency.

---

[1]   Examples include the Departments of religious studies at Obafemi Awolowo University, Ile-Ife, University of Ibadan, Ibadan, and Lagos State University, Ojoo.

[2]   This writer is an apposite example having graduated from the department of religions with a B.A. (Hons), M.A. in Christian Studies, and a Ph.D. in Philosophy; and lectured in the same department for the past 20 years

Worthy of mention, however, is the fact that more male scholars of religions are employed whereas female scholars are few. Though it is true that the number of students applying for the study of religions in Nigerian universities has continued to decrease, in recent years, the percentage of males to females has been nearly 50/50 in some universities.[3] This may be attributed to the increasing attention paid to the education of girls by government and non-governmental organizations. Again, some states in Nigeria now operate free and compulsory education at the primary level; these include Akwa Ibom and Lagos States. Career opportunities for women are at par with those for their male counterparts in the Nigerian polity. The only challenge for woman who aspires to teach in the university is the ability to combine domestic expectations with rigorous academic work; and though challenging, it can be done. This stance is buttressed by the female lecturers in Nigerian universities who successfully combine domestic expectations with academic pursuits. Consequently, reasons for the low employment of female scholars of religions in Nigerian universities would have to be sought beyond the non-availability of suitably qualified experts. I would like to place on record the dire need for in-house training for scholars of religions in Nigerian universities, especially in the area of theory and methodology because there is a gap in the theoretical analysis of religious studies in many academic papers presented at conferences of associations of religious studies scholars in Nigeria. This is crucial for effective teaching of the subjects by lecturers. This training could take the form of workshops, symposia ,or retreats in which experts from within and from outside Nigeria are frequently invited to teach young scholars in these areas. I would lay the onus of doing this at the door of associations concerned about the teaching of religions in higher institutions in Nigeria. Examples include the Nigerian Association for the Study of Religions (NASR), the National Association for the Study of Religion and Education (NASRED), the Nigerian Association for Biblical Studies (NABIS), the Nigerian Association for Teachers of Islamic Studies (NATAIS), and the African Association for the Study of Religions (AASR), which is a regional association.

Teaching

The atmosphere in which religions are taught in Nigerian universities could be described as challenging. Lecturers are stressed to the limit due to a number of avoidable problems. These include, but are not limited to, demands to engage in administrative work in departments, a lack of books and journals, social conditions—irregular supply of electricity, crowded classrooms, cultism, threats on the job, sexual harassment (male and female)—and inadequate funding. The most crucial has been described as the "book famine" (Olupona 1996). An attempt by lecturers to ameliorate this famine through the production of handouts (prepared notes) was allegedly abused and this resulted in an official ban on handouts in

---

[3]   This is true of the University of Ilorin, Ilorin.

some universities. Again, Nigerian universities enjoyed acquiring new books at the expense of the World Bank under the World Bank book project, but this initiative has not been sustained. Invariably, teaching in our lecture rooms continues the tradition of students putting down everything the lecturer says, only to regurgitate the same materials at the exams. Certain changes are, however, worthy of mention in this regard. Due to the opportunities of foreign fellowships and sponsorships, some young scholars of religions who travel for short stays outside the country return with current books in their area of study and utilize materials from these books for their lectures. Some of these books are also made available for the use of students. In addition, these young scholars on returning home introduced their students to the use of the Internet through assignments from the web. The infinite materials on the web has reduced the negative impact of the "book famine" on the study of religion significantly, but then the Internet and its use are not available to everyone in Nigeria. Students are also encouraged to embark on fieldtrips as a method of learning and research. This is in addition to passing a course on research methods, which encompasses techniques on the collection of oral and written data, literature review, and choice of topic, the language of research, and reference materials. The situation concerning the teaching of religions in Nigerian universities is therefore improving, but more needs to be done to enhance it.

Gender and the Teaching of Religions in Nigerian Universities

Curriculum

The emergence of gender as an analytical tool for scholarly enquiry in the study of religions in Nigerian universities is yet to be fully grasped. In fact the few glimpses of the cognizance of gender in the teaching of religions in Nigerian universities could best be described as efforts by individual scholars (mostly female) rather than any clear prescription by the curricula. Some general courses on the role of women in specific religions may be found in the curricula of some universities, but then gender issues are not entirely synonymous with women's role in any specific religion. Moreover, to effectively integrate gender as an analytical tool in the study of religions, there is a need for some ground-breaking understanding of theories and methodologies in gender studies and these are lacking. The situation is made compelling by the fact that in Africa religion is the basic principle from which gender construction is derived. Consequently, it becomes imperative for scholars of religions to prioritize the understanding and utilization of gender as a concept for research and teaching. A lack of this stance is reflected in the latent patriarchal coloring of the scientific study of religion, which has been described as being "enmeshed in notions of male cultural dominance and female passivity." (Braun and McCutcheon 2000: 150).

The question to ask at this juncture is why has the curricula for teaching religions in Nigerian universities undermined "gender" in spite of the global awareness of gender as a crucial tool for understanding human societies and social relations? Responses to this question may vary, but underlying these would be the realization that events in the universities only reflect the disposition of the host societies. The will to change perceptions and orientations could prove challenging and this may account for the slow response to gender issues in the study of religions in Nigeria. Added to this is the dual problem of the availability of relevant books and experts in the area of gender studies. I would argue that there is the need to move beyond the stage where individual lecturers innovatively imbue gender perspectives into their teachings of religions in the classrooms, as is the case presently in Nigerian universities. I would advocate that gender as a concept should be integrated into the curricula of the study and teaching of religions in Nigerian universities. This would compel the provision of all that is needed (books, training of experts, logistics) to facilitate the entrenchment of gender into the mainstream study of religions in Nigerian universities.

Personnel

Male lecturers of religions outnumber female lecturers in Nigerian universities and some reasons can be adduced for this. First, until recently, few women applied for the study of religions in Nigerian universities. In the University of Ilorin for instance, female enrollment between 1990 and 2002 ranged from 0 per cent to 30 per cent of the population of students in the department of religions. Moreover, the percentage of female students decreases even further during graduate studies. Second, there are very few role models for upcoming female lecturers. This has undermined the potential for aiming to succeed. Role models could serve as sustaining forces in the face of intimidating challenges in the bid to attain set goals in any profession. Third, the absence of mentoring arises out of the lack of role models. However, mention needs to be made of male lecturers who are committed to rectifying the imbalance in the recruitments of male and female scholars of religion in Nigerian universities. Such male scholars serve as mentors to upcoming female scholars,[4] but this often opens up such female scholars to uncomplimentary remarks in a society where male–female relationships are usually construed in sexual terms. If a female scholar is not resilient and well focused, such mentoring may end unceremoniously. Fourth, there is an unspoken but inherent assumption of society that women are best suited for marriage and childbearing rather than graduate studies and the building of a career. Some female scholars who brave the combination of building a career and childbearing have stories to tell. This is because married women often find the combination of domestic work and graduate studies cumbersome.

Female lecturers may be found in nearly all departments of religions/religious studies in Nigerian universities. All, except a very few, of these female scholars of

---

4   A commendable example is the unflinching support of Prof. Jacob Kehinde Olupona for the training of female scholars of religion in Africa but especially in Nigeria.

religions specialize in Christian and comparative religious studies. The Lagos State University, Ojoo has the largest number of female lecturers of religions, five in all,[5] whereas the University of Ilorin has four,[6] Ambrose Alli University Ekpoma has three,[7] the University of Jos has two,[8] as does the University of Ibadan.[9] Obafemi Awolowo University, Benue State University, and Ahmadu Bello University have one female scholar of religion each.[10] Female scholars of Islamic studies are very few and far between, which may be taken as a fair reflection of the prescribed roles for women in Islam.

Publications by female scholars of religions in Nigerian Universities comprise articles in journals (local and international) and a few books.[11] These publications are few but increasing every year. The National Association of Scholars of Religions has proved to be a veritable avenue of publication for female scholars of religion. Thus, female scholars contribute to book projects and thereby provide academic materials on gender studies in religions. This is in addition to the contributions of international associations of scholars of religions, especially in the African sub-region. The agenda of these projects include attempts to examine how African religions construct gender and to offer a feminist analysis of this enterprise. This could result in new feminist interpretations of old normative and patriarchal narratives. In addition, these projects attempt to give a "voice" to women and utilize women's stories for academic research work.

Challenges

The basic challenge to integrating "gender" into the mainstream study of religions in Nigerian universities is to improve the training of scholars. This could be through short-term courses, workshops, and symposia (local and international). The provision of books and reputable journals that focus on gender should also be pursued. A review of the current curricula for the study of religions in Nigerian universities is imperative if gender is to be an important academic paradigm of discourse. Once the curriculum is reviewed along this line, gender as an analytical tool of academic discourse in religion would move from the margin

---

[5] These are Peju Bashua, N. Mbisike, K. Amosu, and O. Oyinlola.

[6] These include O. Olademo, B. Akinfenwa, M. Daramola, and B. Dopamu.

[7] These are C.O. Isiramen, B.G. Ogedengbe. and F. Falaiye.

[8] These are Kate Torkwembe and Pauline Lire.

[9] Drs. Akintunde and Labeodan.

[10] B.O. Bateye, V.W. Pepetua, and N.N.P. Digga respectively.

[11] Examples include Isiramen (1998: 44), Akintunde (2001), Internet sources: www.foundation-partnership.org "Gender in the Making of Nigerian University System" by Charmaine Pereira, accessed on February 17, 2010. www.nuc.edu.ng List of Nigerian Universities, accessed on May 2, 2010. www.thecircleawt.org Circle of Concerned African Women Theologians, accessed on February 15, 2010.

to the mainstream. Such a development would also inevitably change the latent patriarchal coloring of religious studies and its teaching in Nigerian universities. Mentoring is another challenge that could be addressed by a correct orientation of female scholars who need to maintain their focus on academic professionalism rather than giving cognizance to side comments and distractions, whether the mentor is male or female.

Conclusion

This chapter has offered a primary overview of the place of gender and female scholars in the teaching of religions in Nigerian universities. It has shown that challenges exist in this regard in the areas of the curriculum, teaching, research, and the general welfare of scholars. The will to integrate gender into the mainstream study of religions is a pertinent and compelling one that should engage the attention of the authorities in charge of higher education in Nigeria.

Bibliography

Akintunde, Dorcas (ed.), *African Culture and the Quest for Women's Rights* (Ibadan: Sefer, 2001).

Braun, W. and R.T. McCutcheon (eds.), *Guide to the Study of Religion* (London: Cassell, 2000).

Friedan, B., *Feminine Mystique* (New York: Dell Publishers, 1983).

Isiramen, C.O., "The Social and Religious Vices of Abortion," in D. Asaju and C. Isiramen (eds.), *Issues in Ethics and Religion: Contemporary Trends* (Ado-Ekiti, Nigeria: De-Gabson Publishers, 1998).

King, U. (ed.), *Religion and Gender* (Oxford: Blackwell, 1995).

Malson, R.M.O., J.F. Barr, S. Westphal-Wihl, and M. Wyer (eds.), *Feminist Theory in Practice and Process* (Chicago: University of Chicago Press, 1989).

Oduyoye, M.A., *Daughters of Anowa: African Women and Patriarchy* (New York: Orbis, 1995).

Ogundipe-Leslie, O., *African Women and Critical Transformation* (Trenton, NJ: African World Press, 1994).

Olademo, Oyeronke, *Gender in Yoruba Oral Traditions* (Lagos: CBAAC, 2009).

Olajubu, Oyeronke, *Women in the Yoruba Religious Sphere* (Albany: State University of New York Press, 2003).

Olupona, Jacob Kehinde, "The Study of Religions in Nigeria: Past, Present, and Future," in J. Platvoet, James Cox, and Jacob Oupona (eds.), *The Study of Religions in Africa: Past, Present and Prospects* (Cambridge: Roots and Branches, 1996), pp. 185–210.

Sharman, A. and K.K. Young (eds.), *Feminism and World Religions* (New York: State University of New York Press, 1999).

Steady, F.C., *The Black Woman Cross-Culturally* (Cambridge, MA: Schenkman Publishers, 1994).

Surdakasa, N., *The Strength of Our Mothers* (Trenton, NJ: Africa World Press, 1996).

Chapter 5
Mainstreaming HIV/AIDS in African Religious and Theological Studies

Musa W. Dube

Introduction: Fifty Years of HIV/AIDS Work

> Friends, we are at a time of great opportunity and great hope. Because of all that we have achieved, we now have the opportunity to build long-term sustainability onto our current crisis management efforts. We must plan and act not just for today but for the next 25 years. With every ounce of our intelligence, innovation and determination, we must advance both social change and science in the fight against AIDS. (Peter Piot, Toronto August 2006)

> The silence of African Indigenous Religions on HIV and AIDS is eloquent. (Chitando 2007: 188)

At the Toronto International AIDS conference of 2006, Peter Piot challenged the international community, saying: "we must plan and act not just for today, but for the next twenty five years…" He called the international community to move its response to HIV/AIDS from a crisis approach of the first 25 years to a long-term plan for the next 25 years. Consequently, I had originally entitled this chapter "Twenty-Five Years of Living with HIV/AIDS and the Next Twenty-Five Years of Studying Religion in the HIV/AIDS Context: Where Do We Go from Here?" The title might be quite misleading since it may suggest that in the academy we have been grappling with studying religion/theology in the first 25 years with HIV/AIDS and that we are now at a point where we are able to make an evidence-based analysis about where we need to go in the second 25 years. It has been repeatedly said that faith-based institutions were slow in responding to HIV/AIDS (Chitando 2007: 19–37), but I am wondering if it may be said that in the first 25 years academic institutions of religion/theology were even more silent, indifferent and less responsive in their research, teaching, and community engagement by failing to design programs that situate theological/religious education in the HIV/AIDS context (Maluleke 2003: 63). Those of us who are located in academic institutions studying religion are in a better position to examine ourselves and to assess how much we have done in the area of curriculum transformation in the first 25 years of HIV/AIDS and what we are putting in place for the current 25 years.

I think that one significant step towards charting the way forward in HIV/AIDS and theological studies must begin with all of us taking note of our lives and our engagement with the HIV/AIDS context in the first 25 years and planning our studies in religion/theological education/training for the current 25 years within an HIV/AIDS context. It is this approach that will assist us concretely to come to terms with the amount of work that we have done, how much more we still need to do, and how we need to do it. Since I am one of those who have been actively involved in seeking to situate my work in the context of HIV/AIDS and to invite others to the same, I will spend a significant part of this chapter telling you my story of the past 25 years. But my story is only told to invite academic scholars of religion/theology to situate their work in the context of HIV/AIDS in the past 25 years: to retrace their own stories on how they have engaged with HIV/AIDS and how they can engage HIV/AIDS in the next 25 years.

Living and Working in the HIV/AIDS-Positive World

One thing for sure, 25 years ago, I was only 18 years old. And another sure thing is that 25 years from now, I will be retired. I think this speaks for itself. Most of us have and will live most of our working lives in the HIV/AIDS context. I remember that I was doing my Form Three in Shashe River Secondary School, in the central part of Botswana, when our biology teacher, whom I only remember as Mrs Wright, told us that a new virus was discovered and it was causing incurable illness. I remember the moment of announcement in the laboratory, but I had plenty of time to forget this announcement as I went on to do my next two years of high school, finishing in 1983. I passed and I went to the University of Botswana where I registered for a degree in Humanities, majoring in environmental science, theology, and religious studies between 1984 and 1988. By then, of course, there were frequent government advertisements or talks on the radio about HIV/AIDS and the need to condomise, the need to screen all blood for HIV/AIDS in the hospital, and the use of disposable needles. But as a student of theology and environmental science, never, at that point, did HIV/AIDS come to have any bearing on the contents of my curriculum. There was no lecturer who ever brought us to think about HIV/AIDS in relation to our theological training or environmental science. And neither did I ever think anything was amiss (Kgalemang 2004: 141).

In 1989–90, I registered for my graduate studies in Durham, where I did my MA in New Testament Studies. Again I read Greek, the Gospels, feminist theology, Pauline letters and wrote my thesis on Mary as our Ancestor, from an African feminist perspective. Yet, once again, in the whole program HIV/AIDS never became an issue for consideration or discussion. I returned to the University of Botswana in 1990 now as a lecturer, while applying for a place to do my Ph.D. studies. I taught the Gospels, Greek, Church History, Introduction to biblical studies, and I believe at no point did I think I should link HIV/AIDS with my work. In the public media the HIV/AIDS campaign was being intensified. Each one of us was now thinking about HIV/AIDS, silently wondering if one is already positive, if one will get infected, if one will die of AIDS, if one's child or partner would be positive. HIV testing centers were rare then. The atmosphere therefore was of growing fear, growing insecurity, growing uncertainty about the future and growing stigmatization as people living with HIV were regarded as immoral and reaping what they sow. By then HIV/AIDS was a gathering storm above our heads, and every warning said, "prepare for it will be a very heavy storm." Most of the time it seemed like a baseless myth. But that time we had an option to think that maybe the storm would pass by, maybe it would be diverted, maybe it would not be so bad. Many of us by then had never seen someone with AIDS in our families, villages, churches, neighborhood, or workplace.

Between 1992 and 1997, I went away to Vanderbilt University in the U.S.A. to do my Ph.D. in New Testament Studies. This was an exciting time for my training in the academic study of religion. I was learning such exciting and stimulating histories, methods, and theories of reading the Bible. I was also reading classical Greek, Koine Greek, Ancient Hebrew, French, and the like. I had inspiring lecturers who made me look forward to being a scholar of the Bible and to make an impact in the academic world. Consistent with the rest of my theological education, I heard nothing about HIV/AIDS in the academic halls. Neither did I notice that something was missing.

There was one difference about this time, however. The story of HIV/AIDS had moved on from a smoldering storm at a distance and had begun to hit the ground in my country. I received letters, messages, telephone calls that "so and so is sick"; "so and so is dead." During those days there were no antiretroviral drugs (ARVs), (or if they were there, it was something we heard from the likes of Magic Johnson, who said his blood tested clear of HIV. What a huge surprise to the world when Magic Johnson made this announcement in 1996/97). The storm had begun to hit the ground, and every house was hit hard in Botswana. I was away and had to grieve alone in a foreign land. As I wrote elsewhere, this, perhaps, is the point where I began to link my academic training in religion with HIV/AIDS—though I must confess it was quite indirect: I still did not see what HIV/AIDS required of us. I had begun to write gospel songs about HIV/AIDS, about healing, about hope, mostly to deal with my grief in a foreign land (see Dube 2003b). Most of the songs I wrote during this time went into the book *Africa Praying: A Handbook of HIV&AIDS Sensitive Sermon Guidelines*. One of the songs that I wrote after a devastating telephone message informed me that a friend of mine had died of AIDS went as follows:

Jabulani Africa inkosi ikhona ... rejoice Africa Your Lord God liveth.
Jabulani lonke, Jabulani Sizwe ... rejoice all, rejoice nation
Jabula mama loba baba ... rejoice mothers and Fathers
Inkosi ikhona ... Our God is with us. (Dube 2003b: 4)

The song was a typical expression of hope in the face of hopelessness, that's what the song was about. At that point, I thought when I got back home I would teach these songs to my interdenominational choir, Hope for Today. The plan was that we would produce an album that would raise money for orphaned children. Even at this point I still did not see that HIV/AIDS required more from me as a scholar and educator of religion. I did not realize that HIV/AIDS could not be compartmentalized; that in fact it was permeating everything and required the response of all sectors, all departments, all disciplines, including academic theology and religious studies.

And so I came back to Botswana with my Ph.D. in New Testament Studies and with my head packed with dreams. Career dreams—the books I wanted to write from a postcolonial feminist perspective, which was the line I explored in my dissertation, were roaming and roving in my head, ready to be born. Little did I realize that perhaps the course of my career had already been redefined by HIV/AIDS. I began teaching the Synoptic Gospels, Johannine literature, Pauline Letters, Biblical Exegesis, and Greek in the University of Botswana. Still I had not found a way of adding HIV/AIDS in/to my teaching, although by now I was an HIV/AIDS activist. I was busy trying to find sponsors for the album that I wanted to produce in order to raise money for orphaned children. Meanwhile the public HIV/AIDS campaign was repeatedly underlining that HIV/AIDS is everybody's business; that each one of us must ask herself or himself how they can be part of promoting prevention, quality care, breaking the stigma, and minimizing the impact.

For me, what finally brought the whole thing together were a number of issues: First, the statistics by then were rating the infection rate as 37 per cent among young and sexually active populations in Botswana. Second, I was teaching my Synoptic Gospels to a class that had about 250 students and I looked across the class and said to myself: "Thirty-seven per cent of these students may not be alive in the next ten years." This reality just shocked me and threw me into a major career crisis: I began to ask myself: "Why am I talking about the historical context of Jesus, redaction criticism and all this stuff if it will not keep these students alive?" I had a huge crisis of meaning, the meaning of life, the meaning of my career and its purpose (Dube 2003a: 12–13). As if I have not written about this story before, as if I have not told it several times before, when I was writing this chapter, again I wept. Then I said to myself: "Why are you weeping, Musa? Why?"

I was weeping for this history, for this time, for the past, the present, and the future, that brought us to live our lives and do our scholarship in a traumatic context of HIV/AIDS. I was weeping for broken dreams, for lost lives, for a future that we could no longer claim. It is a time that brought us face to face with our shattered dreams. I had spent five years in graduate school splitting my brains for doing scholarship in a certain way and dreaming concrete future dreams of the route I sought to pursue. I arrived home and suddenly discovered I had to relearn how to teach the New Testament and how to do my scholarship in a HIV/AIDS context. I even had to face that moment when I asked myself: "What is the importance of teaching New Testament when people are dying of AIDS?" My whole career was put into a big question mark. As I write elsewhere, I had reached a *cul de sac*, one that called for a "U-turn" and to find another way forward (Dube 2004: 4–12).

In 2006, I went to the Society of Biblical Literature (SBL) in Washington DC and met one African student doing her graduate school, who had been reading my earlier work and she said to me: "Musa why have you changed? Why are you not writing about postcolonial feminist hermeneutics anymore? We need you to continue writing about postcolonial ways of reading the Bible." I said: "Believe me, I am trying. And believe me, I want to, but I just seem not to be getting there since HIV/AIDS has put completely new demands on what I do as a scholar, how I do it and why I do my work. But I still hope that I will write a second book on postcolonial feminist hermeneutics of the Bible." As a matter of fact, I told her: "I have been having book plans and eager publishers for the past few years, without ever getting there." The phenomenon of HIV/AIDS has changed many of us. As Peter Piot observed in his opening speech to the 2006 Toronto conference: "Please, let us have no illusion that one fine day, the world will return to what it was before AIDS. No, AIDS has simply rewritten the rules. And to prevail we too must rewrite these rules."

But let me return to my Synoptic Gospels class in the University of Botswana. As I write elsewhere, one of the things that brought me to a further crisis of meaning in my career was the content of the Gospels (Dube 2003a: 13). During that time, there were no ARVs, or once more, they were so expensive that we preferred not to talk about them, because the majority of people could not afford them. Our governments could not afford them. But then while reading the Gospels in the HIV/AIDS contexts where ARVs were not an option we found that:

> ...the miracles of healing seem to chime throughout the texts. As we read, we became consciously aware that we are reading two very different texts: the ancient biblical text and the text of our lives in the HIV/AIDS context. The merging of these two texts became sharply ironic, for Jesus went around healing all diseases and illness, while on the ground and the historical moment that we lived, there was no healing. (Dube 2003a: 13)

Contrary to the boundless healing in the Gospels, I also pointed out that in the HIV/AIDS context:

> If you had HIV, if your friend, your relative, your neighbour, your classmate was infected—then you knew that there was no healing. What then was the meaning of the healing stories in the gospels in the HIV&AIDS context? How should we be reading them? I really had no answer. If I had to address these questions, I could not really find them in my text books and biblical commentaries. Linking HIV&AIDS with my training had to be an experimental experience in the context that demanded such a connection. (Dube 2002: 122)

Fortunately, the HIV/AIDS Information and Education Campaign underlined that all of us needed to struggle with how they can contribute towards HIV/AIDS prevention, care-giving, breaking stigma, minimizing the impact, and addressing social justice issues. The HIV/AIDS struggle therefore was a multi-sectoral approach; it was everybody's business. My experiment included encouraging students to take the healing miracles and read them with the community (Dube 2002); it included encouraging students to write their theses on HIV/AIDS issues; it involved encouraging my colleagues to begin to think about how they could address HIV/AIDS in their areas of specialization; and it included ensuring that I talked about HIV/AIDS in my public speaking events (Dube 2004). Meanwhile, I was still trying to push the gospel album project and got zero sponsorship save for the educational part. I managed to produce a documentary video for church leaders about the plight of orphans in Botswana. My musical album remains a dream, I must say, but one that pointed me to many avenues for engagement with HIV &AIDS in my academic work.

Ecumenical and Circle Engagement with HIV/AIDS

A big break came in 2001–02, when an Africa-wide ecumenical mobilization of the church culminated in the Plan of Action, which listed theology and ethics as central to constructive response to HIV/AIDS (World Council of Churches 2002b: 7). Two significant things happened. First, given my initiatives on mainstreaming HIV/AIDS in the curriculum, I was asked to be an HIV/AIDS and gender theological consultant, charged with training other academic scholars of religion and theology on mainstreaming HIV/AIDS in their programs. The second significant event was that at its Africa-wide meeting held in Addis Abba in 2002, the Circle of Concerned African Women Theologians adopted the ecumenical Action Plan and drew up its own five-year strategic plan on doing theology as women in the HIV/AIDS context. The strategic plan of the Circle ended in September 2006, but another five-year period of continuing with HIV/AIDS theology was adopted at the all-Africa conference in Yaounde, Cameroon in 2007. From these two events, that came to be closely entwined with my life, I will highlight some of the issues that are needed for the next 25 years of HIV/AIDS theology.

Let me pause here with my story of HIV/AIDS and studies in religion/theological education and reiterate the points or questions behind this storytelling. The questions that we need to put to ourselves as religion/theological educators are: how has religion/theological education engaged HIV/AIDS in the past 25 years? And how was the discipline engaged by HIV/AIDS? Second, what should future developments in academic studies of religion/theology and HIV/AIDS cover? Then, making the personal political (a well-known phrase in feminist discourse): What is your story as theological/religion educator in the context of HIV/AIDS? What is the story of your institution? How have you included HIV/AIDS in your courses? Which programs have you designed to study religion/

theology in the HIV/AIDS context? What research have you, your students, and institutions embarked upon in the past 25 years and what are your plans for the next 25 years? The point of my long and "old" story was to divine myself, our institutions, and our academic programs in religion/theological education. I think each one of us has one way or another of answering these questions. But above all, telling our stories will assist us to hear some of the work that has been going on in our faith and academic institutions and among our students. The narratives will assist us to share our experiences and hence inform and empower each other on the way forward.

If my story is anything to go by, then I am correct to say that academic programs of religion/theology abroad and here on the African continent, have been quite slow in responding programmatically to HIV/AIDS in their teaching, research, and community service. My story has shown that I did all my theological education, from 1984 to 1997, in a world that was already living with HIV/AIDS and yet never even once did HIV/AIDS become a subject of inquiry in theological/ religion studies in the academic halls. This late response of religion/theological education is attested to in Steve de Gruchy's introduction to the *Journal of Theology for Southern Africa special issue on Church, HIV and AIDS in Southern Africa*, published in July 2006. De Gruchy writes: "This double volume of the journal is our small attempt *to begin to respond* to some of these concerns" (de Gruchy 2006: 3). Please note that he frankly says, it is a "small attempt *to begin to respond*" to the concerns of HIV/AIDS. It is a statement that is largely true about academic religion and theology's engagement with HIV/AIDS. Many of us are yet to begin to responding in our small ways. Another eloquent indication is found in the reception of the two books that I edited while working for the World Council of Churches. The first book, *HIV&AIDS and the Curriculum: Methods of Integrating HIV&AIDS in Theological Programmes* was published for academics to give lecturers hints on how the academy can mainstream HIV/AIDS in their programs. The second book, *Africa Praying: A Handbook of HIV/AIDS Sensitive Sermons*, was published to assist faith communities to mainstream HIV/AIDS in their teaching and preaching. The latter went on to its fifth printing within three years, whereas the one for academics has not done nearly as well.

My story also highlighted that as a religion/theological educator my involvement came almost as a result of shock. It occurred when HIV/AIDS stood face to face with me, mockingly asking me about the relevance of my career and my teaching. It was then, only then, that I in fact began to mainstream HIV/AIDS in my teaching and research. From the first 25 years of living and working in an HIV positive world, it was only in the last ten years that I came to realize and accept that the HIV/AIDS context is not supposed to be on the periphery, but central to my work as a scholar of religion/theology. Although some may have had a longer involvement and history of studying religion/theology in the context of HIV/AIDS than most of us, on average, many began to be more actively involved in the last six years of the first 25 years of the outbreak. Yet, our hearts must not be troubled, for this chapter does not seek to take anyone on a guilt trip. There are other reasons why the academic field of religion did not respond early. For example, HIV/AIDS itself was a new epidemic and it was an incubative one for that matter—it thus took more than a decade before people could truly grasp its depth, impact, and demands. Since then,

> HIV and AIDS epidemic has affected and highlighted the limitations of current human knowledge, institutions and structures and called for a much intensified search for better and other ways. It was not only the scientific/medical knowledge that was challenged and shown to be limited by HIV and AIDS epidemic. Rather, just about all human departments and institutions were brought to a test in the face of a new disease—one that turned out to be highly infectious, incurable and to a large extent terminal. The cultural, social, political and economical structures, institutions and their accompanying bodies of knowledge were affected and shown to be limited and limiting. (World Council of Churches 2002a: 6)

Academic programs of religion/theology have had their share of grappling with producing relevant knowledge. Luckily, a lot of work has been done to stand up to this challenge, as exampled by the Circle of Concerned African Women Theologians and others, which gives us useful hints on the demands studying religion/theology in the next 25 years of living in a HIV/AIDS positive world, and the annotated bibliography compiled by the Centre for HIV and AIDS, Religion and Theology (CHART) compiled in the School of religion and theology in the University of KwaZulu Natal.

Lessons from Africa-Wide Training of Academic Theologians on Mainstreaming HIV/AIDS in Theological Education

I therefore want to conclude my story by highlighting what I have learnt in the last ten years of the first 25 years of HIV/AIDS and what it can contribute to the next 25 years of religious/theological education in that context. My suggestions will be drawn first, from my work with the World Council of Churches and, second, from the Circle of African Women Theologians' research.

After joining the World Council of Churches in 2002, I carried out training of training (TOT) workshops from 2002 to 2005. Thereafter this work was taken over by Ezra Chitando, for English-speaking Africa, and Charles Klagba, for French-speaking academic theologians and a third theologian was employed for Portuguese-speaking Africa although they did not last. I have not been able to establish how many other theological lecturers have been trained by Chitando and Klagba so far. During my time with the WCC, I trained up to 740 faith and state-based academic scholars of religion from all over Africa (save for North Africa) on mainstreaming HIV/AIDS in theological programs. During this process, I came to realize that many African religion/theological programs and educators are quite archaic and hardly engage with the issues of their context because of the following reasons:

- Many programs were founded by Westerners or mother churches who transported their programs to Africa.
- Most African theologians and scholars of religion are trained in the West (like myself) and they are much more likely to maintain and reproduce the Eurocentric programs that they learnt, than to engage the issues of their context.
- Many faith-based academic institutions had a board of faith leaders, who had to approve any changes, hence limiting and controlling the freedom of the lecturers in the area of curriculum transformation.
- There are many other cases of laziness, where people felt more comfortable with keeping on teaching what they have always taught than with introducing new courses that demand research. The laziness also reflects heavy teaching loads that people carry and inadequate time, pay, and money for new innovations.
- But of course there were also issues of resources, where people said they had no money to buy new books or hire new teachers, for their programs were too full to add new courses or programs—congested programs were a popular excuse.
- Most faith-based academic institutions tend to have lecturers who are not adequately trained—they do not have doctorates, a factor that can only contribute to low standards in research and curriculum innovation. In fact, in most faith-based institutions research and publication were not required.
- Most faith-based scholars tend to have great trouble dealing with social issues and their structural base, leaning towards paradigms of personal morality. But since HIV/AIDS is an epidemic that is really structural, and one which is so closely intertwined with social evil, lack of social analysis speaks of inadequate engagement or on-surface engagements that can be quite stigmatizing.
- Most faith-based academic institutions do not offer African Indigenous Religions and are not always, if at all, conversant with inculturation, liberation, and African women theologies.
- In general, African religion/theological programs still need a great deal of decolonization in both content and the training of staff (Chitando 2008: 6–8).
- French-speaking public universities do not have departments of religion and theology, which disadvantages them from benefiting from government funds.

Because of the above conditions of work, many participants often said: "The workshop was very useful, but I do not have the power to add, or subtract to the course, let alone design new courses or programs." Of course, we need a more detailed report on the response of academic theologians who underwent TOTs workshops on methods of mainstreaming HIV/AIDS in the curriculum. A detailed analysis of the changes and challenges they confronted in their theological schools would be in order. Unfortunately, I could not get any access to the assessment of the Ecumenical Initiative for HIV and Aids in Africa (EHAIA), since the latest report is not yet officially released. But in his email response to my inquiry, Chitando, one of the people who took over my WCC job, wrote that "While Musa, Charles and I have pushed the agenda in theological institutions; departments of religious studies remain largely unmoved. It is easier to move a cemetery than to move a seminary." Chitando went on to say: "I hazard to suggest that while theology in Africa endeavours to be contextually sensitive, religious studies remains marooned in Euro-American captivity."[1]

From the above observations, a major item on the agenda of the next 25 years of living and studying religion/theology in the HIV+ world is curriculum transformation. African religion/theological education needs to be revamped and reorganized to address issues that are more pertinent to their context and day. Some of the issues are as follows:

- The future of religion/theological education in Africa needs leaders, who are willing to change policy, to guide program review and design new courses that are contextually relevant—this is a major challenge for all who are academic deans, principals, heads of departments, lecturers and board members of theology and religion schools.
- A greater involvement of people living with HIV is central to the study and research in HIV/AIDS, religion and theology in the second 25 years of living with HIV/AIDS. Hearing the voices and stories of people living with HIV is central to informing the kind of scholarship we do and how we do it. Further, academic departments of religion should seek formal collaborative working (research, teaching, and community engagements) relationships with associations of people living with HIV. INERELA+, which has representative chapters in each country, would be good place to begin.
- Future developments in curriculum transformation should make special efforts to give a respectful academic space to African Indigenous Religions. Given that most programs were missionary founded, there was no desire to place African Indigenous Religions in the curriculum or to train staff in the area (Chitando 2008: 187–8). Consequently, many theological institutions do not offer African Indigenous Religions and in places where they do, it is taught from a Christian perspective as something that needs conversion than a religion in its own right. More often than not African Indigenous Religions are taught by people who are not trained in the area.[2] With

---

[1] Email communication from Ezra Chitando, dated April 4, 2007.
[2] See the chapter by Adam arap Chepkwony in this volume.

current Pentecostal/charismatic movements, African Indigenous Religions are receiving one of the worst criticisms (Asamoah-Gyadu 2005: 172–7) that can be equated to that given in colonial times, if not worse. HIV/AIDS, however, has underlined that African Indigenous Religions are and will remain a central framework and resource, informing how people respond to life challenges and the events of their lives. Setting up a fund for the study of African Indigenous Religions and for training staff in the area will be in order.

- We also need institutional commitment towards research-based religion/ theological education from students, lecturers, and their supporters. This commitment should drive people to research and reflect from their specific contexts and to engage the same. It should also be demonstrated in willingness to give academic staff sabbaticals, paid study or research leave and other necessary grants. Institutions also need to make qualitative yearly research output a required part of salary raise and promotion for academic staff.

- Future developments in religion/theological studies and HIV/AIDS also demand commitment to training scholars to acquire the highest education they need and to make available research funds and research leave for lecturers, who, more often than not, are teaching very heavy loads. African scholars of religion/theology need to go away and get time to upgrade themselves.

- Further, curriculum transformation is needed from religion/theological institutions in the area of social engagement. Given that Africa as a whole is saddled with numerous ills such as poverty, violence, corruption, patriarchy, dictatorships, and HIV/AIDS, it is important that lecturers and their students should be equipped with tools of doing socially-engaged scholarship or what I have called "prophetically-healing scholarship" (Dube 2008: 3). Our religion/theological education needs tools of analyzing, addressing, and engaging gender oppression, poverty, violence, ethnicity, climate change, international injustice, national corruption, and discriminations of all forms—class, race, ethnic, health, and sexual identity-based oppression.

- Healthy networking between faith and academic institutions is needed. It was the theological poverty in faith-based institutions that led the WCC to embark on a program of challenging religion/theological educators to revisit their programs in order to empower faith-based leaders to respond constructively to HIV/AIDS. For me, this history underlines that academics constantly need to keep healthy and helpful relationships between the academy, faith institutions, and the community.

- Future developments in HIV/AIDS, religion and theology also demand the establishment of regional centers that will continue to train academicians, and encourage research and curriculum transformation in the area. While the WCC did a massive job to sponsor TOT workshops since 2002 and the production of relevant literature, it seems to me that one way of sustaining the work started is to establish centres and programmes that will continue to bring lecturers, students and faith leaders for training, reflection, dialogue and research on issues of health and social concerns. Indeed it is gratifying to note that such efforts have begun to emerge exemplified by CHART, the Center for HIV& AIDS, Religion and Theology in the University of Kwazulu Natal, and a more interdisciplinary center such as CASHA (Centre for Studies on HIV and AIDS) in the University of Botswana. In terms of graduate studies in HIV/AIDS, St. Paul's College in Limuru, Kenya, and the Ethiopian Graduate School of Theology and Makumira in Tanzania are notable. More efforts from other institutions are needed. In particular, it would be helpful if such efforts were strategically spread into various regions to enable access and affordability. The existence of the above programs, for example, suggests that East Africa is quite advanced in HIV/AIDS programs as compared to other African regions, such as west and central Africa.

- Given the character of HIV/AIDS, which interweaves with various social categories and permeates almost all departments of life, future approaches to religion and theology should be both socially engaged and interdisciplinary.

Circle Engagement with HIV/AIDS

When we ask about the future engagements with HIV/AIDS in academic studies of religion/theology, the Circle of Concerned African Women Theologians (henceforth Circle) will continue to play a key role. Apart from the EHAIA, which sponsored Africa-wide training in religion/theological education, the Circle represents the most deliberate and focused academic and faith engagement with HIV/AIDS in the academy. The Circle programmatically responded to HIV/AIDS under the then new leadership of Isabel Phiri in 2002, by establishing a research strategic plan to engage with HIV/AIDS for five years. The plan ended in 2006 with a review of what transpired and an adoption of another five-year term to continue engaging with HIV/AIDS and religion and gender. Since we are asking about future developments in religion/theological studies and HIV/AIDS, the Circle approach and experience gives many useful pointers. I encourage interested readers to have a look at the current focus on their website (www.the circlecawt. org). So far, the Circle has published at least six theological books since 2002 (see Phiri et al. 2003; Oduyoye and Amoah 2005; Dube and Kanyoro 2004; Amoah et al. 2005; and Phiri and Nadar 2006). They also collaborated closely with the EHAIA in researching, writing, and publishing relevant materials on HIV/ AIDS, religion/theology, and gender (see Phiri 2007; Nadar 2007; and Ntloedibe-Kuswani and Mambuluki 2007).

In 2006, I had the privilege of evaluating the literature that has come out of the Circle engagement with HIV/AIDS. The evaluation produced two long articles on what and how the Circle has been engaging with HIV/AIDS and what the future needs look like. The evaluative articles were in a volume edited by Ezra Chitando and Nontando Hadebe (see Dube 2009). The findings highlight the following strengths:

Strengths

- Circle work is a transformative and prophetic study of religion and theology, hence it engages social evils and seeks justice-oriented world. Patriarchal sin and its entire network of social evils are thoroughly interrogated. This is perhaps captured by the now famous statement of Teresa Okure, who holds that in fact HIV/AIDS consists of two viruses. The first one is the virus that assigns women an inferior status and the second one is the global economic injustice that exposes women to poverty (see Ackermann (2004: 35–6).
- Circle work is perhaps the most intense in engaging African Indigenous Religions, although largely from an inculturation perspective (see Oduyoye and Amoah (2004); Amoah et al. (2005); and Phiri and Nadar (2006).
- Methodologically, Circle theology of the HIV/AIDS era uses storytelling, lament, inculturation, gender, feminist, and liturgical/poetic extensively. They also use fieldwork-based collection of data.
- Thematically, Circle HIV/AIDS theology interrogates gender and sexual constructions, highlights issues and the plight of widows, orphans, the girl-child stigma, care-giving, violence, and poverty.
- Constructively, Circle work demands structural transformation from oppressive cultural institutions, faith institutions and governments, calling for justice-loving communities and institutions.
- Organizationally, the power of Circle HIV/AIDS research is that it involves energetic and continent-wide practitioners, from different areas of religion, from various countries and cultures. They are also both in the academy and faith institutions.

Challenges

In terms of future developments in HIV/AIDS and religion/theological education, Circle work highlights that:

- Capacity building in fieldwork and theories of analysis is needed among Circle academic researchers. Reading their publications indicates that many Circle writers still need further educational training and skills empowerment in the area of research. A research and training fund would be in order to strengthen the quality of their work.
- Availability of research funds for Circle members to carry out solid and data-based fieldwork research is needed.
- Circle work on African Indigenous Religions is largely done from a

Christian inculturation perspective, which still subjugates the former to the latter.

- Construction of HIV/AIDS theology in the Circle needs to engage with available theological categories, frameworks, and themes such as Christology, missiology, liberation, inculturation, and reconstruction.
- More stories are needed about efforts and challenges of curriculum transformation in work places. Although Circle research and publications are a major contribution to mainstreaming HIV/AIDS and gender in religion/theological education, there are very few written stories on how members have implemented curriculum transformation in their work place.
- Future development in the study of HIV/AIDS religion/theology also calls for dialogue between African women of the Circle and African male scholars; between Africans scholars in the continent and those in the diaspora. While African women religion/theological engagement with HIV/ AIDS is deliberate, known, and planned, we do not have documentation and evaluation of African male scholars' work in the area of HIV/AIDS religion/theology. We definitely need a bibliographic compilation and analysis of their contents, methods, and themes.
- The strategic plan of the Circle mentions the need to engage with people living with HIV, but a review of their work indicates that it has not been extensive, although there are several examples. Perhaps stigma has been a hindrance. But definitely in these coming 25 years, and in all HIV/ AIDS religion/theological constructions, the voices of people living with HIV and those affected should be central. Our current religion/theology is dominated by the voices of the affected. One way of bridging this gap is to seek ways of working with INERELA+ (and any other organizations for people living with HIV) which has been an important partner in the struggle against HIV/AIDS, but whose major contribution is largely at the level of activism.

In conclusion, we have come a long way in the struggle against HIV/AIDS, but we have a longer journey to undertake in pursuit of hope and healing ourselves, our communities, and our world in the current 25 years of engaging HIV/AIDS. In the first 25 years, we learnt that we are interconnected as men and women, young people and adults, academic and faith-based institutions, Two Thirds world and First world, as people living with HIV and the affected. As Mandela has said, "My freedom and yours cannot be separated"; our healing cannot be separated from one another. Much as we come from different countries, continents, and cultures, we are one world. In this past four years (2004–08), I have attended a number of ecumenical and academic gatherings that have addressed the theme of health and healing.[3] I have great hope, hope for healing, for it has become clear to us that

---

[3] Some examples include the Afro-Asian Mission Consultation on "Healing, Reconciliation and Power: A Tool for Use in Congregations," held in Bangalore, November

we are responsible for and to one another, that we are interconnected and that my health and your health cannot be separated. At the very core of the study of HIV/ AIDS, religion and theology is therefore the quest for being a healed and healers of people and the world—bodily wise and structurally; individually and communally, nationally and continentally.

Bibliography

Ackermann, Denise, "Tamar's Cry: Re-reading the Ancient Text in the Midst of an HIV and AIDS Pandemic," in M.W. Dube and Musimbi Kanyoro (eds.), *Grant Me Justice: HIV and AIDS & Gender Readings of the Bible* (Pietmaritzberg: Cluster Publications and Maryknoll, NY: Orbis, 2004), pp. 27–59.

Amoah E., Dorcas Akitunde and Dorothy Akoto (eds.), *Cultural Practices and HIV/AIDS: African Women's Voice* (Accra: SWL, 2005).

Asamoah-Gyadu, Kwabena, J. *African Charismatics: Current Developments within Independent Indigenous Pentecostalism in Ghana* (Leiden: E.J. Brill, 2005).

Chitando, E. (ed.), *Mainstreaming HIV and AIDS in Theological Education: Experiences and Explorations* (Geneva: WCC Publications, 2008).

—, *Living & Acting With Hope: African Churches and HIV/AIDS*, Vols. 1 & 2 (Geneva: WCC Publications, 2007).

De Gruchy, Steve (ed.) J*ournal of Theology for Southern Africa special issue on Church, HIV and AIDS in Southern Africa* (July 2006).

Dube, Musa W., "Healing Where there is no Healing: Reading the Miracles of Healing in an AIDS Context," in G.A. Phillips and N.W. Duran (eds.), *Essays in Honor of Daniel Patte* (Harrisburg: Trinity Press International, 2002), pp. 122–33.

— (ed.), *HIV/AIDS and the Curriculum: Methods of Integrating HIV/AIDS in Theological Programmes* (Geneva: WCC Publications, 2003a).

— (ed.), *Africa Praying: A Handbook on HIV/AIDS Sensitive Sermon Guidelines and Liturgy* (Geneva: WCC Publications, 2003b).

—, "Doing Theological/Religious Education in a Paradigm of Shattered Dreams and Cul de Sac/ed Roads," *Ministerial Formation*, 102 (2004): 4–12.

—, *Module 5: Reading the New Testament in the HIV&AIDS Context*, Musa W. Dube (ed.), Theology in the HIV and AIDS Series (Geneva: WCC, 2007).

—, *Module 7: A Theology of Compassion in the HIV/AIDS Context*, Musa W. Dube (ed.), Theology in the HIV and AIDS Series (Geneva: WCC, 2007).

—, *The HIV/AIDS Bible: Some Selected Essays* (Chicago: Scranton Press, 2008).

13–20, 2004; the World Conference on Mission and Evangelism on "Come Holy Spirit— Heal and Reconcile," held in Athens in 2005; the AASR Conference on "Health and Healing and the Academic Study of Religion" held in Gaborone, Botswana in July 2007.

—, "In the Circle of Life: African Women Theologians' Engagement with HIV/ AIDS," in Ezra Chitando and N. Hadebe (eds.), *Compassionate Circles: African Women Theologians Facing HIV&AIDS: New Themes* (Geneva: WCC Publications, 2009), pp. 197–236.

— and Musimbi Kanyoro (eds.), *Grant Me Justice: HIV and AIDS & Gender Readings of the Bible* (Pietmaritzberg: Cluster Publications and Maryknoll, NY: Orbis, 2004).

— and Tinyiko Maluleke (eds.), *Missionalia*, 29 (Special Issue on HIV and AIDS and Theological Education) (August 2001).

Hadebe, Nontando, *A Theology of Healing in the HIV and AIDS Era*, Musa W. Dube (ed.), Theology in the HIV and AIDS Series (Geneva: WCC, 2007).

Kgalemang, Malebogo, "John 9: Deconstructing the HIV/AIDS Stigma," in Dube W. Musa and Musimbi Kanyoro (eds.), *Grant Me Justice: HIV and AIDS & Gender Readings of the Bible* (Pietmaritzberg: Cluster Publications and Maryknoll, NY: Orbis, 2004), pp. 141–68.

Leshota, Paul L. and Nontando Hadebe, *Preaching and Liturgy in the HIV&AIDS Context*, Musa W. Dube (ed.), Theology in the HIV and AIDS Series (Geneva: WCC, 2007).

Maluleke, Tinyiko, S. "Towards an HIV/AIDS-Sensitive Curriculum," in Musa W. Dube (ed.) *HIV/AIDS and the Curriculum: Methods of Integrating HIV/AIDS in Theological Programs* (Geneva: WCC Publications, 2003), pp. 59–76.

Mwangi, M. "Community Transformation: A Case Study of St Paul's Life-Long Learning (SPILL), Master of Arts/Post Graduate Diploma in Community Care and HIV&AIDS Programme," in Ezra Chitando (ed.), *Mainstreaming HIV and AIDS in Theological Education: Experiences and Explorations* (Geneva: WCC Publications, 2008), pp. 19–32.

Nadar, Sarojini, *Module 4: Reading the Hebrew Bible in the HIV&AIDS Context*, Musa W. Dube (ed.), Theology in the HIV and AIDS Series (Geneva: WCC, 2007).

Ntloedibe-Kuswani, Seratwa and Kangwa Mambuluki, *HIV and AIDS Curriculum for TEE Institutions in Africa*, Musa W. Dube (ed.), Theology in the HIV and AIDS Series (Geneva: WCC, 2007).

Oduyoye, Mercy A. and Elizabeth Amoah (eds.), *People of Faith & the Challenge of HIV/AIDS* (Ibadan: Sefer, 2004).

Phiri, Isabel, A. *Module 1: Gender, Religion and HIV&AIDS Prevention*, Musa W. Dube (ed.), Theology in the HIV and AIDS Series (Geneva: WCC, 2007).

—, Beverly Haddad and Madipoane Masenya, *African Women, HIV&AIDS and Faith Communities* (Pietmaritzberg: Cluster Publications 2003).

— and Sarojini Nadar (eds.), *African Women, Religion and Health: Essays in Honor of Mercy Amba Ewudziwa Oduyoye* (Maryknoll, NY: Orbis, 2006).

World Council of Churches, *HIV and AIDS Curriculum for Theological Institutions in Africa* (Geneva: WCC Publications, 2002a).

World Council of Churches, *Plan of Action: The Ecumenical Response to HIV&AIDS in Africa* (Geneva: WCC, 2002b).

PART II
Indigenous Thought and Spirituality

Chapter 6
Women, Narrative Traditions, and African Religious Thought

Anthonia C. Kalu

Introduction: Traditions in Transition

In contemporary African literature, of all the images about the encounter between African religion and European intervention, the one that captured my imagination early, involves Achebe's Oduche and the sacred python of Umuaro in *Arrow of God* (1964). Oduche is one of the sons of Ezeulu, the priest of Ulu, Umuaro's god of war. And, Ezeulu had chosen Oduche to join the new religion:

> At first Oduche did not want to go to church. But Ezeulu called him to his obi and spoke to him as a man would speak to his best friend ... I want one of my sons to join these people and be my eye there. If there is nothing in it, you will come back. But if there is something there you will bring back my share ... My spirit tells me that those who do not befriend the white man today will be saying *had we known* tomorrow ... [a]nd the boy went forth with pride in his heart ....
> (Achebe 1964: 50–1) (Arrangement is mine; emphasis in original)

An exploration of significant aspects of Igbo religious thought, *Arrow of God* examines the trajectory of selected conflicts within communities undergoing political and other institutional changes as a result of social invasion. Although Achebe's focus is on certain aspects of Igbo life, some of the conclusions he reaches in this novel have been echoed by other writers and will bear further examination. Different from outright war, *social invasion* is here defined as the use of culture by an outside force to gradually take over the main social institutions of a society or group through the negation of selected features within the target group. Although social invasion sometimes deploys physical violence, its major strategy involves devaluation of the target society and culture by creating uneasiness in citizens about their society's values. As a phenomenon, social invasion has yet to be studied as a separate but significant tool of colonization.

This chapter uses African verbal arts to examine African traditional religion for the illumination it provides about the location and role of the African woman in selected African communities. Religion and religious consciousness are common denominators of every society's quest for self-knowledge. Across time and cultures, that quest defines efforts to organize and propel a given society into a future with viable institutions recognizable by citizens as part of a valid and revered ancestral legacy. Significant in this regard is the part religion plays in institution-building and the installation or abandonment of certain types of governance structures and power. Among these is the way that every society views and treats its women. For contemporary African nations and with regard to colonization, part of the rupture experienced by citizens in general and leaders in particular is the lessening of the place of women in many aspects of social experience. Consistent with the notion of social invasion above, the problem is not that African women stopped fulfilling their roles and functions in their communities but that the attributes associated with those roles and functions were markedly reduced during and following colonization in Africa.

Growing up in the colonized and Christianized African world, I was introduced to Western religious thought through both church and school. Although distanced from the local communities through prevailing Western educational structures, there were nonetheless opportunities within the local culture for developing familiarity with community deities or their representatives. Consequently, for a long time I perceived Christianity as different from religion and religious beliefs; and church attendance meant making weekly visits to the Christian church. Further, with regard to language in an African world where African traditions were fast gaining popularity as an alternative to Western Christianity and culture, the word "Church" frequently meant the same as the actual building where worship took place, or "Sunday" (see Kalu forthcoming). In the schooling environment, this basic problem of language which was part of the conflict between the Igbo and the Western weekly calendar led to some interesting situations between me and my English composition teachers, especially if they happened to be nuns. Also, since school rules and church dogma demanded disconnection from my non-Christian kindred, I made up with my imagination what I did not know about their daily lives and rituals, especially with regard to sacrifices to the community's gods. Finally, as part of a growing well-educated Christian population in a colonized African homeland, I also referred to my non-Christian relations as "people of nothing" (see Achebe 1975: 65). This new way of referring to one's relations was part of the new culture with its arsenal loaded and ready to invade, unravelling binding ties, and shifting loyalties while teaching about moral strength to individuals and groups. By the time I began to understand the difference between church and religion, I also began to entertain the uncertainty that my ancestors might be spending eternity in some part of the Western Christian hell. However, by then I was already fully absorbed with achieving passing grades in Bible Knowledge which required competent and analytical understandings of the Bible as literature and text for the West African School Certificate Examination; a situation which precluded the examination of local religion, myths, or rituals.

Significant to this work, is the version of Christianity that promises life after death, popular in Nigeria since the colonial period. The contemporary African Christian continues to have the option to subscribe to various alternatives, especially with regards to where the African ancestors spend eternity. Consequently, and given the choices inherent in the eternity doctrine and the certainty and practice of collaboration between the living and the dead in ancestral African belief systems, post-colonial Christian legacies extend to the maintenance of full separation from one's ancestors. The ramifications of these alternatives have yet to be explored with regard to Africa's advancement in general, and specifically the development of leadership skills.

Verbal Arts and Religious Traditions

Like many others who grew up in the newly independent Nigeria, I attended the inevitable boarding school; and, alongside the Bible, Greco-Roman mythology, *Aesop's Fables*, *Grimm's Fairy Tales*, I read children's books by authors like Enid Blyton as well as novels by James Hadley Chase and other "forbidden" books. It would take many years for me to understand that I was reading in search of Africa, African thought, and other Africans. For me, reading was a part of the new African heritage, an undisputable part of the new religion embedded in colonialist thought. Briefly: I lived Africa and read the West. And, although I did not express it in those words, I knew I had found what I was looking for when I encountered my first novel written by an African, Camara Laye's *The African Child* (1954). For the first time, the local blacksmith's prohibitions that only his children could work the bellows during our occasional visits to his shed began to make sense beyond the fact that he was keeping us from being scorched by the red-hot iron which he always struck with such precision and care: reverence.

A cursory study of the world's religions shows that narrative traditions and strategies are important to the inception, maintenance, and continuation of religious thought and practice. Whether it is the narratives from Greco-Roman mythology, Christianity, Islam, or Buddhism, relevant cultures and societies ensure the transference of basic thinking about how citizens perceive and use ideas about the supernatural, especially in terms of that which is larger than humans and current efforts at cultural and social constructions of reality. Always, the narratives are used to maintain hierarchies of power so that order prevails in the society. The same is true of narratives of African societies and cultures within which expansionist paradigms (Mali's *Sundiata*, Zulu's *Chaka*) and innovation (most African folktales, but especially narrative performance itself fall under this category) are embedded alongside ideas about punishment for the wicked, rewards for the kind, nurturing of children and respect for the place, functions, roles, and contributions of women.

Most societies across the world have accepted Western Christian thought about women in general and its impact on African women in particular. Among the most vexing areas in the progression of Western thought and civilization is the role of women. From Plato to postmodernism, discussion about where women belong in society and the role they should or are fit to play remains important to thinking about human advancement. Within that framework, religious thinking about women seems unchanging. In their *Inventors of Ideas: An Introduction to Western Political Philosophy* 1998), Tannenbaum and Schultz examine Western political philosophy from Plato to the present, making occasional references to the relationships between religion, law, politics and important social institutions like the family. In their succinct examination of Sophocles' *Antigone* and with regard to human obligations, they assert the following:

> Sophocles' *Antigone* thus poses the dilemma that our duties to family, religion and politics may not always mutually support one another. *Antigone* demonstrates the need for harmony among these three sets of duties by revealing their potential to clash, possibly with disastrous results … *Antigone* suggests that the universe represents a seamless harmony of duties and obligations, but that human motives can disturb this unity and precipitate "a fall from grace" (as it is later described in the Christian tradition) … [f]orcing conflicted individuals to make choices between their several obligations. (Sophocles 1982: 24)

Eventually and as king, Creon's decision overrides Antigone's efforts to use defiance to provoke change. According to the narrative:

> CREON: Go down below and love, if love you must—love the dead! While I'm alive, no woman will lord it over me. (Sophocles 1982: 86)

Later in the play, Creon continues:

> CREON: Therefore we must defend the men who live by law, never let some women triumph over us. Better to fall from power, if fall we must, at the hands of a man— never be rated inferior to a woman, never. (Sophocles 1982:. 94)

In their examination of human nature and Christian equality, Tannenbaum and Schultz find similar refusals to acknowledge women's and other citizens' participation and engagement after the death of Christ:

> …while another message of Jesus and early Christians seems to recognize women as equal to men, this message is quickly lost or contradicted. In the life of Christ, women such as his mother, Mary, and Mary Magdalene occupy important roles, and Jesus seems to speak to both men and women. *But Paul retracts many of the original gender-neutral or egalitarian claims,* enjoining women to remain subordinate to their husbands. (Tannenbaum and Schultz 1998: 72–3, my emphasis)

Thus despite women's participation and collaborative actions in support of social institutions evidenced in ancient Greek traditions and Christ's teachings, Creon and Paul use politics and social status (Creon as King and Paul as the Apostle of Christ) to assign secondary citizenship to Western women. Later, Athens and

Jerusalem come together, strengthening certain views within Western civilization including the domination of women. Subsequently, that will to political dominance is exported and applied to African society and life during European intervention on the continent. However, rather than direct exclusion and domination as experienced by Antigone and the new Christian communities indicated above, social invasion was used as the primary strategy to effect change in Africa, especially in areas where social changes were already in progress. African verbal arts offer some examples.

In Achebe's *Arrow of God*, Oduche's Christian zeal emboldens him to physically ensnare one of his people's religious objects—the python—exposing Umuaro citizens to emotional and spiritual uncertainty and therefore conversion to the new religion. With reference to this work's focus on social invasion, the point here is that the assault of one of Umuaro's significant religious objects by one convert is not the same as an assault on the whole of Umuaro's religious thought. Although the python was considered sacred, the people of Umuaro did not worship it. Within Umuaro's religious system, the python belonged to Idemili. According to legend, Umuama was one of Umuaro's seven villages but its members were scattered all over the land of Olu. It was said that after six sons of Umuama killed and cooked a python, a fight which ensued during their effort to dish out the meal among themselves quickly spread to include others and almost resulted in the death of all the villagers: extinction. The survivors dispersed and the village itself was abandoned.

The remaining six villages, seeing what had happened to Umuama, went to a seer to find out the reason, and he told them that the royal python was sacred to Idemili; it was this deity which had punished Umuama. From that day the six villages decreed that henceforth the python was not to be killed in Umuaro and that anyone who killed it would be regarded as having killed a kinsman (Achebe 1964: 53–4).

Always looking for ways to maintain life, most traditional communities gathered and maintained extant information in the service of the living, forming stable social institutions including a religious system that, though based on the faith of those responsible for introducing a given aspect of the belief system, helps to sustain current populations. In the above story about Umuaro, the installation of the python as a sacred object is based on the fact that no one really knew what caused six brothers, who together could kill and cook a python, to turn on each other in the course of eating an apparently regular meal. This segment of the novel's story begins with a disagreement between Moses Unachukwu, a convert and a native of Umuaro, and Mr. Goodcountry, the English-speaking new teacher from the far away Niger Delta. Contrary to Mr. Goodcountry's teachings, Unachukwu insists that "…neither the Bible nor the catechism asked converts to kill the python, a beast of ill-omen" (Achebe 1964: 53). But the disagreement escalates as Mr. Goodcountry, whose homeland's sacred iguana had already been assaulted and diminished by the Western missionaries, continues to push the Umuaro converts to test their Christian faith by killing the royal python. He ignores Unachukwu's story about Umuaro's tried and tested effort at using the royal python as a tool for the maintenance of brotherhood and a strong kinship system. Mr. Goodcountry's challenge augments Oduche's Christian zeal, encouraging him to invoke the Bible and the Edenic myth about Eve and the serpent.

But instead of killing the royal python, Oduche imprisons it. Although obvious, the parallels indicated by the two stories are not the subject of this chapter. Rather, of interest is the examination of the ways in which different cultures evoke and maintain faith by invoking, intensifying or ignoring aspects of the unknown. In the case of Africa, the problem posed by social invasion is that its purveyors frequently see only the logic of their own histories, experiences and expectations for the futures they imagine. In the various collaborations and confrontations between religious systems globally, this fact remains the greatest pitfall for citizens of relevant societies. Even as each group announces its uniqueness as part of the quest for self-knowledge, members of different groups seem inadequately equipped to acknowledge others' uniqueness.

By invading aspects of African thinking about social well-being, colonizers and African Christian converts succeeded in holding African heritage at bay, delaying development by denying, through piecemeal negations, the right of citizens to familiar objects, places and individuals with the ability to provide access to other forms of innovative discourse, behavior and insight. Although the silencing of many African deities became a reality during and after the colonial era, it is important to note that part of Umuaro's problem was that both Ulu and Ezeulu were already under scrutiny before the missionaries arrived. Thus colonialism should not bear all the blame for the shelving of Africa's entire ancestral heritage; the complacency and complicity of Africans regarding African heritage must be examined. While the imprisonment of one of Umuaro's royal pythons and the eventual dismissal of Ulu discredited all of Umuaro thought by labeling them evil, continued examination of Sophocles' *Antigone* has enabled further research into different aspects of ancient Greek tradition, religion, culture, and history, helping to unveil advances in Western thought about women over the centuries. Similar results continue to be assessed through re-examination of Eve's story and Paul's various epistles (insights) to the various communities to which he ministered. That agreement to assemble and organize the different insights from several acknowledged events, people, and places from history, legend, and other areas of knowledge, is what upholds the study of Western philosophy and religion, for instance. Recent developments in African Studies are helping to open up areas of knowledge that has been constrained in African life since the colonial period. For example, in most traditional African religious practice women are perceived either as knowledgeable or as participants. Although many myths and epics present men as protagonists, closer analysis reveals that success required the presence of, and sometimes action by, women.

Women and Leadership in African Religious Traditions

However, contemporary studies of women and gender revolve around whether or not the woman's status in African life reflects her significance and power. Given the discussion above about the emergence of a different morality focus during European intervention on the continent, it is obvious that a great deal of work still needs to be done to illuminate the concept of woman in traditional African religion, politics, the arts, and other relevant institutions. There is an urgent need for research on how different groups conceptualized the woman as co-creator of different community endeavors before Western intervention. Whether she is the hunchbacked Sogolon, the mother of Sundiata of old Mali, or the beautiful Moombi who is the favored mother of the Kikuyu, all African communities place her at the beginning and end of life. As wife, mother, sister or priestess, her knowledge of the hills, caves, rivers, fish, and fauna endorsed her participation in all social institutions. A significant part of the problem encountered in many African traditional belief systems was the fact that the woman was perceived as both ritual object and ritual. And, in many instances, she was also a priestess. Although no traditional African community held her and her various life-availing offices in contempt, it was difficult to find a place for her in the predominantly patriarchal European-oriented belief system of colonialism.

In traditional Africa, her main sacred place was her hearthstones (different from her kitchen) and not everyone was welcome to the area where she set those up. Although she was available as a priestess in many communities, her everyday role and function in other areas of community life ensured that she was not always accessible for every sacrifice or ritual. This last idea is expressed in several ways by African narrators. In his discussion about the Ifa orature and sculptural repertoire, Rowland Abiodun's focus on *ìróké* is illuminating:

> ...the priest uses the *ìróké*, or divining tapper, to invoke *Òrúnmìla* during divination. With a clapper or bell at its open end, the *ìróké* is usually carved in ivory and sometimes brass or wood. The tappers range between twenty or sixty centimeters in length. Typically, they have three major parts: a plain pointed end separated from the (usual) equestrian figure in the lower section by a middle section often carved as a human head or a kneeling female nude figure holding her breasts ... The female intervenes on behalf of humanity to ensure the selection of good orí, which must be chosen and "received kneeling down," *akúnlegba*. The kneeling male figure is not as powerful or as sacred as the female figure, who indicates the kneeling called *ikunle-abiyamo*, "the-kneeling-of-the-pains-at-childbirth." Linked to the greatest act of reverence that humans give to the *orisa* are the special qualities and status of women as those through whom all have come into the world. (Abiodun 2008: 57)

In general, this ritualized perspective about woman-as-woman in African thought remains a puzzle for the contemporary African thinker. Part of the problem resides in the refusal to engage traditional African thought on its own terms; resulting in the marginalization of African philosophy by contemporary African scholars. However, as the narrator of the Sundiata epic insists:

> Griots know the history of kings and kingdoms and that is why they are the best counselors of king ..., for it is the griot who rescues the memories of kings from oblivion ..., and seers who probe the future know it. They have knowledge of the future, whereas we griots are depositories of the knowledge of the past. But whoever knows the history of a country can read its future. (Niane 1965: 40–1)

Indeed self-knowledge for both individuals and communities has always resided in the ability of the narrator to depict and store events and the dreams of nations and citizens alike in local lore and using relevant languages. Although and predominantly, the woman trained her children in the basics of story types, form, structure, and style, this art is quickly losing ground in contemporary Africa as the art of storytelling has moved to the writing of novels and the creation of video-films. While participation in capitalist venues predicted by expertise in this art is of interest to writers, removal of the woman from the story-circle in the family does not augur well for Africans and Africa. During several recent (2005, 2006, 2008) research trips to two West African countries in search of oral narratives, I could find very few women who, like Achebe's Ekwefi in *Things Fall Apart* (1959), could hold the basic oral narrative story line and performance together. Rather, in several places and since I was looking for a specific oral narrative type, I was directed to male chiefs of the villages! The same is true of the local priestesses. Also, although traditionally, both men and women were griots, current trends in telling Africa's story continue to exclude women and the few published children's stories languish on the shelves of the even fewer bookstores, because despite the lessons taught previous generations using stories like those of Moombi, Sundiata, and Chaka, the education of Africa's children is no longer based on the need to build and maintain local communities. Most importantly, ignoring ancestral heritage and working in the tradition of colonialism, most contemporary African institutions either openly exclude the African woman or bring her in as an afterthought.

A brief examination of the African woman's place and role in contemporary African religious thought reveals that during colonialism, like the continent, she also gained the reputation of collaborating with darkness and having access to evil. Though the female principle is considered both potent and productive in ancestral African thought, European interventions on the continent place those attributes in opposition to the new teachings. A closer look at Africa's traditional narratives and religious thought shows that although the African woman is perceived as knowing darkness, she does not collaborate with it; a distinction that made it possible for traditional African thinkers to respect the place of woman at the crossroads of human existence. This last idea is evidenced in Achebe's *Things Fall Apart* when Chielo, the priestess, takes Okonkwo's daughter, Ezinma, for that nocturnal journey to the Oracle of the Hills and Caves. When she arrives at Okonkwo's compound and announces her errand and Okonkwo demurs, Chielo screams: "Beware, Okonkwo! ... Beware of exchanging words with Agbala. Does a man speak when a god speaks? Beware!" However, Ezinma's mother Ekwefi gives the child over after a brief exchange and follows Chielo into the night. During that visit, Chielo runs through Umuofia carrying Ezimma on her back, calling out greetings to Agbala and the villagers she passes. Okonkwo, the great warrior and man of titles, goes straight to the place of Agbala and not finding any sign of the priestess goes back home to wait until the women complete the night's run through Umuofia.

Everyone knew that Ezinma was an *ogbanje*, a spirit child born to die many times by the same mother. When Chielo begins her journey that night, most families including Okonwo's had finished the evening meal and were telling stories. Ekwefi had just finished telling a story and Ezinma was about to begin hers when Chielo's voice interrupts. Achebe's narrator comments:

> It was Chielo, the priestess of Agbala prophesying. There was nothing new in that ... But tonight she was addressing her prophesy to Okonkwo, and so everyone in his family listened. The folk stories stopped.

> "Agbala do-o-o-o! Agbala ekeneo-o-o-o!" ... "Okonkwo! Agbala ekene gio-o-o-o! Agbala colu ifu ada ya Ezinmao-o-o-o!" ... She walked through Okonkwo's hut into the circular compound and went straight toward Ekwefi's hut ... "Ekwefi," she called, "Agbala greets you. Where is my daughter, Ezinma? Agbala wants to see her." (Achebe 1959: 94–5)

Although different from formal religion and worship, an aspect of Umuofia's religious thought and practice is evident as this scene unfolds. It is important to note how Chielo calls on each individual or group to either agree or disagree with the task of taking Ezinma to the Oracle. is achieved. As the narrator points out, "there is nothing new" (Achebe 1959: 94) here. A danger confronted by a child of Umuofia must be averted, and Chielo will preside over this ritual to its logical conclusion because Umuofia's agreement is already in place. Although people eventually go to sleep that night, it is understood that Chielo's task was not completed in darkness; it is neither secret nor evil. Thus Okonkwo, the warrior who is known to sweep everything and everyone aside in the face of danger or threat to his people, steps aside for Chielo, the priestess, to take his daughter into the night.

In *Sundiata: An Epic of Old Mali* (Niane 1965) the story also unfolds a pattern of agreements involving women's participation in creating and maintaining religious and political institutions, showing the close linkages necessary for the harmonious existence mandated by traditional African communities. Sogolon is introduced to the king as an ugly hunchback maiden with special powers. Her arrival in Nianiba and introduction to the king are prophesied by the hunter-seer long before the event takes place. After he completes the necessary tasks and kills the buffalo that had been ravaging the countryside of Do, killing some of its people, the hunter who brings Sogolon to the king is directed to pick Sogolon out from a crowd. The king of Do had deprived his sister of part of her inheritance. In retaliation she had been ravaging the countryside in the form of a buffalo. Sogolon is her wraith.[1] Vanquished by the kindness of the brothers, she tells them the secret which allows them to kill the buffalo and receive the prize promised by the king of Do, a beautiful maiden of Do for a wife. Eventually, the hunters take Sogolon to the king who has been waiting for a son who will succeed the throne. As promised by the buffalo to the brothers, the king finds that Sogolon is so strong physically that he has to trick her in order to subdue her. She eventually gives birth to Sundiata but has to contend with her co-wife who already has a son.

After the king's death, Sogolon raises Sundiata, nurturing him through exile to full manhood. To accomplish this, she is helped by her daughters. Together, the women obtain information from cunning rulers, including the sorcerer king Sosso king, Soumaoro Kanté. From the beginning the griot describes Sogolon as "ugly in a sturdy sort of way..., a very ugly maid—uglier than you can imagine" (Niane 1965: 7, 8). A hunchback, she is said to have a beautiful character and inner strength and she is also a sorceress. Later, when Sundiata's griot praises him in preparation for war, he says: "You are the son of Naré Maghan, but you are also the son of your mother Sogolon, the buffalo-woman, before whom powerless sorcerers shrank in fear. You have the strength and majesty of the lion, you have the might of the buffalo" (Niane 1965: 63).

According to the griot's rendering of this narrative, not only is Sogolon a king's mother but she is a kingmaker, co-creator of the might of Old Mali. Indeed in many African communities and continuing to contemporary times when the use of surnames refer to one's patrilineage, children are mostly identified with their mothers. Thus the name Sundiata or Sondjata, is derived in the Mandingo language from Sogolon Djata, that is, Djata, son of Sogolon (Niane 1965: 23), indicating the place and role of women in the overall discourse about community and continuity.

A significant portion of Sundiata's story portrays that part of the traditional African belief system frequently referred to as magic. Because narratives of African religious belief systems entered the contemporary global arena through colonialists' perspectives, both Europeans and African converts continue to subscribe to the idea that it is dominated by superstition, magic, and witchcraft. About this, Mbiti says:

> ... there is a mystical order governing the universe. The belief in this order is shown clearly in the practice of traditional medicine, magic, witchcraft and sorcery. It is held in all African societies that there is power in the universe, and

---

[1]   G.D. Pickett's (translator) note in the book reads: "Most West African tribes believe in wraiths or doubles, but beliefs vary and are often difficult to determine even for one tribe." See Trimingham 1959: 58–60.

that it comes from God. It is a mystical power, in the sense that it is hidden and mysterious … Knowledge of this mystical power is used to help other people … or to harm them. When it is used harmfully, it is regarded as evil magic, witchcraft or sorcery. (Mbiti 1975: 41–2)

Given the colonial agenda on church and schooling, women's participation was late and scanty. This produced at least two results: the women held on to ancestral traditions longer than the men in many communities and the intensification of the notion that she was more prone to evil survived on both sides of the colonial divide in Africa. The assignment of the African woman to a place of literary and religious darkness continues to obscure research in this area, with most works insisting that she has always been oppressed and marginalized and further assigning her to oblivion.

A full understanding of the African woman's place and role in African religious thought requires an in-depth exploration of the role of magic in African religious practice. Although the African woman's access to magic and magical objects is evident in legends, myths and epics like *Sundiata*, the *Mwindo Epic*, *Chaka*, and in many folk narratives that contain the images and wisdom that a group compiles about itself in its knowledge base, she is rarely presented as more evil than the male characters. For example, while Sundiata's quest for the throne reaches its height during the magical duel between him and the sorcerer king, his victory depends on information given to him by the women. While Sundiata was in exile, Soumaoro defeated his half-brother Dankaram Touman, who, upon his submission, also gave up his sister Nana Triban to the conqueror. Nana Triban became one of Soumaoro's wives and found out his secrets before she escaped from Soumaoro with Sundiata's griot, Balla Fasséké. As Sundiata was getting ready for the last part of his war with Soumaoro the most famous soothsayers of Mali advised him to

sacrifice a hundred white bulls, a hundred white rams and a hundred white cocks. It was in the middle of this slaughter that it was announced to Sundiata that his sister Nana Triban and Balla Fasséké, having been able to escape from Sosso, had now arrived. Then Sundiata said to Tabon Wana, "If my sister and Balla Fasséké have been able to escape from Sosso, Soumaoro has lost the battle." (Nianae 1965: 56–7)

Eventually, Sundiata's certainty about Mali's victory is well-founded because he wins the war against Soumaoro. Like all great leaders, he knew that recapturing Mali's greatness from the Sosso king required the coming together of Mali's treasures—priests/soothsayers, griot, the intent to sacrifice as well as sacrifice itself, and the woman. The instructions about what must be done are always specific. The specifications point to ethnic unity, helping to differentiate communities and groups. At the same time, those specifications are required within African religious systems, making for an overall unity between the belief systems. For example, Sundiata had to know Soumaoro's *tana*, his hereditary taboo, in order to kill him. Although such knowledge about an individual does not always have fatal results and not all groups have taboos, the existence of a taboo among many groups is a common feature of African belief systems and is usually taken into consideration in significant social interactions. In this case, the sorcerer Soumaoro was forbidden to touch the spur of a cock (Niane 1965: 64). Using this information that Nana Triban brought to him from her encounter with Soumaoro, Sundiata made an arrow "of wood and pointed with the spur of a white cock" (Niane 1965: 63) with which he killed Soumaoro.

Among the Zulu, Thomas Mofolo tells the story of Chaka who also brings together the people using the help of two doctors, female and male. When Chaka was born, a woman doctor foretold that he would

> receive great blessings such as had never been received by a human being. She gave Nandi a medicine horn and said, "Always when the moon is about to die you must bathe this child in the river very early in the morning, before the sun has risen, and then when he has finished bathing he must walk quickly back home, and when the first rays of the sun shine upon the village, you must take some of this medicine with your fingers and anoint his head with it. You must anoint only the center of the head where the child's head throbs; be sure to anoint only this tuft of hair which is never to be shaved off.... Bathe him in a large river, not a small one ...." (Mofolo 1931: 8)

However, after his father Senzangakhona disowned his mother Nandi, she raised Chaka on her own. During the initial period of Chaka's preparation to take over his father's throne, Nandi was not only aware of instructions he must follow to ensure his well-being but she was also nearby as he fulfilled some of the instructions. Later, Chaka met the doctor Isanusi who became his personal mentor. Isanusi's directions were precise and efficient. He not only fortified Chaka with medicines but fashioned for him "the spear with a short handle" which became Chaka's trademark and which his soldiers used in subsequent wars to conquer the people and lands that eventually made up his vast kingdom.

Although both men achieve adulthood through different social norms, Sundiata and Chaka are comparable in many ways. While the details of their cultural norms within their birth societies are different, the religious beliefs are similar and would bear further and deeper examination, especially in terms of the intrinsic computations embedded in both narratives with regards to medical and psychological practices. Like Sundiata, Chaka was prominent, influential and powerful. Both men's lives had far-reaching impacts on their people. But each man's life story evokes images of a strong African heritage deeply entrenched in local religious thought and practice.

Conclusion: Religion and Nation-Building

In traditional Africa, the life of the religious leader was perceived as that of the interpreter of art, symbols and texts of life. In contemporary society, that niche is occupied by the professor of religious traditions and practice as the interpreter of religious texts and life for the laity. The difference is that most of the details in the contemporary text are alien to that laity who, in their mostly tropical existences, have to be taught to think of the tropical heat as punishment (Hell) even as most citizens have no idea of the merits of winter or snow. This deployment of social invasion has been the most successful because of the difficulty it poses for research and development. Like Chaka during his time of troubles, what contemporary Africa needs are individuals such as this "*isanusi* who, … it has been said would come to … and …, if this is he, then truly … affairs were going to take a new turn, because it was quite clear that this *man could feel things with his head…*" (Mofolo 1931: 39, my emphasis).

What remains less explored and explained is how religious beliefs and knowledge systems symbolically or tangibly contribute to the core ideas of state formation and nation-building on the continent. Although African religious thought is embedded in symbols and modes of worship in traditional African thought, in holders of sacred objects, and in other repositories of African religious systems, contemporary African nations continue to encounter problems following in the footsteps of their ancestors; despite the promises of independence in the post-colonial era, they remain unable to follow in the footsteps of the West. However, according to the African narrators, ancestral repositories are always contained, maintained, and dispersed by the language of the culture whose religion is explored. And, since those systems were highly developed in pre-colonial African communities, contemporary African nations, if they are to move forward, must examine the role of religious beliefs and knowledge as part of the core of state formation and nation-building as frameworks for the maintenance of justice. Such a focus will liberate contemporary African nations and set them again on the road to collective advancement and progress, energized by co-participation of its daughters and sons in the search for balanced and just development.

Bibliography

Abiodun, Rowland, "Who Was the First to Speak? Insights from Ifa Orature and Sculptural Repertoire', in Jacob Olupona and Terry Rey (eds.), *Òrìsà Devotion as World Religion: The Globalization of Yoruba Religious Culture* (Madison: University of Wisconsin Press, 2008), pp. 51–69.

Achebe, Chinua, *Arrow of God* (New York: Anchor Books, 1964).

—, *Morning Yet on Creation Day: Essays* (London: Heinemann Educational, 1975).

—, *Things Fall Apart* (New York: Fawcett Crest, 1959).

Haynes, Jeff, *Religion in Third World Politics* (Boulder, CO: Lynne Rienner Publishers, 1994).

Juergensmeyer, Mark (ed.), *Global Religions: An Introduction* (Oxford: Oxford University Press, 2003).

Kalu, Anthonia, "Narrative Traditions and African Religious Thought," in Simeon Ilesanmi, et al. *(*Forthcoming).

Kaufmann, Walter, *Nietzsche: Philosopher, Psychologist, Antichrist* (Princeton, NJ and London: Princeton University Press, 1950).

Kenyatta, Jomo, *Facing Mount Kenya* (New York: Vintage Books, 1965).

Laye, Camara, *The African Child* (London: Fontana Press, 1954).

Mbiti, John S., *Introduction to African Religion* (Oxford: Heinemann Educational, 1975).

Mofolo, Thomas, *Chaka* (Oxford: Heinemann Educational, 1931).

Niane, D.T. *Sundiata: An Epic of Old Mali*, trans. G.D. Pickett (London: Longman, 1965).

Sophocles, *Antigone*, in *The Three Theban Plays*, trans. R. Fagles (New York: Penguin Books, 1982).

Tannenbaum, Donald, and David Schultz. *Inventors of Ideas: An Introduction to Western Political Philosophy* (New York: St. Martin's Press, 1998).

Trimingham, J. Spencer, *Islam in West Africa* (Oxford: Clarendon Press, 1959).

Chapter 7

African Spirituality from "Noise, Dust, Darkness and Dancing"

Lilian Dube

Introduction

One among many outstanding contributions that Jacob Olupona has made to the study of African religions is condensed in his volume on *African Spirituality* (Olupona 2000). It is evident from this work that the search for the spiritual core where the person is open to the transcendent dimension to experience the ultimate reality is not hidden away in complex religious maze in most African societies, but is revealed in the "noise, dust, darkness and dancing" of the African peoples. African spirituality is embedded in the living traditions and cultures of the African people which this volume formally organizes in logical categories that relate to other spiritualities in the world without being measured through or by them. This opens fresh avenues in the study of African religions which this work attempts to illustrate in Jacob Olupona's most deserving honor.

African Spirituality provides a guide for the search of emerging African traditions in the study of African religions in myths, rituals, and human agents who undergo ritual apprenticeship like priests, diviners, herbalists, kings, chiefs, and artists. The search for African traditions that could influence the study of religion in Africa draws extensively from art and performative, personal, and lyrical acts of human agents in Africa. This chapter is inspired by Kathleen O'Brien Wicker's observation that African religions and life are co-extensive (O' Brien Wicker 2000: 198). It proposes art, music, and dance as emerging African traditions in the study of African religions.

The chapter appreciates the steps that have been taken to Africanize the study of religion in Africa. It also acknowledges the influence of African traditions on newer religions in Africa and the African Diaspora, where folk music has not only translated vernacular traditions to deconstruct and interrogate racism but folk aesthetic has been used as a vehicle for social activism and cultural autobiography. To disregard their contribution to the study of religion in Africa would make little sense. Music has ethnographical power to restore communal identity and tradition. In her analysis of the cultural production of black women's folklore, Billingslea-Brown also explains: "For African Americans, the conditions for the formation of a functional identity assumed urgent and collective overtones during the 1960s and were linked, not only to history and socioeconomic and political power, but also to the spheres of art and aesthetics" (Bilingslea-Brown 1999: 10).

Singing the Oral Traditions of Africa

Songs are a part of the dynamic African oral tradition that permeate time, place and purpose. In places with limited literacy skills, African folk music relates stories of historic interest, poetry, and tradition, giving the singer a central place they have not lost even in contemporary society where folk music has changed. The adaptation of African culture to urban life has created new spaces in the cities for the African singer in night clubs and churches but has not altered the highly social functional role of African music.

More generally, songs in Africa have various functions that reflect people's social history and allow the performer to make a commentary on society, altering it in accordance with contemporary situations and needs. This process is always received with mixed feelings. While it is beyond the scope of this chapter fully to discuss the various forms of functional songs, attention will be paid to gender because women play an important role in traditional religions and in the contemporary religious setting in Africa where the role of religious songs in African struggle is for protest, praise, and morale raising and entertainment.

There has been extensive research on cultural music, popular music, and gospel music by African scholars of religion. The scope if this chapter will limit my research to southern Africa for the sake of detail. In his extensive study of Gospel music in Zimbabwe, Chitando notes that there has been much interest by ethnomusicologists such as the late Dumisani Maraire in folk music and the significance of music for the ancestral cult ..., a focus on specific indigenous instruments such as the *mbira* ..., the use of folk songs during the liberation struggle ..., the development of popular music ..., music instruments in general ..., protest by established artists like Thomas Mapfumo ... who is currently in the USA in self-exile in protest against Mugabe's corrupt regime, the impact of nationalism and other ideologies on popular music ..., as well as investigations into fear and self-censorship ... There exists substantial research on developments within the Church that has analysed the importance of Christian poetry and music drama, and the history of hymnody in Zimbabwe (Chitando 2002: 6). In this study, Chitando explores gospel music in Zimbabwe in the 1990s and responds to pertinent questions about adaptation, for example music with a fast, danceable beat and utilizing Christian themes (to gain popularity), the dominant socio-political and cultural themes in Zimbabwean gospel music.

Chitando makes an accurate observation in his study when he argues that gospel music has created alternative space for social groups that had been rendered invisible, such as women and children in a society where music performances had been dominated by middle-aged male artists, especially in African Initiated Churches more than in mission churches due to the latter's emphasis on the "gifts of the Holy Spirit to all people regardless of gender." He also discusses the numerous hurdles female musicians still encounter as they articulate notions of despair over the economic and political struggles encountered by many Zimbabweans. Their songs of protest and despair are also songs of hope for Christ's intervention in the sorrows of the people (Chitando 2002: 74). His portrayal of women as agents of social change for their communities partially sheds some light on the gist of this chapter's argument but fails to highlight the important aspect of their own liberation as they find their own voices in the public spaces of their nation. However, he fails to expound on their new identities, in which they become agents of change. The significance of their acceptance as musicians in patriarchal settings marked by the record-breaking sales of their music and the awards conferred to women singers in his research (Chitando 2002: 74) is indicative of something larger that Chitando fails to recognize but Ojo clearly identifies, namely, "a means of enhancing self expression and self determination" (Ojo 1998: 222–3). He does not delve deeper into a gender analysis of the effect of public performances on these women artistes and on their audiences, an aspect that this chapter identifies as vital in correcting gender imbalances. The politics of power involved when women, young women for that, stand up and interpret, critique, and prescribe solutions within the larger context of political, economic, cultural, social, and other national events, calamities and despairs using gospel public song performances cannot be underestimated or glossed over. As women "singing preachers" address a variety of issues on religion and culture, good governance, HIV/AIDS and other health issues, human rights, and sexuality issues their self-image evolves. They ascend social hierarchies they would ordinarily never dare. Ojo contends that by commenting on issues that are most important to Nigerians, women are transcending their parochial world (Ojo 1998: 225).

Embodied Spirituality of Nudity and Dance

Dance has been defined as cultural behaviour which accurately mirrors the different people of Africa's values, attitudes, and beliefs (Asante 1998: 64). Pearl Primus, quoted by Kariamu Weish Asante, argued that dance rituals in Africa express the very heartbeat of communal living and claims, "The true African dance is basic in subject matter: birth, death, puberty, marriage, hailing new chief, discovering evil spirits, detecting criminals, praying for rain, sun, strong children, good harvest, good hunting, victory in warfare, success in love, revenge, protection of the gods, honoring the ancestors, and play… " (Asante 1998: 64).

A logical conclusion to this line of thought is that dance(s) can credibly inform the study of African religion. This section will only highlight one aspect of dance for emphasis, namely female ritual dances in private spaces, for self-expression, empowerment, and spiritual growth within the larger community of others.

Gender Dynamics

The role of private song and dance in women's lives is present in Asian cultures as illustrated by the Asian feminist theologian Hyun Kyung. In a moment of sanity and liberation a mother bathes in a deep forest river, sings and dances naked in the forest as she reclaimes her childhood freedom that had been locked away in her memory following years of a loveless marriage. She is natural and spiritual as she connects with the deepest center of her person and ultimate reality. She is open to the transcendent dimension as she discovers this core on her physical and spiritual journey described by her daughter:

> "Mum, stop it!" I screamed at her, but she did not look at me. She continued her dance, moving nearly naked in the forest. I felt ashamed for her; I wished she were not my mother. There was nothing to hide the scene before me. There was a deathly silence around us, except for Mother's singing and the sound of the river.

> Under the hot sun of August, the forest seemed to be taking a nap. There were no villagers moving about, only Mother and I. She looked like a person who did not belong to this world. I saw real happiness in her face while she was singing and dancing. I could see her breasts, the lines of her body—large, like a whale's—through her wet underwear. I did not want anyone in the world to see that shape, my mother's body that had worked and lived. I finally started to cry out of extreme embarrassment. I wanted to hide from her. She did not look anymore like the noble mother of whom I was always proud. But in spite of my crying, she continued singing and dancing, twirling the forest as a child might, twirling and dancing in a space of her own.

> ... "Mom, stop it, stop it!" I screamed, but she continued to dance and sing, her body flopping and straining against the dampened clothes. I could not stop the tears from coming, and we stayed like that—me crying and her dancing—for some time. After a while, because of my continuous crying, she stopped her dance and put on her clothes and we took up our journey again. (Ching Hyun 1998: 54–5)

The striking similarity with *chinamwali,* a growing-up ritual in Malawi (Chitando 2009: 36) that uses song and dance to instruct girls and women about religio-cultural gender relations and their own sexual power as they discover their embodied selves in nudity within sacred and safe spaces for women. These sacred spaces are usually deep in the forest, which in many African traditions, are spirited. As Wyatt MacGaffey rightly observes about the Yoruba and the Luba beliefs: "the spirits reside in the forest, in the deep of the earth, and in the inner space of the person" (Olupona 2000: 230). Thus the connection between the deep forest and the spiritual awakening in girls and women undergoing initiation rituals in secluded forests is intriguing. Fulata Moyo describes the graduation celebration of the initiates who are in touch with their own bodies and spirits at a tender age as follows: "Bare-foot and only in underwear, with a thick band of beads of all colors around the waist, they make rhythmic gyrations and sensual vibrations from their waists to their bottoms, corresponding to their singing and drumming" (Olupona 2000: 41). They emerge with their signature dance which will characterize them throughout their lives without limiting their creativity. Thus when each girl becomes a person through the control of their bodies, it is a liberation moment which unfortunately is not allowed to continue in the distorted gender imbalanced contemporary cultures that Moyo critiques. In this narrative, Moyo acknowledges song and dance as a holistic media for ritual instruction: "this involves not just one's ears and other hearing organs but the whole body singing and dancing, the psychological, sociological as well as the mental elements of the instructed and the instructor." She also acknowledges that it is one of the most effective means of doing liberation theology among women to break the barriers of sexuality taboos (Moyo 2002: 406).

Dance Politics

The significant role of traditional "private" dancers in the study of religion in Africa is not undermined by this section on "public" dancers for money, politics, or worship which characterizes contemporary Africa. Song and dance are still loaded with culturally symbolic meaning and religious overtones even when performed in the glitter of modernity by Africa prophets and prophetess. They leave them with the power of self-expression as they relate their own experiences of power and powerlessness in the new spheres. The self-embodied performer redefines the community's political, cultural, social, and religious values as well as their personal visions that could be explored in the study of religion in Africa. Thus, when African women still emerge as prophets, visionaries, teachers, and entertainers outside their cultural spaces in contemporary African settings to bring out the rich traditions of Africa, the study of religion in Africa could be enriched. Stella Chiweshe and Miriam Makeba top the ranks of female singer-dancers from Southern Africa who embody rich African traditions and culture. They have the oral scripts of African traditions and history inscribed in their lyrics and in their swaying and swirling bodies.

Miriam Makeba (1932–2008)

Miriam Makeba did not only sing in protest, she also acted on her words. Singing in her native Xhosa language in New York back in the 1960s, Makeba was not only an exotic archive of South African beauty, but a professor of African culture and religious experience and an ardent activist against the apartheid politics of the time. She embodied a rich African style through her dress, braided hair, the clicks of her tongue and her body movement to the African rhythm while simultaneously lambasting an evil system of racial segregation of the black majority in her home country. She is a good example of how aesthetics can inform the study of religion in Africa.

Milton Bracker, writing in the *New York Times*, finely describes Makeba's dual personalities "onstage" and "offstage" thus:

> In daytime conversation, Miss Makeba is soft-spoken and reticent as to suggest a roll of extremely delicate paper ribbon. She can be unwound, but the most meticulous care must be exercised, lest the roll tear and the process have to begin all over again. A dozen hours later, however, facing a nightclub crowd, she has complete confidence and an electrical manner. Her style is simple, original and assured. ... she can insinuate a song into the mike. Or she can stand far back, with a male trio and belt out "Wimoweh," a symbolic number about a lion hunt. (Bracker 1960).

African prophets on the world stage like Zimbabwe's Mbuya Stella Chiweshe[1] use traditional dance and folk music to teach African spirituality.

Sculpture and Spirituality

Indigenous expressive and figurative art reflects the wealth of Shona traditional culture and religion and because their sculptors emerge from a cultural heritage rich in spiritual imagery Mack 2000: 210)it makes the discipline a reliable source for the study of religion in Africa. Zimbabwean Shona sculpture captures familiar patterns and recreates the lost rhythms of a people's culture and religion that could be very well revisited for the study of African religions. They depict hidden treasures, philosophies, and memories for those searching for new awakenings and messages by considering the spirituality defined by sculpture. An understanding of the body as a work of art among the Luba of south-eastern Congo explains why the female body undergoes modification "to enhance their sexual attractiveness and thus their fitness to become vessels to contain and transmit political power" (MacGaffey 2000: 230). This embodiment of art mirrors the work of the sculptor: "The modified body, eroticized by rich scarification, elongated labia and intricate coiffures, is itself a work of art, imitated in sculpture" (MacGaffey 2000: 230). Thus ritual bodies of men and women have whole traditions inscribed on them, and are embodied spiritual sources, human agents, reliable informers about religion in Africa. This venture will take the scholar right back to oral sources and living traditions and not necessarily historical archival material stored away in lofty places. This point is clearly reiterated in several places:

---

[1]   Mbuya Stella Chiweshe is a leading traditional *mbira* player in Africa who performed in forbidden spiritual ceremonies under the danger of imprisonment during the colonial Rhodesian government.

African art is produced in an enchanted world—a world in which a community of believers endows their ritual objects with spiritual values which are seemingly incommensurate with their physical properties. Oceans away, in a geographically separate and culturally distant corner of the globe, African art is being consumed today in a totally different, yet, I would argue, equally enchanted world. (Steiner 1994: 164)

MacGaffey discusses how African art in the hands of art collectors, in museums or galleries conceals its true meaning, and only the natural environment with "the noise, dust, darkness, and dancing" brings out its true identity because "African art is often deliberately concealed or partly visible, and the sight of it is accompanied by a variety of other sensual stimuli" (MacGaffey 2000: 225). It seems more apparent that the study of religion in Africa should seriously consider images depicted in the "noise, dust, darkness and dancing" of their origins as more authentic sources of religion than the clean, polished and shiny art on display in gallant museum spaces of distant lands. My experience at Hartsfield-Jackson Airport underscores the unique scope of ethnographic research while appreciating the evolutions and transformations of African religious artifacts. The latter inspire reinterpretations of the familiar images in distant lands as new sources of African Diaspora religious scholarship.

Conclusion

My outward journey on the red-eye flight had been rough and delayed, leaving very little time for the connection which sent me scurrying across Atlanta International Airport towards gate T4. I slowed down and stopped to the sound of *mbira* music that filled the spotless corridor that connects concourse T and A. My eyes were fixed on the gallant giant Zimbabwean poetic sculptures created from life and myths that are placed several meters apart in the corridor. This homecoming is overwhelming in creating a rollercoaster of emotions in me as I lose myself in this wonder walk. This is Zimbabwe, this space at Hartsfield-Jackson is indeed Zimbabwe graced by the native stone carved by Zimbabwean sculptors depicting local and international themes, created for me, and others to enjoy and understand the importance of the spiritual and of relationships. The clean, polished giant Shona sculpture are both alienating and inviting to the Zimbabwean migrant who is equally removed from the African natural rhythms, vitality and struggles captured in "noise, dust, darkness and dancing." Though estranged by these glamorous displays, the lure to sit and rediscover these new identities is stronger. I reach for a pen and quickly scroll the old and contemporary themes depicting "lovers" and "children," "the elegant Shona queen," "a subdued woman receiving instructions," "happy dancers," "talkative women," "travellers," "family protected by spirits," "a bird embracing a man," "water spirit *(njuzu)*", etc. Without the "noise, dust, darkness and dancing" they are estranged, especially without the sculptor and his community, including me, to interpret the religion and cultural value of these huge stone carvings and the spirituality they are imbued with in Zimbabwe.

The primacy of music and art among African peoples is unquestionable. They function in the religious, political, social, and economic structure of most African societies. As Bebey, a Cameroonian musician, argues, music is an integral part of African life from the moment of one's birth to one's death. He also notes: "African music is fundamentally a collective art. It is a communal property whose spiritual qualities are shared and experienced by all." (Bebey 1969/ 1975)

Therefore, this chapter builds upon and extends the scholarship of African traditions of art, music and dance in the study of religion in Africa. This can be done using a multi-layered theoretical framework that includes but is not limited to feminism/womanism, phenomenological, historical, and sociological approaches. As demonstrated by Peter Connolly cited in Chitando (2002: 105), religion can be studied from multiple perspectives of anthropological, psychological, phenomenological, sociological, theological, and feminist approaches.

Bibliography

Asante, K.W., *African Dance: An Artistic, Historical and Philosophical Inquiry* (Trenton, NJ: Africa World Press, 1998).

Bebey, F., *African Music, A People's Art*, 1969, trans. Josephine Bennett (New York: Lawrence Hill, 1975).

Billingslea-Brown, A.J., *Crossing Borders Through Folklore: African American Women's Fiction and Art* (Columbia: University of Missouri Press, 1999).

Bracker, Milton, "Xhosa Songstress: A former housemaid from South Africa brings her exotic songs to New York," *New York Times* (February 28, 1960): SM32.

Steiner Christopher B., *African Art in Transit: The Production of Value and Mediation of Knowledge in the African Art Trade* (Cambridge: Cambridge University Press, 1994).

Chitando, E., *Singing Culture: A Study of Gospel Music in Zimbabwe* (Uppsala: Nordic African Institute, 2002).

—, *Troubled But Not Destroyed* (Geneva: WCC Publications, 2009).

Ching Hyun, K., "Following Naked Dancing and Long Dreaming," in L.M. Russell, K. Pui-lan, A.M. Isazi Diaz, and K.G. Cannon (eds.), *Inheriting Our Mothers' Gardens: Feminist Theology in Third World Perspective* (Louisville: Westminster Press, 1988), pp. 54–5.

MacGaffey, W., "Art and Spirituality," in J. Olupona (ed.), *African Spirituality: Forms, Meaning, and Expressions* (New York: Crossroad, 2000), pp. 223–56.

Mack J. (ed.), *Africa: Arts and Culture* (New York: Oxford University Press, 2000).

Moyo, F., "'Singing and Dancing Women's Liberation': My Story of Faith," in I.A. Phiri, D.B. Govinden and S. Nadar (eds.), *Her-Stories: Hidden Histories of Women of Faith in Africa* (Pietermaritzburg: Cluster Publications, 2002), pp. 389–408.

O'Brien Wicker K., "Mami Water in African Religion and Spirituality," in J. Olupona (ed.), *African Spirituality: Forms, Meaning, and Expressions*, New York: Crossroad, 2000), pp. 198–222.

Ojo, M., "Indigenous Gospel Music and Social Reconstruction in Modern Nigeria," *Missionalia*, 26.2 (1998): 210–31.

Olupona, J. (ed.), *African Spirituality: Forms, Meaning, and Expressions* (New York: Crossroad, 2000).

Steiner Burghard C., *African Art in Transit: The Production of Value and Mediation of Knowledge in the African Art Trade* (Cambridge: Cambridge University Press, 1994).

Chapter 8
Tribes Without Rulers? Indigenous Systems of Governance and Sustainable Rural Development

Rose Mary Amenga-Etego

Introduction

The designation *Tribes Without Rulers* was used by John Middleton and David Tait for their edited work on African segmentary systems (1958). In their introductory chapter, they identified six African societies, including the Komkomba of Northern Ghana, the closest neighbours among the named societies to the Upper East Region (UER). Their book dealt with "the maintenance of social order within certain societies in Africa that have no centralized political authority" (Middleton and Tait 1958: 1). They note that the chosen six "represent certain types of uncentralized African societies only" (1958: 1), implying there were others within that typology that were not included in the collection. Besides, they were quick to point out: "We consider them as indigenous systems, unaffected by European contact" (1958: 1). Although the above identifiable statements may be considered normal within this field of study (anthropology and political science), they nevertheless bring to the fore a number of issues. Not only was their aim well defined and focused, one in which they sought to conform to and authenticate the existing methodological and theoretical frameworks of the time (Evans-Pritchard 1958: x); as E.E. Evans-Pritchard pointed out, their work fell in line with the "classification of types of African societies" and "the functions of African institutions" (1958: xi). Moreover, were these scholars suggesting that the system of governance in these societies would have been different if they had come into contact with Europe? Or, were they saying that it was their lack of contact that enabled them to be considered indigenous?

This leads me to ask the questions, "What is indigenous?" "What does it mean to be indigenous or better still, what is indigenous in the African context?" "Will the mere contact with Europe disqualify an African society, its institutional systems or practices from being classified as indigenous?" Whatever the case may be, my aim in this chapter is not to engage in the discourse of what it means to be "indigenous," but to question such an ascription in the light of contemporary notions of good governance. It is also to show how the indigenous systems of governance previously labelled "stateless" are comparable to the concept of decentralization. Thus, in the light of current discourses in the area of decentralization and sustainable rural development in Africa, these indigenous systems of governance, which are still functioning in their respective rural communities in Ghana, can be a good avenue for sustainable rural development.

Even so, the question remains as to what it means to declare a people as "tribes without rulers," "stateless," "uncentralized," or "acephalous." In one of the seminal works in this area of classification, *African Political Systems*, three distinct types of political systems were identified. Among them is the uncentralized system, which I am concerned with in this chapter. By "uncentralized," Middleton and Tait are of the view that "there is no holder of political power at the centre, and specialized roles with clearly defined authority are less easy to find" (1958: 2). This viewpoint is rather questionable. What do they mean by "no holder of political power at the centre"? Who defines the center or what is meant by political power in this religio-cultural context? The situation becomes clearer when Meyer Fortes draws his conclusion on the basis that, prior to the British occupation of the area, the people in the north-eastern corridors of the then Gold Coast had no individual person in central authority to exact tax, tribute, and services from the rest of the inhabitants or to rally them together for the purposes of war. Consequently, Fortes drew a conclusion that "They had, in short, no 'tribal' government or 'tribal' citizenship, no centralized State exercising legislative, administrative, juridical and military functions in the interest of the whole society" (Fortes 1940: 241).

As we deduce from David Kimble, the problem was not simply limited to "the absence of "really big chiefs"" or "the official ignorance of local traditions and customs," but, most importantly, the anthropological gaze. For even though there was inadequate knowledge "about the mystical functions of the *Ten'dana*, or priest-king, and his powers over land" by 1924, anthropologists still went ahead to ascribe the titles "stateless," "uncentralized," and "tribes without rulers" to these indigenous societies (Kimble 1963: 488). Kimble may simply refer to the process of disruption and ascription of new identities or labelling as "the more revolutionary invasion of the white man with his preconceived ideas" (1963: 489), but with the current system of decentralization alongside local governance, should these earlier misunderstandings of the indigenous system be allowed to linger on, resulting in the duplication of institutions of governance at the local community level with its attendant waste of scarce national resources?

Colonial Anthropological Findings

Evans-Pritchard's preface to Middleton and Tait's edited volume on *Tribes Without Rulers* clearly established the view that their collection was in line with the issues of the day. These included the desire to satisfy "the growing interest in African ethnography and to show the advancement of anthropology in method and theory" (Evans-Pritchard 1958: x). For me, questions remain as to whether such growing interest and the desire to satisfy it (as we now gather from scholars like

A.W. Cardinall, Rattray, and Fortes and their studies on the institutions, customs, and folklores of the people now constituting the UER) form part of the agenda to colonize, to project their own power to classify and name the "exotic other" or, in short, the Western imperialist interest (P'Bitek 1990: 1–7).

In their bid to systematically construct and classify these indigenous institutions of governance, anthropologists inadvertently created a hierarchical structure. Not only were these indigenous institutions of governance generally viewed in contrast to the Western system of governance; some of these systems were gradually relegated to the background. That is to say, whereas we may find discussions on chiefs and the institution of chieftaincy within the indigenous systems of governance today, the specific case of the *tindana* and *tindanaship* is contained within the former ascription as an ethnic symbol or identity (Olsen 2004: 31). In other words, *tindanaship* is to northern Ghana as chieftaincy is to other indigenous societies. It is, perhaps, in these areas of their findings that their assistance was highly sought for by colonial administrators, in their bid to rule or effectively colonize the African continent.

Although the power to read meanings into other people's ways of life and to ascribe labels or names to them were part of scholarship (Cohen and Middleton 1967: x–xii), these labels are still being used, even by indigenous African scholars (Solanke 1982: 33), without serious questioning, except some occasional reassessments and realignments of societies from one form of classification to another (Sahlins 1967: 89). This notwithstanding, I return to the words of Jolayemi Solanke which state:

> African societies developed remarkably viable and enduring social and political institutions, many of which are surviving the relentless onslaught of the twentieth century. The changes in the traditional ways of life wrought by the incursions of Western technology, modernisation and political independence are themselves legitimate subject for study, but they are not the focus of the present chapter (1982: 33).

Indigenous Governance in the Upper East Region

Even though every community in the UER has its own story about the history of its chieftaincy, there are similarities between the key components of this as an indigenous religio-cultural and socio-political institution (Awedoba 2006: 409). As A.R. Radcliffe-Brown pointed out: "In Africa it is often hardly possible to separate, even in thought, political office from ritual or religious office" (1940: xxi). For a better understanding of these interconnected institutions, a brief overview, reconstructed from various snapshots on the *tindanaship* and chieftaincy systems in the region, is outlined below.

The *Tindanaship*

Translated literally from the local language, Tait describes the *otindaa* (*tindana*) as the "landowner" (1958: 171). However, in explaining that the *otindaa* "stands in a special relation to the land, and the Land Shrine," based on what Tait refers to as his first settler right, he has helped to defuse any notion of outright ownership as the English word landowner connotes. Traditionally, people do not own land. Rather, they possess user rights based on a general understanding of their mutual interrelationship or interdependence with the land and other beings on it. This sort of relationship is enhanced by a ritual enactment or agreement initiated at the beginning of the settlement. In the case of the Dagbamba, John M. Chernoff makes this distinction when he explained that even though the word *tindana* connotes ownership, in reality, it conveys "the notion of stewardship of the well-being of the town predominates over the notion of ownership, for the notion of the *tina* includes the land within and around the town that is related to the god or shrine of the place" (Chernoff 2000: 259–60).

Tindana Alagmbange, the *tindana* of Zuarungo, explained in an interview with Milton Aberinga[1] that a *tindana* (*sic Tindaana* or *tendana*) is the founder or leader of all the settlers in a given community or land. In other interviews, the *tindanas/tindan-duma* (plural of *tindana*) made reference to their ancestors as the heads of the first families who founded their respective communities (Cardinall 1920: 16). The latter explanation is, however, misleading because the core issue surrounding the *tindanaship* is not simply based on leadership, but on the fact that as a leader of his group he led his people into a kind of natural or wild space to create a human habitat for the first time. In doing so, he and his people may not have only interrupted the natural rhythm of life in the place but could possibly have displaced other beings, beings other-than-human (Harvey 2005), from the particular location that was being settled. It is for this reason that the leader assumes a responsibility of pacifying the spirits of the area for the interruption of its normal life, created as a result of his or their presence. It is believed that the original ritual is a propitiatory one.

Today the *tindanas* have become known as the spiritual owners ("liaisons") of their respective community lands. In addition, the original settlements and their descendants are referred to as *tindaama* (early settlement and the owners of the lands). Succession to this leadership is therefore limited to this group. As the *tindana* of Sumburungo explained, a *tindana* does not really own the land. He owns the right of leading all official rituals related to the spirits of the land as a result of the special relationship he secured for his people (Tait 1958: 171). It

---

[1]   Milton Aberinga is my field research assistant based in Bolgatanga. A graduate in Social Work with Sociology from the University of Ghana, Legon, his assistance was particularly valuable in this patriarchal and patrilineal society which both of us come from. Together, we are able to navigate as well as interrogate some of the gender-based restrictions within society.

is within this context that he performs rituals to the spiritual entities dwelling on the land to ensure peaceful coexistence between them and the people. It is also by virtue of this special relationship that permission must be sought from him before any piece of land can be released for new settlements, the creation of new farm lands or any other major project. In the case of new settlement, especially in larger communities or land areas like Naga, new or subsequent migrant communities to the area may be allowed by the first *tindana* to establish their own spiritual relationship with the spirits of the area of allocation or enclave. In such communities, the *tindanbibsi* (smaller *tindanas*) function as sub or divisional *tindanas*. These see to the immediate needs of their units and may have distinct beliefs and practices from the other units in the overall community. As is the case of Naga, the Chaba unit and its earth spirit abhor witchcraft or the practice of witchcraft within its sacred space; hence, there are unique ritual practices within that unit (Chaba clan) that are absent from the rest of the Naga community. This notwithstanding, the unit *tindanas*, like the Chaba *tindana*, together with his colleague divisional *tindanas*, must work with the overall *tindana* (Naga *tindana*) for the well-being of the entire community. Perhaps it was structures such as these that led some anthropologists to suggest that the priest-kingship role of the *tindana* could have eventually developed into a kingship system if it was given the chance (Kimble 1963: 488–9).

The *tindana* communicates with the spirit of the land and performs the sacrifices necessary to bring peace, good health, and a bumper harvest for its inhabitants. At the beginning of the farming season he undertakes a number of rituals to ensure a good yield. In consultation with a diviner, he determines the type(s) of ritual(s) needed for each season or occasion. In situations where a ritual involves a sacrificial animal he is incapable of supplying, he calls on his council of elders, divisional *tindanas*, to support him by supplying the ritual requirements(s).

With the advent of the chieftaincy institution to all parts of the region, there has been a greater collaboration between the chiefs and the *tindanas* in this area of ritual performance. In these instances, some chiefs support their *tindana* with his ritual requirements. Sometimes, the community members are called upon to contribute to provide the necessary items for the ritual sacrifice(s). Usually, after the harvest, the *tindana* carries out a thanks-giving ritual, where there is a bumper harvest. These thanks-giving ritual seasons have been transformed into harvest festivals and organized on large scales for tourism and development purposes. Examples of these festivals include the *Adaarikoya* of the Bolgatanga area, the *Fao* of the Kasena-Nankanas, and the *Feok* of the Bulsas. On the other hand, when the yield is poor, the *tindana* undertakes a fact-finding mission to determine the cause and to provide solutions, mostly in the form of pacification or appeasement. This is carried out with the hope of a better harvest in the following season.

The main tenets of the institution of *tindanaship* have not been seriously affected by contemporary social change. The mode of installation has remained the same. The qualifications for the office of *tindanaship* have also not changed. According to the *tindana* of Sumborongo, "I was in Accra when through consultations the spirit directed that I become the next *tindana*. I was then brought home for the installation."[2] Sacrifices are still also carried out and they are honored by members of the community. He explained that "as the spiritual head I ensure that frequent consultations with the earth spirit is held. With this the right sacrifices are made and blessings are brought to the community. I also appeal to family and clan heads to release land, whenever the need arises, for development projects".[3]

This notwithstanding, the power of the institution has weakened as a result of the chieftaincy institution and the modern system of governance. Additionally, people's perception of the efficacy of its rituals as well as their participation has declined as a result of contemporary social change. This includes the influence of other religions, education, migration, and urbanization. In November 2006, the *tindana* of Tindunsobligo stated that "people no longer show keen interest in the sacrifices I make and some are not willing to contribute. This makes things difficult for me in terms of cost. Sometimes I have to bear the cost solely. Meanwhile, blessings from the sacrifices are for every community member."[4]

The Chieftaincy Institution

Unlike the *tindanship* which has been relegated to the background, chieftaincy is an important religio-cultural and governing institution in Ghana. Its significance is especially crucial in rural communities where the national government is considered far removed from the specific socio-cultural reality of the people (Garuru VI 2000: 30). In the rural areas of the UER for instance, the chiefs' palaces are the first points of call for political, judicial, socio-cultural, or development issues. The chieftaincy institution is a system of or a religio-cultural right to rule over a people. Writing on "Chieftaincy Politics in Ghana: Historical Dimensions," Irene Odotei observed that "The term 'chief' is used in Ghana to describe traditional rulers of varied stature, from the village head to the paramount ruler" (2003: 324). Even though her observation is true, as a recognized institution, it refers to such categories as the sub-chiefs, divisional chiefs, and paramount chiefs. For many communities in the region, the chieftaincy institution is quite recent and is also viewed as an additional leadership institution to the more indigenous *tindanaship* (Allman and Parker 2005: 81–5). In contrast to the stool systems in southern Ghana, the symbol of the chieftaincy institution in the north is the skin; hence, instead of "enstoolment," the process of becoming a chief is referred to as "enskinment."

---

[2] Interviewed at his home by Aberinga on June 13, 2009. No specific date was given except the reference "the years have gone by very quickly and one tends to lose count with time."

[3] Ibid.

[4] Interviewed by Aberinga at his home on November 26, 2006. The purpose of this interview was to obtain some comparative data for my Ph.D. dissertation on "Mending the Broken Pieces."

In the UER, the right to chiefship (*naam*) is through the male line, that is to say, the skin is patrilineal. This right is obtained by the possession of a *dongo* perceived by some as a goddess. As with a goddess, the process of becoming a chief is described in terms of courtship and marriage. It is said that the goddess is courted and married spiritually by the intended chief. In return she imbues her spouse with grace, charisma, honour, majesty, wisdom, wealth, power, and all that is required to make him outstanding to appear as a leader of the people in the land. One common favour that the *dongo* offers the chief is wives. With respect to the latter, the first wife of the chief after his enskinment is the *naam poka*. The chief also sits on materials made from animal (cow) skins. It is believed the first skin is made drom the ritual cow after *naam poka*. This is why the term "enskinment" is used to denote the process. The cow is a symbol of wealth and honour in Northern Ghana and thus, it seeks to illustrate what the *dongo* endows the new chief with . The chief, therefore, is expected to sit on wealth for his entire life.

There are different ways of becoming a chief in the region. For communities like Tongo and Bongo, the chiefs go to Nalerigo for enskinment. Having acquired his authority, the chief of Tongo, who is a paramount chief, has obtained the right to enskin the divisional chiefs in his area, including Balungo. But there is another method in parts of the Kasena-Nankani area, examples of this include the Kologo and Naga chieftaincies (paramountcies), where the family that enskins the new chiefs is not chiefly. Besides, the latter entails a combination of the indigenous owner of the *dongo* and an electoral system from the District Assembly. Traditionally, those endowed with the original spirit of the chieftaincy or possess the right to enskin others are referred to as the owners or parents of the *dongo*. They are not only crucial in the selection of the candidate and the enskinment processes, they are also important at the death of a reigning chief. At death, the *dongo* returns to them (her parent, owner, or next of kin). When the chief is buried and the funeral is performed, the *dongo* becomes available to be contested for by a new set of princes from the prevailing patrilineal royal line. Therefore, the owner of the *dongo* is always involved in all the processes related to their brand of chieftaincy, especially at any time a fresh claim is made to possess the *dongo*.

With particular reference to the latter example, a new chief is sought for and enskinned only after the death of a previous one. The election or selection is initiated in the form of a request to the *dongo* to obtain her preference among a number of competing princes. To obtain the results, two independent enquiries are made through *bakoloko* (divination): one by the royal family and the other by the owner or parent of the *dongo*. The results are then compared. As long as there are disparities or inconsistencies in their findings, the enquiry process will be repeated until both parties produce the same prince as the preference of the *dongo* for marriage, and for that matter, the chieftaincy. The selected prince begins his journey to become the chief by first going through a period of intense indoctrination and the acquisition of knowledge. This training session includes the history and secrets of the community as well as of the skin (chieftaincy). It is at this point that the prince is taught the dictates of his *dongo*; hence, it is during this period that the prince becomes acquainted with the goddess and all that she represents.

During this period, only the skin makers (kingmakers) are allowed to see the prince. They are considered the most knowledgeable in this area of affairs. The head of the skin makers is the owner or parent of the *dongo*. The prince is accompanied through this special and most crucial ritual period by the *dongo poka* (*dongo*'s wife). The *dongo poka* is the woman who is enskinned together with the chief. She is usually the first or senior wife of the prince. She goes through the period of instruction and fortification "side by side with the chief." She is expected to know what the chief knows with regards to the ways of the *dongo* so that she can prompt or advise him when he is straying. Unlike the chief's other wives, therefore, she has a spiritual bond with both the chief and the *dongo*. In my view, this title is quite complicated and controversial since the *dongo* is feminine and the process is described in the symbolic frame of a marriage. In other words, how can a married man go with his wife into a ritual process to marry another woman (*dongo* goddess) but at the end, emerges as a chief and his wife, the *dongo poka*? How come the man becomes the chief and the wife, the *dongo*'s wife (the literal translation of *dongo poka*)? Is there some form of ritual or symbolic exchange between the woman and goddess? Even though these questions require further investigation, this is not the focus of the current study.

At the end of the period of spiritual and physical instruction, and the acquisition of all the attributes required for ruling the people, the new chief is shown to the people. During this ceremony, the horn (symbol) representing the *dongo* is ritually invoked in a process known as *ngme dongo ti ba nyu* (beat the *dongo* and let them drink). This ritual is the period of swearing the oath of allegiance to the new chief. The people involved in this ritual include the skin makers and the princes. The process is immediately followed by the swearing of the oath of allegiance by the new chief to the people of the land and a promise to obey the rules of the *dongo*. It is the general belief that anyone who swears the oath and goes contrary to its tenets will immediately die. As a result, all contestants are expected to rally behind and support the winner or new chief to restore peace and unity in the community.

Chiefs who violate the rules or taboos of the *dongo* become victims of her wrath. Her favors are withdrawn and, in the worst cases, the chief loses control of the people and eventually appears ordinary before the people. He loses his good sense of judgment. This culminates in the demise of the chief, leading to the search for a new chief. It is said that the rules of the *dongo* seek to make the chief live a righteous life. They enable the chief to do what is right, just, and fair. Compliance to the rules of the *dongo* offer several favours to the chief and his subjects. On the other hand, disobedience does not go unpunished.

As a female spirit or goddess, the *dongo* demands sacrifices from the chief and his people. She also demands strict adherence to the rules and regulations governing the possession of her power and benevolence. In line with this she possesses enormous power to inflict her wrath on any person in the community who goes contrary to her ideals: most especially, the chief. The *dongo* is cared for by the chief and his subjects. Together with the *tingani* (earth/land spirit), which is cared for by the *tindana* (earth priest), these two spirits have joint responsibility to protect and inform the people of the land about iminent dangers. Thus, they form a spiritual anchor in times of war, famine, or drought or even in times of abundance and success. The *tindana* is the spiritual head of the land but is a subject to the chief of the community. As a result, the *tindana* and the chief are partners. Together, they form the spiritual and political leaders of their communities. While the chief rules over the *tindana* and the rest of his subjects as their political leader, the *tindana* is the spiritual leader of everyone dwelling in the community. He plays his leadership role from the background by providing the necessary spiritual services to the land on behalf of the people. Since the *dongo* dwells in the land, and the *tindana* is the landlord, it goes without saying that the *tindana* is the spiritual head of the land.

This form of power-sharing system (spiritual and political) is not limited to the religio-political institutions governing *tindanaship* and chieftaincy, as exemplified in the case of the Kologo and Naga scenarios presented above. According to the indigenous belief systems of the region, spiritual power is not vested in one spiritual being. This is irrespective of the traditional view that *Wine* (the Supreme Being) is the creator of the universe and all its spiritual entities. It is generally held that *Wine* shares this great resource through a self-styled delegated system with other beings and entities known the *yan-duma* (ancestors), *baga* (divinities) and a host of other spiritual beings and objects (Awolalu and Dopamu 1979: 68–71). S.A. Thorpe refers to this relationship as a "'senate' of deities" (1991: 105), and it is these other spirits who are responsible for the daily administration of the universe. With this system of power sharing, one's ardent belief in or preference for one of these spiritual entities does not necessarily exclude him or her from benefiting from the others. As evidently displayed in the description of both institutions of *tindanaship* and chieftaincy, even though the rights of eligibility is obtained through the lineage system (which is vested on the individuals through their ancestors), the main power sources are the *tingani* and *naam dongo*, both of which are divinities. This creates a system of interdependence and collaboration which complement and balance one another. This state of affairs is reflected in the culture of the people, as can be seen in their way of life (Hulsether 2005: 491). If, therefore, the religio-cultural sources of power are shared, one wonders why these earlier anthropologists expected the political system to be different (centralized)?

Governance in Contemporary Ghana

In Odotei's contribution to the book on *Indigenous Political Structures and Governance in Africa*, she clearly outlined the various encounters between the pre-colonial governing institutions of traditional societies (chieftaincy) in Africa and the modern system of governance with specific reference to Ghana. As a historian, she identified each principal intersection and its impact on the chieftaincy institution. Observing that some sort of a consensus was and is still built around maintaining this institution as a part of our indigenous heritage, she also drew upon the prevailing popular desire for some form of a working link between the traditional authorities and the modern system of governance in the country (Odotei 2003: 324–5). The latter, however, is bedevilled with controversies that are not of concern to this chapter.

The most important thing to note is that governance in African societies is no longer dependent on the indigenous institutional structures and authorities, and their related religio-cultural value systems which are coded in taboos. Instead, governance is dependent on laws that are nationally formulated and enforced through external powers and structures such as legislators, lawyers and the law courts, and prison officers and the prisons that are not physically present in most communities. Yet, even though the gradual exclusion of traditional leaders from the mainstay of governance is pronounced in urban centres where their authority is less visible, their authority is essential for the maintenance of law and order as well as development in their respective rural communities.

As illustrated by Odotei, there have been some reforms in the chieftaincy institution to enable it conform to the democratic tenets of the country (Amenga-Etego 2007: 80–82). Some of these reforms, however, have been to the detriment of this traditional institution. Some of the conflicts related to the chieftaincy institution are observed to be a direct result of these reforms. Yet the search for good governance continues to take a toll on the indigenous systems as various concepts are being experimented with on the African continent. For instance, the concept of good governance as defined by the World Bank is "the exercise of political power to manage a nation's affairs" (World Bank 1981: 60–1). This definition is based on the Western democratic system, the key indicators of which include multiparty politics, participatory governance, respect for human rights, and anti-corruption policies and practices. This conceptual framework has also become a key factor in both development cooperation and discourses. But good governance does not necessarily result in development and wealth creation. This is because if these indices are not backed up by good social and fiscal policies, their presence would not necessarily result in development. Besides, does it imply the indigenous systems have no avenues for such a concept?

There are also pertinent questions regarding the import of the above World Bank definition on non-Western countries. In Africa, where the concept has become a crucial index on the development agenda, it is often employed as an analytical tool for the assessment of her underdevelopment and poverty status. It stands to question the place of indigenous systems of governance which, in the case of Ghana, continue to function in some respect, with the modern system of governance. African societies have socio-political institutions and tenets that, to some degree, ensure participatory governance and individual self-expression, as illustrated under the *tindanaship* system above. In other words, the current call for decentralization, which seeks to defuse the power structure so as to delegate some of its authority for the essential governance and development of the various segments of society, reflects the indigenous system of *tindanaship*, as in the Naga example. Therefore, it could be argued that this supposedly new system (decentralization) is a readjustment or amalgamation of the indigenous systems of governance. However, because of the inability to properly adjust or align the two systems of governance (indigenous and modern), the creation of such bodies like District Assembly Members and Unit Committee Members has, in some cases, led to power struggles at the local level, instead of facilitating good governance and sustainable development.

Indigenous Systems of Governance and Socio-Economic Development

Writing on the modes of succession, one of the major issues surrounding traditional leadership in contemporary society in the UER in 2006, Albert K. Awedoba added that:

> The primary objective of traditional leadership has been to effect development, as it is understood in the community. This could be through the exploitation of the religious, economic, political and other strategies and resources available, including warfare if need be. On the question of effective leadership: it would seem that these days not only is a chief expected to lead the community to attract developers and win the community's share of the national cake, the loyalty of the chief to his people, to his region and to the nation and even the government of the day is highly valued by stakeholders. (Awedoba 2006: 423)

If this was the case, why is the region still grappling with serious poverty and underdevelopment, even after the 2000 Population and Housing Census report (Ghana Statistical Service 2005) had categorically outlined the key indicators to include education, health, agriculture, environment, infrastructure and social amenities as part of its problem areas? Is it to say that the communities' understanding of these identifiable manifestations of poverty and underdevelopment, categorized according to the demands of modernity, are incompatible? Or are the leaders ineffective in attracting the requisite developers and in their demand for the people's share of the national cake as indicated? Among the many questions raised by this quotation from Awedoba is the issue of loyalty and whether or not traditional leaders are able to cope with and navigate the different strands of loyalties needed by the stakeholders involved. All these questions put considerable pressure on traditional authorities, the majority of whom are either illiterate or semi-illiterate, yet are called upon by these diverse stakeholders and demands within the frameworks of tradition and modernity.

Traditionally, the role of the *tindanas* as spiritual leaders of their respective communities imposes on them the responsibility of seeking spiritual favours from the spiritual beings, in and around their communities, for their people. These spiritual favours include petitions for peace and unity, good health, the warding off of evil and disasters, high fertility in humans and animals as well as bumper harvest. Additionally, their special relationship and sensitivity to the environment as a spiritual entity enables them to seek ways of living that promote sustainability, a key concept in modern development discourse since the 1980s. Besides, as custodians of the land, *tindanas* have greater control over the use of the land as an important resource in contemporary sustainable development (Seini 2006: 552). In their relationship with the land as a spiritual entity, *tindanas* can be important allies in the fight against environmental degradation in the communities (Alhassan 2006: 527–8).

Similarly, the chief who is currently "an embodiment of the cultural identity of his people" (Odotei 2003: 325), not only wields military, legislative, judiciary, and executive powers; his co-tenureship with the *tindana* enables him to exercise some socio-economic control over the land and natural resources in his area of jurisdiction for development (Alhassan 2006: 534–6). Chiefs often use their positions as the religio-political leaders of their communities to mobilize their subjects and their resources for their communities' well-being. In the past, these community-based actions were directed into rituals, construction of homes or new settlements and farming. In addition to these, today's mobilization efforts are channelled into building schools, community and market centers as well as the establishment of development funds for subsequent action. For instance, the paramount chief of Bongo explained that

> when I am on the skin that is where my voice is best heard. Even though I have been an assemblyman [of Akunduo], I had limited powers as an assemblyman. As God has given me this opportunity I think that I want to spearhead development and my priority is going to be education. The second is health, the third one is the environment.

Identifying education as his first priority is an important step, but he will have to collaborate effectively with the District Chief Executive and District Director of Education of his community for their support. Even so, his immediate focus on education should not be narrowly skewed toward formal education. This is because educational programmes can be organized on various pertinent topics in the community's health and environmental issues.

On the religio-cultural front, the chief indicated the use of the traditional harvest thanksgiving festival, the *Zambeene*, to generate the initial fund to start an educational development fund to support brilliant but needy students, with priority for girls. This is a laudable idea because it has the potential of addressing both his socio-cultural and educational visions. This is because Arhin Brempong has explained how the "proliferation of festivals centred around traditional rule as symbolic statements of ethnic or sub-ethnic identities and autonomy in the area of traditional rule but also as a means for mobilizing resources within and without the political community for the purpose of advancing material welfare" (2001: x).

Conclusion

Even though the indigenous system of governance, made up of *tindanas* and chiefs, bears some resemblance to the modern democratic system because of the representations, the two systems are uniquely different. While the former is religio-culturally enshrined, the latter is secular. That is, the nature of indigenous leaders, although based on the lineage systems of their respective communities, is imbued with sacred rituals, and this sets them apart from the multi-party system of modern governance. This is not to say that they have not influenced each other. It is quite easy to see snapshots of community-based or ethnic-based inclinations and support systems in the current democratic structure. It is for these reasons that the duplication of the structures of governance, especially in rural African communities, is not only breeding conflicts as a result of internal power struggles, but is inadvertently stalling development. The latter is clearly visible where the parties involved are unable to collaborate and coordinate their efforts effectively to utilize their limited resources. There is, therefore, a need to undertake a comprehensive examination of governance in Africa so as to carve out a suitable system for the continent. As of now, some of the new concepts that are being introduced on to the scene seem like a simple repackaging of the indigenous African system that was hitherto viewed with prejudice under the guise of civilization.

Even so, this proposed stock-taking exercise needs to pay significant attention to the current divergent views expressed within the African continent. For instance, there were conflicting answers to my question on the future of these indigenous institutions. For some people, the institutions must not only be preserved and empowered; they should be strategically included in the modern democratic system of governance to preserve our continental identity, stressing that such a move was crucial even in this era of globalization. Others, however, argued that given the manner in which some of these indigenous institutions are handled, they are nothing but iconic relics of our heritage. To this group of people, the future of these institutions is not important. They argued that their future should be left to the natural trend of events, stating that "what will be shall be." Yet for others, these indigenous institutions, like other religio-cultural practices, ought to be seen as our heritage's living museums; hence, in this age of commercialization and globalization, it is not only relevant to preserve them; they should be repackaged and marketed as tourist attractions. One section of this group noted that the proceeds could be channelled to the development of their respective communities. The other section of the group added that the move could be seen as part of the modern call for sustainable development. A few individuals likened such a process to the proverbial "killing two birds with one stone."

Irrespective of the above observations, the reality on the ground provides significant data for consideration. It is quite clear that while the *tindanaship* is basically relegated to the background, perhaps as a boundary marker (Olsen

2004: 33),[5] the current state of the chieftaincy institution is still the second most important indigenous system and practice in Ghana, second only to the general traditional belief systems, which are deeply enshrined in peoples' worldviews. As a matter of fact, it is the most organized and visible establishment of our indigenous heritage. Even though contemporary socio-political changes have turned it into some form of a tourist attraction, having lost its military role as well as much of its executive and judicial power to the modern democratic system and law courts, its absorption into a modern administrative structure continues to provide a glimmer of hope. Currently identified under the Ministry of Chieftaincy and Culture, these institutions may continue to wield power in their local communities, most especially, in the rural areas. This is because, the "Customary law" of Ghana; so defined as "the rules of law which by custom are applicable to particular communities in Ghana",[6] provides an immediate avenue of justice to those who need it most. Besides, they continue to be the most immediate source of both spiritual and material development to the people. Thus, unlike the ad hoc forms of developmental provisions of the external political system, these indigenous institutions which are part of the environment seek and provide a more sustainable form of development for their communities.

It is reasonably clear from the above discussion that the religio-cultural systems provided the necessary social cohesion and political harmony for some of these indigenous African societies hitherto described as "stateless" or "tribes without rulers." With respect to the example drawn from the Kologo and Naga communities, the *tindanas* and later, together with the chiefs, were the major religio-cultural institutions exercising the relevant physical decentralized political system of governance in the area. They did this by balancing their positions and duties efficiently through diverse systems of control mechanisms, including ritual performances, mediation, and arbitration. In these capacities, they were capable of mobilizing social and religious resources within their communities for their important and immediate needs, hence they saw to the overall development of their communities.

Bibliography

Alhassan, Osman, "Traditional Authorities and Sustainable Development: Chiefs and Resource Management," in Irene K. Odotei and Albert K. Awedoba (eds.), *Chieftaincy in Ghana: Culture, Government and Development* (Legon: Sub-Saharan Publishers, 2006), pp. 527–46.

---

[5]   Unlike Olsen's view, however, the *tindanaship* is not as much "important ethnic marker" as it is a boundary issue, creating a clear difference between the varied ethnic groups of the north from the south whose boundary marker may be seen in the queen mother.

[6]   Article 11 (3), *The Constitution of the Republic of Ghana*, 1992.

Allman, Jean and John Parker, *Tongnaab: The History of a West African God* (Bloomington and Indianapolis: Indiana University Press, 2005).

Amenga-Etego, Rose Mary, "Mending the Broken Pieces: Religion and Sustainable Rural Development among the Nankani of Northern Ghana," PhD Diss., University of Edinburgh (2007).

Awedoba, A.K., "Modes of Succession in the Upper East Region of Ghana," in Irene K. Odotei and Albert K. Awedoba (eds.), *Chieftaincy in Ghana: Culture, Government and Development* (Legon: Sub-Saharan Publishers, 2006), pp. 409–27.

Awolalu, J. Omosade and P. Adelumo Dopamu, *West African Traditional Religion* (Nigeria: Onibonoje Press & Book Industries (Nig.) Ltd., 1979).

Brempong, Arhin, *Transformations in Traditional Rule in Ghana (1951–1996)* (Accra: Sedco 2001).

Cardinall, A.W., *The Natives of the Northern Territories of the Gold Coast: Their Customs, Religion and Folklore* (London: George Routledge and Sons, 1920).

Chernoff, John M., "Spiritual Foundations of Dagbamba Religion and Culture," in Jacob K. Olupona (ed.), *African Spirituality: Forms, Meanings, and Expressions* (New York: Crossroad, 2000), pp. 257–74.

Cohen, Ronald and John Middleton, "Introduction", in Ronald Cohen and John Middleton (eds.), *Comparative Political Systems* (New York: The Natural History Press, 1967), pp. ix–xiv.

Evans-Pritchard, E.E. "Preface", in John Middleton and David Tait (eds.), *Tribes Without Rulers: Studies in African Segmentary Systems* (London: Routledge and Kegan Paul, 1958), pp. ix–xi.

Fortes, M. "The Political System of the Tallensi of the Northern Territories of the Gold Coast," in M. Fortes and E.E. Evans-Pritchard (eds.), *African Political Systems* (London: Oxford University Press, 1940), pp. 239–71.

Garuru VI, Togbega, "Traditional Ruler (A Man): The role of women in the Ghanaian Culture," in Elizabeth Amoah and Mercy Amba Oduyoye (eds.), *When Silence is no Longer an Option* (Accra-North: Sam-Woode Ltd, 2000), pp. 27–30.

Ghana Statistical Service, *Population Data Analysis Report* Vol. 2, Population and Housing Census 2000. (August 2005). Available at www.statsghana.gov.gh/nada/index.php/ddibrowser/3, accessed on November 1, 2011.

Harvey, Graham, *Animism: Respecting the Living World* (London: Hurst and Company, 2005).

Hulsether, Mark, "Religion and Culture," in John R. Hinnells (ed.), *The Routledge Companion to the Study of Religion* (London and New York: Routledge, 2005), pp. 487–508.

Kimble, David, *A Political History of Ghana: The Rise of Gold Coast Nationalism 1850–1928* (Oxford: Clarendon Press, 1963).

Middleton, John and David Tait, "Introduction," in John Middleton and David Tait (eds.), *Tribes Without Rulers: Studies in African Segmentary Systems* (London: Routledge and Kegan Paul, 1958), pp. 1–31.

Odotei, Irene, "Chieftaincy Politics in Ghana: Historical Dimensions," in Olufemi Vaughan (ed.), *Indigenous Political Structures and Governance in Africa* (Ibadan: Sefer, 2003), pp. 322–45.

Olsen, Kjell, "Heritage, Religion and the Deficit of Meaning in Institutionalized Discourse," in Anna-Leena Siikala, Barbro Klein and Stein Mathisen (eds.), *Creating Diversities: Folklore, Religion and the Politics of Heritage* (Helsinki: Finnish Literature Society, 2004), pp. 31–42.

P'Bitek, Okot, *African Religions in European Scholarship* (New York and Chesapeake, ECA Associates, 1990).

Radcliffe-Brown, A.R., "Preface", in M. Fortes and E. E. Evans-Pritchard (eds.), *African Political Systems* (London: Oxford University Press, 1940), pp. xi–xxiii.

Sahlins, Marshall D., "The Segmentary Lineage: An Organization of Predatory Expansion," in Ronald Cohen and John Middleton (eds.), *Comparative Political Systems* (New York: The Natural History Press, 1967), pp. 89–119.

Seini, A. Wayo, "The Role of Traditional Authorities in Rural Development," in Irene K. Odotei and Albert K. Awedoba (eds.), *Chieftaincy in Ghana: Culture, Government and Development* (Legon: Sub-Saharan Publishers, 2006), pp. 547–64.

Solanke, Jolayemi, "Traditional Social and Political Institutions," in Richard Olaniyan (ed.), *African History and Culture* (Lagos: Longman Nigeria, 1982), pp. 27–37.

Tait, David, "The Territorial Pattern and Lineage System of Konkomba," in John Middleton and David Tait (eds.), *Tribes Without Rulers: Studies in African Segmentary Systems* (London: Routledge and Kegan Paul, 1958), pp. 167–202.

Thorpe, S.A., *African Traditional Religions: An Introduction* (Pretoria: University of South Africa Press, 1991).

World Bank, *Sub-Saharan Africa: From Crisis to Sustainable Growth* (Washington, 1981).

Chapter 9
"Life is Superior to Wealth?": Indigenous Healers in an African Community, Amasiri, Nigeria

Elijah Obinna

Introduction

An examination of the conceptions of health and healing among the Amasiri offers an interesting basis for interacting with ambivalences surrounding definitions of knowledge and the concept of disease. Indigenous healing reveals a process in which the healer, client, and the social and cosmological order of the Amasiri interact to bring about meaningful, desired results of healing to individuals, groups, or community. The Amasiri clan has three autonomous communities which include Ezeke, Ndukwe, and Opi (which is an acronym for Ohaechara, Poperi, and Ihie). The villages that make up Amasiri clan are compact, with populations in the thousands (Oko 1993: 15). Although Amasiri villages belong to the matrilineal system (*Ikwu nne*), the organization of the villages and compounds is built up around patrilineal lineages (*Umudi*), thus every individual member of the clan belongs to a double descent. This family network plays a key role in the sustenance of the indigenous worldview and quest for holistic well-being.

Indigenous healers appear to be the key health resource for several Nigerian groups, including the Amasiri clan. Although there are also a good number of Western medical practitioners, in many cases indigenous healers are the preferred source of health care (Adegoke 2007: 223–32). Indigenous healers as respected members of the community function in multiple capacities. Their leadership and services play a major role in the field of health, governance, family disputes, marriage/divorce, sexuality/infertility, and guidance of children. Their advice is often sought, believed, and acted upon by many community members. Their geographical distribution often provides access that appears unattainable by the modern providers and health dispensaries. The influence of some indigenous healers on policy makers and religious leaders appears to assure an additional important avenue of impact.

Furthermore, among the Amasiri, indigenous healers serve not only as healers but also as consultants on family, village, and clan matters. They also take an interest in ecological issues and, as such, are often consulted when there appears to be a delay in the coming of the rains and also when there is a flood or drought. Irrespective of these huge roles played by indigenous healers, there remains increasing misrepresentation by both the government and even by some of their clients.

In view of the above, this chapter seeks to engage with the following questions: Why are many people among the Amasiri attached to indigenous medicine even upon conversion to Christianity? What reasons have informed the continuity of indigenous medicine and the belief of many people among the Amasiri in its efficacy? How are indigenous healers negotiating or renegotiating modernity and what challenges does that hold for both the government and the people of Amasiri? Are these practices related to poverty—some people seeking out indigenous healing instead of Western medicine due to financial constraints?

In order to engage with these issues, there is the need for a wider understanding of the general roles of healers that are integral for the effective functioning of an indigenous society. This chapter shows the nature and reasons for the resilience of indigenous medicine among the Amasiri. Furthermore, the chapter argues that an understanding of the socio-religious context of the Amasiri is crucial in order to value the extent to which the services of indigenous healers are sought, even in contemporary times. For many within the Amasiri, life has no duplicate and it is more precious than wealth so it has to be preserved through whatever means possible.

Understanding Health and Illness

Among the Amasiri, health appears to be valued above wealth. This is evidenced by many adages including *Ahafu ndu kpa eku nonye iro erie ye*, meaning that wealth accumulated at the expense of one's health is mere vanity and savings for one's enemies. This strong attachment to good health is also revealed through the names that the Amasiri people bear: *Ndubuisi* meaning "life is the ultimate," *Ndukaku* meaning "life is greater than wealth," and *Ndukwe* "if life permits." Thus health for the traditional Amasiri is the foundation of societal development and individual greatness. It is considered a shameful thing to die of a disease owing to lack of funds to receive the medication required. To this end, many individuals and families often sell their land or property in order to receive treatment during illnesses. In some cases, individuals who are not able to pay the healer end up living with and serving the healer for an agreed period in order to indemnify their bills. In other cases, daughters of patients are sometimes given in marriage to the healer as payment for successful treatment.

Health for many Amasiri therefore does not merely entail a healthy body or a healthy mind. Health is a sum first, of a person's relations with the family and community members including the living dead (Iroegbu 2005: 81). Disease is thus not just a physical or mental malfunctioning of the body system, but it is a religious matter. Therefore "health and illnesses" are inextricably connected with socially approved behavior and moral conduct. Sickness implies that there is an imbalance between the metaphysical and the human world as the flow of supernatural life force may have been disturbed. Thus, disease is often conceived as resulting either from a failure to uphold some religious rituals or ceremonies such as initiation into the Ogo society or from revealing the secrets of that society.

Ogo society is an institution into which every Amasiri male is expected to be initiated. It is believed that a male initiated into the society cannot be attacked by malevolent spirits, witches, or sorcerers as long as such a person lives by the rules. Often within the Amasiri patients are brought home from cities for healing. Sometimes parents, on hearing of their child's illness in the city, would say *Unu Ihilatie ezi,*, meaning he or she should be brought home; implying with a high sense of confidence that there will be a sure healing once the person is brought home.

Within contemporary Amasiri society there are diseases thought to be curable by modern medicine and others not, and in the light of such a division one knows what kind of healer to consult. This differentiation between sicknesses in medical anthropology is referred to as hierarchy of resort or, the customizing of practice—a decision process that includes moral spheres of reference (Narayanan 2004). Most common diseases like the common cold, stomach ache, and headaches are often interpreted as a "fault in the physical system," and are treated with herbal medicine or modern tablets from dispensaries. However, persistent headaches, intermittent fever, continued stomach disorder, menstrual troubles, repeated miscarriage, etc. are often attributed to unseen forces. Such cases are taken to indigenous healers for cure. Even in contemporary Amasiri society, Western medicine may be considered first, but if the illness persists, indigenous healers are consulted. In some cases, medical cures as well as propitiation of the unseen powers are undertaken simultaneously.

Similarly, calamities such as the failure of crops, total blindness, repeated failures in undertakings, or inability to find a loving and stable marital partner, or the death of children or adults in quick succession, are taken to indicate "misfortune" and the handiwork of malevolent forces. These forces include witches, sorcerers, and spirits; they have unlimited influence and control in the affairs of humans in the world. Smallpox, cholera, and plagues are always attributed to the wrath of various unseen forces, and for such diseases sacrifices are often carried out. The Amasiri indigenous worldview considers disease to be a state of disharmony in the body as a whole and not only a result of external factors and causes. Thus, treatment should aim not only at the finding of appropriate internal remedies, but the employment of all available means to restore normal balance or equilibrium.

This indigenous view of diseases is much more widely held among Christians. Several diseases are often seen as "attacks" from the devil, for which intensive prayers, sometimes with fasting, should be observed. Thus there appears to be an intersection of the indigenous and Christian worldviews. The intersection involves, first, acceptance of the idea that lesser spiritual entities play a part in the material world and, second, that prayers as ritual can influence these powers. Western medicine has chiefly considered disease as the result of outside agencies like microbes; while the indigenous understanding perceives disease as a result of complex malfunction. Within this scenario prayer is not only words recited or sung, but action as well, and is supposed to do things—attract and drive out different forces. Through the performative force of ritual speech and action, benevolent forces are attracted, while malevolent forces are repelled (Adogame 2005: 3). Two planes of spiritual warfare—horizontal and vertical axis—are clearly marked out for the encounter. Members are charged to enact intensive prayer rituals as a potent tool for deliverance from this "spiritual warfare zone" and "Satan's strongholds."

While some Christians reject the indigenous system of divination and sacrifice, they have retained belief in the influence of lesser spiritual entities over the material world and the efficacy of prayer as the key ritual for influencing the powers (Ray 1993: 267–8). Robbins (2004: 128–9) refers to this tendency "to preserve people's beliefs in the reality and power of the spiritual worlds from which they have broken" as perhaps the most distinctive quality of global Pentecostalism generally in comparison with other forces of cultural change, and one that distinguishes it from other forms of Christianity. It is important to ask if Christians in Amasiri could possibly break from belief in the spiritual world as suggested by Robbins. Rather, what is seen appears to be a reconstruction of the past in the present. Thus boundaries appear fixed, but actually fluid, between exclusive reliance on Christian resources and recourse to indigenous healers.

Furthermore, as Robbins points out, Pentecostals tend to demonize the indigenous spirit world and then devote much of their energy to struggling against it, thus reinforcing its existence and its relevance to post-conversion life. Peel (2000: 314–15) refers to the way Nigerian Christians—especially the new Pentecostals—regard these "hidden forces" as potential hazards, impeding personal progress and preventing individuals from achieving their destinies. Within the contemporary Presbyterian Church of Nigeria (PCN) at Amasiri, which shares many Pentecostal and charismatic features, there are healing services held every Wednesday and night prayers. Common at such services are prophecies, revelations, speaking in tongues, spiritual songs, and loud shouts of "halleluiah" and "Amen." Spiritual healing involving laying on of hands, anointing oil, and prophetic prayers are also prominent therapeutic options among the PCN.

Furthermore, some Christians within Amasiri continue to patronize indigenous healers directly or through their families. Severe misfortunes like sickness, death, and spirit possession are developments that often motivate religious conversion and the continuity of such beliefs. It does appear that indigenous healers exhibit greater success in the alleviation of psychological disturbances than Western-trained psychotherapists. Indigenous healers are often very conscious of social order and group cohesion, and particularly family harmony and group dependency (Cheetham and Griffiths 1982: 957). Indigenous healers therefore operate within the specific social pattern of the people and also within the context of their religious experiences. These give indigenous healers a priestly role, consulting the ancestors and discovering their prescriptions for problems.

Furthermore, some Pentecostal, charismatic, and even some mission churches appear to appropriate some of the practices of these indigenous healers in their worship. Idowu (1973: 205) underscores the ongoing religious reconstructions by some Amasiri Christians in attempts to solve existing life problems. Although

Christians, they are not exempt from the harsh realities of life and so solutions are often sought from multiple sources. Within the PCN, as well as other Christian groups in Amasiri, members with one problem or another often turn first to their pastors or prayer (warriors) groups for solution. Unfortunately if those consultations do not yield the needed quick result, such persons often feel they have no choice but to return to indigenous diviners or healers for solutions. They could, directly or through agents, consult diviners and follow their advice to perform rituals in the village, family, or in some other sacred spaces. When the problems are over, such Christians sometimes return to Christianity and continue from where they stopped. This shuttle or window shopping in the spiritual market place is often described as "attempting to go where it works." Thus the bottom line is based on the individual's and group's notion of what it means to say that something has worked. Furthermore, it involves a related engagement with pursuing whatever means that will bring that form of efficacy.

Despite a tendency to demonize indigenous culture and to present themselves as modern individuals, many Amasiri Christians continue to interpret Christianity through the lens of existing religious categories and especially the indigenous search for spiritual power (Okorocha 1987: 206, 278). For the Igbo, the quest for power (*agbara*) to enhance life is the hermeneutical key to understanding their attraction to all religion.

Some Amasiri Christians attach a variety of meanings to the experience of suffering. Sometimes it is regarded as an enemy to be overcome through faith and prayer, especially if it is believed to be satanic in origin. In this case, problems such as sickness, barrenness, poverty, and failure are believed to be caused by human or spiritual agents of Satan, who are then counteracted by means of aggressive spiritual warfare. This presents elements of continuity with indigenous belief such as that present among the Igbo. Affliction is often blamed on the activities of malicious agents, such as witches or evil spirits, and various preventative and purificatory rites are performed to immunize potential victims against their attacks (Peel 2000: 166; Okorocha 1987: 131).

Belief in the powers of witchcraft is held by both Christians and adherents of the indigenous religion. It is often common to hear comments such as *Choch erukwe ghi naya onwani a*, meaning that a particular situation cannot be undermined or explained through a Christian lens. This indicates relative assignment of authority, contingent on the nature of the affliction. Witches are thus persons or mediums empowered by diabolic spirits to cause evil and disaster. Witches are individuals who have access to the spirit realm and are able to use their knowledge of the spirit world to inflict disease on others (Olupona 2004: 113). It is believed that certain illnesses which defy scientific treatment can be transmitted through witchcraft, including barrenness, infertility, accidents, disasters, attacks by dangerous animals, and bites by dangerous snakes.

Indigenous Healing

The divergent views of various cultures produce different concepts and perceptions of health, physical well-being, and religion. Indigenous healers often share their client's cultural norms and are therefore individuals from whom people seek various forms of assistance, healing, and guidance (Helms and Cook 1999; Sue and Sue 1999). Sue and Sue (1999) assert that from the beginning of human existence, all cultural groups had developed not only their own explanations of abnormal behaviours, but also cultural-specific ways of dealing with human problems and distresses.

These culturally bound methods could be termed indigenous forms of healing. In addition, societies like the Amasiri have designated individuals or families considered to be gifted in healing. Their duties involve not only curing physical ailments, but also addressing problems that relate to psychological malfunctions. Helms and Cook (1999) also note that indigenous healing refers to helpful beliefs and practices that originate within a culture or society, that are not transported from other regions, and that are designed to treat the inhabitants of a given group.

Helms and Cook's thoughts on indigenous healing are helpful but limited in their scope. Contrary to their views, healing methods and materials used may not necessarily originate from the same community; there are also possibilities of learning and borrowing from other clans, sometime in exchange for gifts. Moreover, indigenous healers do not only treat clients from within their own areas as often their services are also sought by people from a wide range of locations. Hardly would an indigenous healer among the Amasiri decline to offer such services. It is often thought that a wider patronage of indigenous medicine implies its wide acceptance and efficacy. Some healers may sometimes not require any cash deposit before treatment, implying that they trust the potency of their medicine and that payment should be made after the healing has been effected.

These processes involve healing by creating and validating a narrative or history of affliction for the client that contributes to resolving the problems. Indigenous medicine covers a wide range of therapies and practices, healers might specialize in particular areas or combine various specializations. Examples include the Indigenous Birth Attendant (IBA). In 1978, the World Health Organization (WHO) recognized the traditional birth attendants (TBA) as important allies in the expansion of primary health care. The TBA is defined as "a person (usually a woman) who assists the mother at childbirth and who initially acquired her skills delivering babies by herself or by working with other Traditional Birth Attendants (TBA)" (Oakley and Houd 1990: 23).

Among the Amasiri, TBA are often elderly women aged 60–85; without formal training. They learned the craft from a member of their family or kin group or under the tutelage of older attendants. Once their reputations are established, they might begin to draw clients from beyond their immediate groups. Indigenous birth attendants are more than just useful source of physical help to families. They speak in languages and concepts that their clients understand and often accept.

This is because they have learnt through experience the proper approach to take to village people. Furthermore, the influence of the attendant is felt in the daily life of the families and the clan because there is a family-like relationship between them and their clients. With experienced birth attendants, childbirth through caesarean operation is not common. If there is a difficult or prolonged labor, the attendants would massage and press on the woman's abdomen. Sometimes they administer plant-prepared medicine before the delivery day in order to reduce the pains.

Izugbara and Ukwayi (2003) have shown that clients of indigenous birth attendants are not merely women in labour, but also those in search of abortion, who suffer from vaginal bleeding, sexually transmitted diseases (STDs), neonatal conditions and serial miscarriages. Their studies further show that medical health service providers in several Nigerian hospitals openly advise patients to seek indigenous treatment when Western medicine fails. Izugbara (2002), further notes that many Nigerians also believe that indigenous medicine is capable of healing all categories of diseases and misfortune including HIV and AIDS. However, it must be pointed out that there has been the problem of evidence and authenticity, yet belief in the powers of the healers often remain undaunted. As earlier mentioned, such beliefs about the powers of indigenous healers over diseases are also held about some pastors popularly called "Men of God." It is often believed that the prayers of many of them are capable of healing all manners of sicknesses including HIV and AIDS. Many sick people are brought to their churches and programmes for what is often called "the anointing touch." While such claims have been contested, questions of authenticity become blurred with value judgements.

Another group of healers are the indigenous surgeons. This group is made up other varying groups which perform specific duties which include the cutting of facial marks, especially on new-born babies. After such cutting the healer applies charred herbal products to the bleeding areas in order to effect healing. In the past ten years it was a common practice among the Amasiri to leave such marks on children as it was believed to serve as protection from evil spirits. Other indigenous surgeons perform male and female circumcision. They use special knives and scissors and the wounds are treated with specially prepared fluid from plants. Other indigenous surgeons undertake the treatment of whitlow and other boil-related diseases. Others pierce the ears, especially for females, to allow the fixing of earrings; extraction and treatment of infected teeth with indigenous medicine prepared with local gin also falls within the roles of the indigenous surgeons.

Another group of indigenous healers are the bone setters or orthopaedic surgeons. This group is gifted in the practice of repairing fractures and other orthopaedic injuries. It is recognized to have attained a higher level of success than Western medicine in Nigeria. Such healers are knowledgeable in the art and skill of setting broken bones, thereby bringing about the uniting and healing of compound or simple fractures. They use extracts from plants to stop the bleeding, while patients are subjected to radiant heat treatments or hot applications to reduce inflammation and swelling. Often their treatment is such that deformities or abnormal shapes of post-treatment limbs are very rare. With the bone setters, cases of amputations are rare, as they are capable of treating deteriorating gangrenous limbs. Sometimes, patients with fractures or dislocations or other orthopaedic-related problems are withdrawn from hospitals to be treated by the bone setters.

Furthermore, there are the indigenous psychiatrists who specialize in the treatment of lunatics and those with mental problems (Chukwuemeka 2009: 36). While some believe that insanity or madness is hereditary, others see it as an ailment resulting from a gross disregard of the gods' warnings. It is also seen as a means through which the gods execute judgement in revealing the guilty in a dispute. In some other cases, depending on the gender of the victim, madness is often associated with *Ogbanje* (marine spirit) possession. *Ogbanje* refers to people who are believed to cycle rapidly and repeatedly through birth and death (Ilechukwu 2006: 239). Among the Amasiri *Ogbanje* is perceived as resulting from the subversion of human destiny by wilful alliance of the newborn with deities who guard the postulated interface between the birth and pre-birth (spirit) existence. Chukwuemeka (2009: 38) observes that among the Igbo, fair complexioned and beautiful women are more prone to marine spirit possession. Nonetheless, there are also cases where "ugly" women fall within the group. While the question of authenticity often arises, it is my contention that such spirit possession may not be limited to women but is also present among males. However, it is often said that the presence of such marine spirits in males are the worst cases. Lunatics are usually restrained from going wild or violent by chaining them with iron or by clamping them down with wooden shackles. Interestingly, some diseases, especially mental and psychological disorders which defy modern medical cures, are being treated by indigenous healers (Abimbola 1991: 57).

The indigenous diviners (*dibia*) or fortune tellers form the next group of indigenous healers. Divination can be viewed as a way to access information that is normally beyond the reach and control of the rational mind. Almost by definition, diviners base their knowledge claims on communication with spiritual forces, such as ancestors, spirit guides, and deities. The service of diviners are usually sought in order for clients to receive diagnoses of diseases, which include explanations, predictions, and treatment of disease through the lens of divination. Causation might be tied to past history, in ancestors, in forgotten actions, in accidental behaviours, or even in conscious but not yet regretted actions or words. Establishing this history, by diagnosis, the diviner identifies the particular deity connected with his or her client's problems and then prescribes sacrificial rituals to appease malevolent spirits and/or herbal medicines which are prepared using empowering incantations. As in Olupona's (2004: 103–4) studies on Ifa diviners, "healing takes place when the diviner successfully diagnoses the source of the client's illness and carries out necessary sacrifice". It is as if by revealing the past causes of the present, one's path is made right.

Olupona's point is crucial as it highlights the central role of sacrifice in indigenous healing. Sacrifice is thus meant to counteract the evil machinations of the malevolent spiritual beings on humans and to invoke the benevolence of the deities, ancestors, and spirits in order to ensure and maintain cosmic balance and cohesion in society. Thus sacrifice is expected to express faith, repentance, pleas for forgiveness, and adoration. Sacrifice is a religious act in which offering is made to ancestors or spirits in order to attain, restore, maintain, or celebrate friendly relations with the deities. Based on the diviner's abilities to deal with the unseen, they are usually held in high esteem within the community as they are perceived as having extra-sensory perception and understanding. Through these processes the diviner among the Amasiri serves as a mediator between worlds, a translator of messages and a healer providing explanation and remedy for illness and misfortune. The social and religious dynamics of diviners and other healers earlier examined places individual and group circumstances in context, contributing to the wholeness of the community. As a result of this, indigenous healers continue to assert themselves within the contemporary indigenous Amasiri clan.

Engaging with Biomedical and Indigenous Healing

The paradoxes and contradictions in a biomedical "world view" have been noted by Comaroff (1982) among others. She argues that while biomedical knowledge is based on "empirical objectivity," in practice its underlying epistemology remains a "cultural construct" existing in "dialectical relationship with its wider social context." Comaroff contends that central to biomedicine's cultural construction is "rational individualism," a view of "man" as a "self-determining, biologically contrived individual" existing in a context of "palpable facts and material things" (1982: 57). It is, however, my contention that biomedicine may not necessarily coincide with the worldviews of its patients, even in "Western culture." Experiences of sickness and afflictions disconcertingly challenge the adequacy of tacitly assumed material individualism.

Such assumed individualism is never the case among the Amasiri. When a person is ill, the person turns to relations who live in the same family or compound. These may consult other relations in the village or in the clan, depending on the nature of the illness. The role of such networks is noticing and taking care of and comforting the sick person and making them know that they are available to support them in their suffering. If home remedies do not yield the needed result, the relations would decide to invite a specialist—an indigenous healer. Members of the family are often present during such consultation and readily carry out whatever treatment may be prescribed. The way symptoms are identified and interpreted thus determines the type of therapy to be sought. Often treatment is accessed from the cheapest and most accessible form of treatment to the most expensive.

Relations often pay the bills for such treatment as it is considered irrational to disturb a sick person with money problems. If the treatment is not successful, the relations would consult the healer again and may decide to try another healer or go to a biomedical hospital. This illustration underlines the close identification of the family with a sick member from the onset of their illness. The group takes a decision about treatment and participates in it; patients therefore rely on and are dependent on their group for support and help. At the same time the family feels the illness of one of its members to be a crisis for them all and the members' obligation and readiness to help are a measure of their sense of the danger to the whole group. It is arguable that this complex interpersonal relation among the Amasiri mediates people's health choices and decisions. The networks provide pathways through which patients access information and healing destinations. Many people rely on these networks and ties to mediate difficult situations.

Another level of problem which biomedicine faced in its establishment among the Amasiri was that of physician–patient communication. This was because of wide difference in culture with respect to concepts of bodily diseases as earlier discussed. The barrier of language related to concepts of illness appears formidable to physicians and health personnel, even when they share the same spoken language as their patients, and in intercultural situations it is obviously still more difficult.

Fletcher (1973: 17) has asked: "How can we improve our communication with patients?" The first thing he observes is the need to recognize the problem. Few doctors realize how little of what they tell their patients may be understood or remembered. That notwithstanding, the business of communication with the patient is something much more complex than the indigenous means of communication.

On the other hand, cultural norms are reflected in resistance to hospitalization and isolation in cases of epidemics. Thus the health worker who has been trained in an urban hospital needs a reorientation in two important directions in order to grasp the significance of the family and community background to the physical and mental health of an indigenous community. The second direction in which health workers need reorientation is towards understanding the people's attitude to their life in the clan as a "whole."

The traditional Amasiri hold the concept of the integration of social relationships and cultural ways of living to be central and this informs the responses of local people to public health and welfare programs. This communal ideology remains inherent among the traditional Amasiri despite the severity and sustained duration of the colonial impact and modernity. This communal sense of living does not only lend itself to human relationships but also even more importantly to those with one's ancestors. The ancestors provide spiritual guidance embodied in the Creator, the giver of live, harmony, peace, and healing. An understanding of this dynamic relationship between the traditional Amasiri and their world is very necessary for engaging in health and healing discourses.

However, within the framework of this chapter, there is the issue of how indigenous healers are represented from official perspectives within Nigeria. Indigenous methodologies are not always respected for the integrity inherent in them. Rather, Western scientific paradigms are often used to deny or refute valuable and successful indigenous practices. Interestingly, for instance, even though the majority of the African population utilizes indigenous medicine services, in many African nations indigenous medicine technically remains illegal.

The World Health Organization's 2001 survey of the legal status of indigenous and complementary/alternative medicine revealed that of the 44 African nations surveyed, 61 per cent had legal statutes regarding indigenous medicine (World Health Organization 2001). However, even with legal statutes in place, national policies have not always been implemented. Often the certifying or authorization mandate is assigned to a local governmental authority without national uniformity.

While on the one hand there appears to be a concern and commitment by the government to incorporate indigenous means of healing, on the other hand it seems that the definition and interpretation of what is "lawful" still resides within the government machinery which could impinge on the effective practices of indigenous healers. In order to engage with this problem, there is a need for a wider understanding and appreciation of indigenous forms of healing and especially of the general roles of some healers which are integral for the effective functioning of an indigenous society.

A dialogue with indigenous healers has become crucial, given the central role which religion plays in their healing processes and how such are appreciated by many people today. It must be pointed out that the option of dialogue is not without some complications. On the one hand, there appears to be no shared foundational therapeutic paradigm and, on the other hand, many shared dimensions of lived worlds and worldviews. Within these interwoven and complex tensions and synergies, many of them situational and existential, are polysemous symbols and meanings.

Nonetheless, this dialogue is imperative because whatever biomedical health professionals think of indigenous healers and their belief system, it is largely to these practitioners that many people turn in time of illness. They are generally respected health care providers and opinion leaders in their communities. National health services in Nigeria lack adequate numbers of personnel and these are unevenly distributed, with nearly all doctors in the major cities. The resulting rural outreach is poor. The indigenous healers are the main providers of primary health care among the Amasiri. The healers often share the cognitive understandings and cultural values of those they treat. At the local or village level, indigenous healers enjoy greater prestige and credibility in health and socio-religious matters.

Indigenous healers may not be wished away or legislated out of existence; attempts to do so by both colonial and post-independence governments have often failed. These healers, as earlier observed, occupy a critically important role among the Amasiri clan. They perform functions broader and more complex than those of their medical counterparts in the modern sector. Indigenous healers are priests, religious ritual leaders, family and community therapists, moral and social philosophers, teachers, visionaries, and perhaps political leaders, in addition to being healers in the more restricted, Western sense. Their existence and resilience stand as evidence that they meet important social needs, and these needs are in no way diminished as the clients they serve urbanize and undergo rapid socio-cultural change. Rapid socio-cultural change has been shown to lead to a variety of psychosocial problems, and healers who have experienced these problems themselves may be especially adept at helping people who are torn by the conflicting expectations of their changing worlds. Indigenous healers are highly motivated to learn about Western medicine, to attend training workshops, and to cooperate with modern health sector personnel; they are open, not closed, to techniques and concepts characteristic of cosmopolitan medicine.

Initiatives that promote cooperation would improve communication between the indigenous and medical health sectors, allowing access to the beliefs and practices found among healers and presumably their clients. This in turn would allow for the development of creative, culturally-appropriate, and effective health education strategies. It may also facilitate interventions aimed at discouraging practices proved to be harmful. Freedom of religion and other fundamental rights are often undermined when there are attempts to directly or indirectly legislate against indigenous healers. An efficient, cost-effective training-of-trainers approach is possible by focusing public health training efforts on leaders of healer associations and on senior healers under whom novice healers apprentice. Members and especially leaders of indigenous healer associations may be especially open to new ideas. A great and unprecedented opportunity now exists for including public health ideas and methods in the indigenous curriculum of healer training.

The shift away from hospital-based health services to community-based primary health care and culturally-appropriate approaches brings health planners face-to-face with the contribution of indigenous healers. This therefore requires a restructuring of the scope of health care planning in order to make it more inclusive of the inputs of these healers. Such collaboration could lead to new discoveries, which could lead to the development of new, useful medications. The central roles of the indigenous healers earlier discussed are hard to be dismissed; there is always a sustained and insatiable demand for healing, the elimination of evil agents, and a quest for power, protection, good health, and increase in prosperity in day-to-day life. As long as these realities which require the reassurance of supernatural goodwill are met by indigenous healers, indigenous medicine will continue to be relevant to the contemporary Amasiri clan.

Bibliography

Abimbola, W., "The Place of African Traditional Religion in Contemporary Africa: The Yoruba Example," in J.K. Olupona (ed.), *African Traditional Religion in Contemporary Society* (St. Paul, MN: Paragon House, 1991), pp. 51–8.

Adegoke, T.G., "Socio-Cultural Factors Influencing the Use of Spiritual Healing Churches in Ibadan Metropolis, Nigeria," *Anthropologist*, 9.3 (2007): 223–32.

Adogame, A., "Dealing with Local Satanic Technology: Deliverance Rhetoric in the Mountain of Fire and Miracles Ministries," paper presented at the CESNUR International Conference on *Religious Movements, Globalization and Conflict: Transnational Perspectives*, Palermo, Sicily: June 2–5, 2005.

Cheetham, R.W.S. and J.A. Griffiths, "The Traditional Healer/Diviner as Psychotherapist," *South African Medical Journal*, 62 (1982): 957–8.

Chukwuemeka, N.K., "Traditional Psychiatric Healing in Igbo Land, Southeastern Nigeria," *African Journal of History and Culture*, 1.2 (2009): 36–43.

Comaroff, J., "Medicine: Symbols and Ideology," in P. Wright and A. Treacher (eds.), *The Problem of Medical Knowledge: Examining the Social Construction of Medicine* (Edinburgh: Edinburgh University Press, 1982), pp. 49–69.

Fletcher, C.M., *Communication in Medicine* (London: Nuffield Hospitals Trust, 1973).

Helms, J.E. and D.A. Cook, *Using Race and Culture in Counselling and Psychotherapy: Theory and Process* (Boston, MA: Allyn and Bacon, 1999).

Idowu, E.B., *African Traditional Religion: A Definition* (London: SCM Press, 1973).

Ilechukwu, S.T.C., "Ogbanje/Abiaku and Cultural Conceptualizations of Psychopathology in Nigeria," *Mental Health, Religion and Culture*, 10.3 (2006): 239–55.

Iroegbu, P., "Healing Insanity: Skills and Expert Knowledge of Igbo Healer," *Africa Development*, 30.3 (2005): 78–92.

Izugbara, C.O., "Notions of Sex, Sexuality, and Relationship among Adolescent Boys in Rural Southeastern Nigeria," *Sex Education*, 4.1 (2002): 63–81.

— and J.K. Ukwayi, "The Clientele of Traditional Birth Homes in South-Eastern Nigeria," *Healthcare for Women International*, 24.3 (2003): 177–92.

Narayanan, V., *Understanding Hinduism: Origins, Beliefs, Practices, Holy Texts, Sacred Places* (London: Duncan Baird, 2004).

Oakley, A. and S. Houd, *Helpers in Childbirth: Midwifery Today* (New York: Hemisphere Publishing Corporation, 1990).

Oko, A.I., *Amasiri: A Legacy* (Onitsha: Nap Publishers Co., 1993).

Okorocha, C.C., *The Meaning of Religious Conversion in Africa: The Case of the Igbo of Nigeria* (Aldershot: Avebury, 1987).

Olupona, J.K., "Owner of the Day and Regulator of the Universe: Ifa Divination and Healing among the Yoruba of South-Western Nigeria," in M. Winkelman and P.M. Peek (eds.), *Divination and Healing: Potent Vision* (Tucson: University of Arizona Press), pp. 103–17.

Peel, J.D.Y., *Religious Encounter and the Making of the Yoruba* (Bloomington and Indianapolis: Indiana University Press, 2000).

Ray, B.C., "Aladura Christianity," *Journal of Religion in Africa*, 23.3 (1993): 266–91.

Robbins, J., "The Globalization of Pentecostal and Charismatic Christianity," *Annual Review of Anthropology*, 33 (2004): 117–43.

Sue, D.W., and D. Sue, *Counselling the Culturally Diverse: Theory and Practice*, 4th edn (Oxford: John Wiley & Sons, 1999).

World Health Organization, *Legal Status of Traditional Medicine and Complementary/Alternative Medicine: A Worldwide Review* (Geneva: WHO, 2001).

Chapter 10

Christianity and the Negotiation of Cultures: A Case Study of Yakurr Festivals in Nigeria

Dodeye U. Williams

Introduction

The Yakurr people of Nigeria were deeply rooted in their indigenous religious cultures prior to the encounter with Christianity. The rituals performed during their festivals are of symbolic importance and reveal their core values. Victor Turner (1968: 2) notes that "rituals are a storehouse of meaningful symbols by which information is revealed as authoritative, as dealing with crucial values of the community." Over time, Christianity has become a preferred alternative over traditional practices. Using information drawn from participant observation and oral histories, this chapter shows the extent to which the choice of Christianity alters the meanings of indigenous religious practices that were once held sacred. What implications do these changes have and how are the changes negotiated? I explore two festivals—*Leboku* and *Ledu*, and I suggest that although these festivals and the beliefs associated with them still form a part of Yakurr life, Christianity has significantly altered the way some rituals are performed owing to the fact that most Yakurr people, including religious adepts (the chief priests), many of whom have converted to Christianity, no longer hold sacred the meanings, nor the socio-religious values, attached to them.

Generally, African cultures are tied very much to a religious dimension. The values and meanings of the systematic and symbolic activities that characterize these cultures are anchored on certain beliefs. These beliefs include the following: (1) belief in "deities" of the land as symbolized by inanimate objects chosen for their special characteristics, e.g. trees, rocks, stones, animals etc.; (2) belief in ancestors as the cornerstone of African traditional and religious consciousness: ancestors are believed to have the power to inflict pain, enhance life, bring good fortune, and generally affect human destiny; and (3) belief in the power of supernatural forces to influence human action. These supernatural forces act and operate through the elders of the land or the chief priests as representatives of the deities.

The systematic and symbolic way and pattern that these beliefs are ceremoniously expressed and repeated are called rituals. As members of the community grow up seeing certain rituals performed, the meanings they convey are embedded in the consciousness of the people and their entire lives are shaped by the myths that govern the rituals. However, these practices have undergone several changes in the course of history, perhaps not in terms of content, but in terms of intensity and levels of meaning. One of the factors responsible for these changes is the influx of Christianity. It is the direct impact of Christianity on some of these rituals that this chapter explores.

Methodology

The data, especially with regards to the festivals, on which this chapter is based, are drawn from oral histories through interviews conducted in Idomi, one of the Yakurr communities. Using this data, I intend to describe some of the ways through which Christianity has altered the meaning of ritual practices that were held sacred in the past and to also show how these changes are negotiated or, in some cases, resisted. The Yakurr community in Nigeria is composed of five clans—Idomi, Nko, Nkpani, Ekori, and Ugep.The *Leboku* and *Ledu* ceremonies, explored in this chapter, are performed by all five clans. Although the sequence of events may differ, the meanings associated with the rituals performed are more or less uniform.

Overview of Yakurr Cultures

The Yakurr inhabit a territory that lies approximately between latitude 050 40' and -060 10' North and longitude 080 and 080 50' East in the geographical center of the Cross River State, Nigeria (Obono 2001). They live in five compact towns (Ugep, Ekori, Nko, Mkpani, and Idomi) situated 140 kilometers north-west of Calabar in the Yakurr local government area (Obono 2001). The Yakurr are related by strong linguistic and historical ties established by a tradition of common origin and reinforced by frequent intermarriages and "a continual interchange of visitors and permanent migrants" (Forde 1964: 3). Yakurr people are mainly yam farmers. Other crops grown by these farmers include corn, palm oil, okra, and pumpkin. At the center of Yakurr belief system are deities and divinities whose beneficence includes promoting peace, productivity, fertility, and the general economic well-being of the people. It is around the ritual activities of the priests of these deities that the entire social, religious, and political process revolves.

Christianity and Its Influence on Yakurr Cultures

The rituals that African cultural practices throw up as believers conduct their "worship," dramatic as they may seem, have embedded in them irrefutable spiritual significance. They are believed to have been handed down by the ancestors as inviolable and its custodians have the responsibility of preserving them and handing them over to generations after them. For this reason, any attempt to water down the import of these meanings or question their authenticity has always been strongly resisted. Nevertheless, the resistance has weakened with time in some circles, especially where Christianity has been the opposing force. In the discourse on the influence of Christianity on African cultures, three main positions emerge. The first is that Western culture, using Christianity as a disguise, is trying to make Africans abandon their traditions in exchange for foreign cultures. Those who hold this perspective argue that this situation should be resisted strongly in order to preserve African cultures. As such they resist Christianity. The second position is that Christianity is a welcome way of getting rid of "idolatry" on the continent. Christianity, they argue, is the best way to bring enlightenment to Africans and a way of purging the continent of "demonic" practices. The third group believes that there can be a compromise where the two, Christianity and African cultures can exist side by side. For them, the two must not be antagonistic but should be allowed to exist side by side and produce a blend. One thing, though, is common to these three arguments and that is they agree that a change is taking place. As Salami (2003) rightly observes, careful examination of Yakurr traditions reveals that over the past sixty years Yakurr ritual protocol has changed significantly and that all that remains of originally spiritually important customs are those facets which involve public display, e.g. pouring of libations at public shrines and processions of priest-chiefs through towns.

What does Christianity preach as opposed to African cultures and religious practices? The basic tenets of the Christian faith as contained in the Holy Bible, can be summarised as belief in Jesus Christ as the son of God and the Messiah; belief in Jesus Christ as the only true God who must alone be worshipped; belief in the Trinity—Father, Son, and the Holy Spirit; belief in salvation through faith in Jesus alone not by works; belief in the inerrancy of the Bible as the word of God as containing basic principles that should guide the life of mankind; and belief in eternal damnation for sinners and eternal life or believers in Christ. This content of the Christian message sometimes creates a change in the worldview of those who accept and "experience" it and it is seen as a liberating force from the "bondage" that comes from holding on to the traditional forms of worship. Those who choose Christianity over traditional religions believe that Christianity will bring some benefits revolving around freedom from fear of unknown spirits, especially evil spirits; freedom from fear of ancestors who are believed to be able to cause harm or do good; and freedom from fear of witchcraft, magic, or divination.

The freedom here is the language of those who have embraced Christ as the controller of their destiny as many will ask whether this "freedom" is a reality or merely something that is believed as a requirement of the new faith. When the Christian message is received and experienced, it begins to express itself in certain ways and in different aspects of the people's local tradition. It is against this backdrop that this chapter shows how the core foundations and meanings of some rituals in African cultures/religion have been altered by Christianity and how these changes are accommodated or resisted using two main Yakurr festivals in Nigeria as a case study.

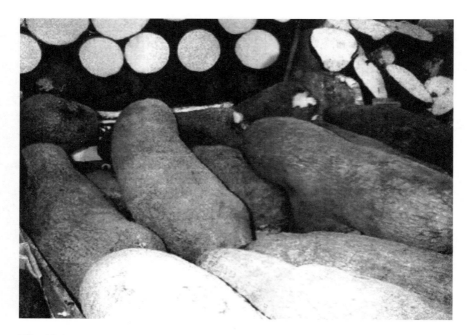

Fig. 10.1   A yam harvest

Leboku

The *Leboku* festival is a celebration of the yam harvest (see Figure 10.1). Yam is
the common name for some species in the *Dioscorea* family. They are important
for their starchy tubers in Africa, Asia, Latin America and Oceania. *Dioscorea
rotunda* (white yam) is a primary agricultural commodity in West Africa in general
and for the Yakurr people in particular. Yakurr belief is that it takes the blessing
of the "deities" for one to have a fruitful planting season. For this reason new
yam should not be eaten without due acknowledgment of the role of the gods
and ancestors in making the farming season profitable. There are at least twenty
ritual motions that characterize this ritual festival of *Leboku*. This chapter only
discusses three of these rituals and shows how they have changed in the intensity
of meaning and in some cases in the actual display. They include *Leboku Kepili*,
Zanenboku, and *Okondel,*. The first ritual is the *Leboku Kepili*. It is the practice
in Yakurr communities to abstain from eating new yams until the blessing of
the local deities has been obtained. It is only when the announcement has been
made for the commencement of the festival that farmers are permitted to openly
bring yams into the village and eat them. This announcement is what is known as
Leboku Kepili. It is believed that it is disrespectful to the "deities" for the villagers
to harvest their yams and eat them before their blessings have been received.

In contemporary Yakurr society however, there is an open disregard for this prohibition. As soon as the yams are ready for harvest, farmers begin to harvest and eat them and even bring them openly into the village. One of the key reasons is a change in worldview from a traditional religious worldview to a Christian worldview where the gods are no longer seen and revered as being responsible for a bountiful harvest but it is now attributed to the "Obase Woden" (Almighty God) who owns the universe and causes rain to water the ground to bless the farmers in order to produce a great harvest. The churches organize harvest thanksgiving services where farmers bring their farm produce to "give God thanks" for the harvest.

The second ritual is the *Zanenboku*. The second day of the *Leboku* festival is called *Zanenboku*, which literally means "women's festival day." The young women adorn themselves to be ready for the actual *Leboku* the following day. This ritual is symbolic of the blessings for fertility and in honour of the earth goddess and the ancestral gods of fertility. The young women in the community dress very beautifully with brass rings called *liman* (money) on their ankles. These brass rings give a musical rhythm as the maidens move one step after the other. According to Salami (2009: 19) they "reinforce the liminal state" of these festival maidens who parade the town, "spinning a web of ancestral support around the community in order to access the spirit world." On this day, gifts are given to women by their loved ones and friends and some traditional dances also take place. However, in recent years and with the promotion of tourism in Cross River State in general, tourists on the night of *Zanenboku* are faced with two options – the traditional carnival-like drumming and dancing to the rhythm of the Ekoi drums to usher in the *Ledemboku* (the mens' festival day), held in the playground or the modern-day Miss Leboku Beauty Pageant, held in one of the hotels within the town. The ritual has become a mere symbolic display. In fact, as Figure 10.2 suggests, it has metamorphosed into a grand beauty pageant. Prizes are awarded for the most beautiful maiden during the festival and so it has become more or less a competition among the young women. The meanings that this ritual once carried seem to have been lost. Again, one of the major reasons is that there is the prevailing belief that the Christian God is the one that gives and enhances fertility and gives children and so all the worship must go to him. Although some Christian members of the community see the entire activity as "idolatry," others take part in them and actually wear the *liman* merely as a cultural display. Sometimes, members of the Christian community are invited to the village square by the leadership of the festival to pray for the festival and this is often done after the traditional libation has been poured out in reverence for the communities' deities. This accommodates both the traditional adherents and the Christian community.

Another ritual worthy of mention is *Okondel*. This has to do with the thank offering of yams to the deities at certain hours of the night. The choice of the night hours could be attributed to the quietness and the privacy/secrecy that the darkness offers the chief priests to carry out these rituals. It is done by selected chief priests and no member of the community must be seen outside at such hours. The chief priests sacrifice yams to ancestors at night while other villagers remain indoors and

Fig. 10.2   Maidens at the Leboku Festival in Idomi (*Picture taken by Elder Akpan, Idomi*)

must not be seen outside to avoid the wrath of the deities. However, this curfew is violated as the chief priests merely collect bottles of wine, kola nuts, money, etc. from offenders as punishment for their violation. This act further emboldens the Christians who already feel they owe allegiance to the "Obase Woden" who is superior to the local deities and so cannot be punished by them. Rather than offer thanks to the local deities, the Christians choose to offer their thanks in church to God whom they believe is the reason for their bountiful harvest. These two practices have obvious similarities as they both involve offering of thanks and worship. It could be argued, therefore, that the act of harvest thanksgiving in the churches is an indigenous ritual that has been Christianized.

Finally, at the end of the ritual celebrations, the Obol Lopon, the village head and the chief priests walk through designated points in the community, locking hands as symbolic of building a wall of protection around the village (see Figures 10.3 and 10.4). The procession is not to be intercepted by anyone. In fact, watching the procession should to be done from a great distance to avoid encroaching on the sacred space meant for this ritual activity. In recent years however, it has become a mere activity as the majority of the members of the community believe that protection comes from the "Obase Woden" alone. The presence of video cameras, tourists, etc. during such processions shows again a narrowing down of the sacred space that was once very well delineated. This procession is one of the highly

Fig. 10.3   The Procession by the Priest Chiefs Led by the Obol Lopon of Idomi (*Picture taken by Elder Akpan, Idomi*)

disregarded rituals in recent times. Although the chief priests still go through motions that were hitherto imbued with immense spiritual significance, people no longer see the mystery in this protection – the awe and dread seems to be fading in such a way that this is fast becoming merely a public display.

The *Ledu* Celebration

The *Ledu* title ceremony is a prestigious one. *Ledu* is the highest title of the land, given to successful male farmers who have demonstrated the wealth, ability, and capacity to feed lots of people. It requires, among other things, the redistribution of the titleholder"s entire wealth through philanthropic acts (Salami 2009). One criterion for the title is that a farmer must have up to 14,000 large tubers of yam in his yam barn. The farmer must organize these yams into lines of 35 yams each tied to a stick in the barn and these lines must be up to 400. There are several rituals that must be performed before a farmer receives the title. However, the layers of meanings and intensity of these rituals have been watered down and some cases lost altogether in the process of time. The entire process of initiation of new members into the *Ledu* society is wrapped in rituals, from eating certain foods at midnight at specific locations to the final coronation as a titled member of the society. It

Fig. 10.4   The Okpebili of Idomi (Prime Minister) (*Picture taken by Elder Akpan, Idomi*)

Fig. 10.5   A Ledu Initiation Ceremony (*Picture from the archives of Elder Okoi Obeten, Idomi*)

is difficult to observe changes that have taken place inside these initiations but other changes can be observed. Christianity has played a huge role in altering the perceptions of members of the Yakurr community towards these rituals.

In the past, a very important part of the requirements for the male farmer who wanted the *Ledu* title was the purchase of a person (usually a female) from a neighboring village, often outside of the Yakurr communities. It usually involved a huge amount of money and was symbolic of the farmers' ability to feed an extra mouth. With the abolition of slavery the practice had to be modified. It could not be entirely abolished because it was a significant part of the requirements for the title. It was modified and called marriage. However, for some members of the community who had become Christians and were already married, marrying a second wife was not an option for them as the church permitted them to marry only one wife. To accommodate this category of farmers, the practice became more or less "adoption," where the person is brought into the family and just lives there as a part of the new family and eventually grows up to marry and raise her own family.

As far as the *Ledu* title is concerned, Christianity has a large part to play in the changes that have occurred, but we must not lose sight of the role that urbanization and maybe environmental changes have played in making the *Ledu* society less attractive. It is becoming more difficult to be a member as a Christian because the society is seen as not being compatible with Christian living. As a matter of fact those who joined the society even as Christians get to a point where they feel they have to denounce the society. Again, the type of Christianity they affiliate to plays a huge role here. The orthodox Christians tend to accommodate members of the society, but the Pentecostal Christians demonize the society and would have nothing to do with it. Many members of the *Ledu* society go to church; they make donations to churches out of the funds raised from new or intending members and old members also. They contribute to encouraging hard work in the society in order to make their impact felt. Although members are still respected, the urge to join the society has dwindled over the years and it is no longer very attractive to young people.

Conclusion

The festivals and the attendant rituals discussed here reveal a pattern of changes taking place in Yakurr communities. Scholars like Salami (2009) rightly argue that these changes can be attributed to a large-scale conversion to Christianity. In contemporary Yakurr culture, the original purposes of the rituals have given way to mere performances and in some cases they have been totally eradicated. Some will perceive these changes as negative and others as positive, depending on their worldview. The ritual format is changing, sacred spaces are narrowing, ritual behaviour is being altered with each passing year and the major explanation can be attributed to large-scale conversion to Christianity. It does not appear that this is the only factor of change, but Christianity has made it easier for any other factor, including the ever-growing rate of urbanization, to express itself.

Bibliography

Forde, Darryl, *Yakö Studies* (London: Oxford University Press, 1964).

Obono, Oka, "Matriclan Priests and Fertility among the Yakurr of South Eastern Nigeria." Paper prepared for the IUSSP XXIV General Population Conference (Session S23: Value Orientations and Reproductive Behavior), Salvador, Brazil, 18–24 August, 2001.

Salami, Gitti, "Corrugated Cardboard is What I Have for Right Now: An African Teenager"s Pursuit of a Future in Aesthetics." Paper presented at the 46th annual meeting of the African Studies Association, Boston, Massachusetts, October 30 – November 2, 2003.

—, "Towards "Radical Contemporaneity" in African Art History: The "Glocal" Facet of a Kinship-Based Artistic Genre," *Critical Interventions: Journal of African Art and Visual Culture*, 3/4 (2009): 78–99.

Turner, Victor, *The Ritual Process: Structure and Anti-Structure* (Chicago: Aldine Press, 1968).

PART III
Christianity, Islam, Hinduism

Chapter 11

"From Prophetism to Pentecostalism": Religious Innovation in Africa and African Religious Scholarship

J. Kwabena Asamoah-Gyadu

Introdution

Jacob Olupona has contributed immensely to the academic study of religion in Africa, with extensive research covering various aspects of Christianity on the continent. In addition to his several works, he also surveyed "West African Pentecostalism" in the revised and expanded edition of the widely acclaimed *International Dictionary of Pentecostal and Charismatic Movements* (Olupona 2002). Africa has within the last half-century, emerged as a hotbed of contemporary Pentecostalism in both its classical and neo-Pentecostal versions. Not only has African Christianity become very Pentecostal, but also by the end of the twentieth century, the largest Christian congregations in Europe—both East and West—were led by Africans. In spite of this, the first edition of that dictionary neither considered developments within the region nor among Africans in the Diaspora.

This made the dictionary unrepresentative of global Pentecostalism because the movement has clearly emerged as the representative face of Christianity among Africans. This religious innovation in Africa, which is usually of a decidedly pneumatic character, has not occurred through a monolithic movement. Nevertheless, it is interesting to note that within the Christian context most African religious movements have had this pneumatic orientation and they have developed under charismatic leadership. Jacob Olupona has written on all aspects of it, including on the immigrant forms of African Christianity. An essay focusing on the subject matter of "changes within Pentecostal/charismatic Christianity in Africa" should therefore serve as a fitting honour to Jacob Olupona for his labours in the field of African religious scholarship. With that as backdrop, this chapter examines some of the changes and selected critical issues arising out of Christian religious innovation in sub-Saharan Africa.

Religious Innovation in Africa

Three main issues affecting African indigenous Christianity and occurring within the scholarship dedicated to its study will engage our attention. First, we will look at some of the terms and expressions that have been used in describing the groups concerned. Second, we will discuss the reinvention of prophetism, and related to that, healing as an important part of African Christianity; and third, we will look at the relationship between the classical or older African independent church movements and the neo-Pentecostal or newer charismatic churches. The two main movements have both been driven by belief in the experience of the Holy Spirit. However, whereas the older independent churches were led by prophets and charismatic figures who literally became custodians of the Spirit and power, in the newer independent or neo-Pentecostal churches, charisma seems to have been democratized. There are prophets here too, but individual access to the Spirit means that churches now revolve not just around a single personality—although founders still possess the charisma in higher measure—but each member has a ministry that is exercised within the group to make the church charismatically functional.

Religious innovation in Africa could be said to have started with the rise of Ethiopianist/Nationalist churches at the end of the nineteenth century. Except for its indigenous leadership and the use of the vernaculars, the Nationalist churches in sub-Saharan Africa never developed into mass movements. They were significant only to the extent that they virtually became the Christian equivalent of movements agitating for cultural recognition, political independence, and ecclesial administrative control. "The battle at the time," Ogbu Kalu points out, "was the recovery of African identity through religious power" (Kalu 2008: viii). The leadership, consisting mainly of the African Christian elite then, was scandalized by the lack of recognition and opportunity from the missionaries and decided to establish local denominations that would be free of missionary influence. These churches, beginning with Mojola Agbebi's Native Baptist Church in Nigeria formed around 1880 and the Nigritian Church in Ghana are still historically and religiously significant as the first set of new churches to emerge within Christianity in Africa. Ethiopianist/Nationalist churches have remained within the shadows of other forms of African initiated Christianity and would not form part of the Christian new religious movements discussed in this chapter.

Independent Indigenous Pentecostalism

In my writings, I have sometimes classed all the Christian movements that came after the Ethiopianist/Nationalist churches as independent indigenous Pentecostal/charismatic movements and churches. They have manifested in five broad categories as:

1. Early twentieth century itinerant prophetic movements led by such charismatic figures as William Wadé Harris of Liberia, Garrick Sokari Braide of the Niger Delta, Simon Kimbangu of the DR Congo, and Isaiah Shembe of South Africa. These prophets, Ogbu Kalu would argue, "tilled the soil on which modern Pentecostalism thrives. They were closer to the grain of African culture in their responses to the gospel and so felt the resonance between charismatic indigenous worldviews and the equally charismatic biblical worldview" (Kalu 2008: x).

2. African independent/initiated/instituted churches arising directly through the evangelistic efforts of the itinerant prophets. At the centre of the African prophetic churches, as Olupona chooses to call those in this category, is the role of the charismatic founders and leaders. They were the custodians of charismatic power. "The visions, prophecies, utterances, and actual practices of these leaders help define the identity and character of their churches and the Pentecostal African movement in general" (Olupona 2002: 12).

3. Neo-Pentecostal or charismatic churches and movements that have burgeoned in urban Africa since the late 1970s. These have been greatly inspired by North American televangelism in particular and display such characteristics as an attraction for Africa's upwardly mobile youth, internationalism, modern outlook and relaxed sense of dress code, extensive appropriation of modern media technologies, and the gospel of prosperity.

4. Trans-denominational fellowships like the Full Gospel Businessmen's Fellowship International and the Women Aglow movement.

5. Renewal movements that have emerged within historic mission denominations.

I class all of the movements listed above as "independent" because they are usually free of Western mission control. They are "indigenous" on account of their coming into being through African initiatives led by local charismatic figures and they could generally be described as being of a "Pentecostal/charismatic" orientation because of the keenness with which they all seek to integrate and normalize charismatic experiences in Christian life and worship.

Marthinus L. Daneel writes that even though the classical AICs do not overtly describe their churches as Pentecostal, they "reveal definite Pentecostal traits, in that the Holy Spirit features prominently in their worship and daily activities" (Daneel 2007: 21). It is the reason for which Daneel refers to these older AICs as "Spirit-type" churches. The last two groups listed in the category also belong to the neo-Pentecostal stream of African Christianity. They are historically younger than both the AICs and the classical Pentecostal denominations and possess a certain religious and theological versatility that has come to be associated with the independent neo-Pentecostal or charismatic churches. Although both the renewal movements within the historic mission denominations and trans-denominational fellowships are led by indigenous Christians, the trans-denominational fellowships are not usually of indigenous origins. Both the Full Gospel Businessmen's Fellowship International and its female version Women Aglow originate from the USA although they were introduced to sub-Saharan Africa by local Christians. Their encouragement of "responsible church membership" even for members belonging to non-Pentecostal churches has done a lot to introduce charismatic renewal into existing historic mission denominations.

"Pentecostalization" and "Charismatization" of African Christianity

Perhaps the most important development within African initiated Christianity is the rise of the autochthonous neo-Pentecostal, charismatic, or as they are called in Nigeria, Born-again churches. Mega-size urban-centred and modern independent charismatic churches such as Enoch Adeboye's Redeemed Christian Church of God, David O. Oyedepo's Word of Faith or Winners' Chapel International, William F. Kumuyi's Deeper Life Christian Church, all based in Nigeria, and Mensa Otabil's International Central Gospel Church and Nicholas Duncan-Williams' Christian Action Faith Ministries International based in Ghana, have taken over from the older AICs as the growing edges of African Christianity. Olupona's description of this new phenomenon is most revealing:

> Charismatic churches are evangelical churches founded by African leaders who have adopted radical spiritual conversion, often called "born again," through baptism of the Holy Spirit, recalling the day of Pentecost. As in the prophetic independent African churches before them, the charismatic churches emphasize speaking in tongues, divine healing, and miracles. In addition, they profess that the material success and prosperity of their members are signs of divine grace and benevolence. (Olupona 2002: 14)

Their presence together with those of the other neo-Pentecostals has been so forceful especially through their media ministries that in recent years, this has led to higher levels of "pentecostalization" or "charismatization" of Christianity in Africa. The public face of African Christianity, I have noted earlier, has become the Pentecostal/charismatic versions of it. I use "pentecostalization" and "charismatization" in this essay, to describe situations in which non-Pentecostal and non-charismatic churches are pressured into adopting charismatic tendencies to help stem the tide of their own members drifting into some Pentecostal or charismatic church. In Africa, Pentecostalism has done well but usually in places where the ground has been "softened" through missionary work and historic mission church activities. Indeed, this is the main reason why the historic mission churches started tolerating charismatic renewal movements within their denominations. Thus charismatic renewal movements have been acknowledged in both African religious scholarship and by mission church authority as helping to restore vitality into churches that were losing members because people found them dull, staid, unattractive, and their theologies, non-interventionist.

Today, one of the critical marks of indigenous Pentecostalism in Africa is the integration and normalization of charismatic experiences in Christian life and worship. Furthermore, all the movements listed, in spite of the resonances of their worldviews with those of African religious cultures, aim primarily to be biblical in their spirituality. The experiences of the Holy Spirit, healing and miracles are cherished because they are biblical and the God who was active in the New Testament is also active in Christianity today. However, in the quest for relevant ways of expressing their faith, African independent Pentecostal/charismatic movements and churches have remained indigenous by working within African religious ideas. Olupona writes:

> The central distinguishing element of these churches is that they take the African cosmological world seriously, including the reality of witchcraft, predestination, the world of spirits and ancestors, and so on. In their liturgical practices and social ethics as well, they often combine elements of Christian tradition with indigenous African culture (Olupona 2002: 12)

This has led them into taking seriously confrontation with evil and the creation of ritual spaces to deal with its effects in the lives of adherents and patrons.

Historical Developments and Nomenclature

The quantitative proliferation of independent indigenous Pentecostal/charismatic movements and churches has changed the qualitative face of Christianity in Africa. In their various regions of origin these churches and movements have usually been called by their local names. Thus for example, the classical AICs are referred to in Ghana as *Sunsum Sorè*, meaning "churches of the Spirit" or as they are commonly referred to, "Spiritual churches." This same group of churches are in Nigeria generically called the *Aladura* (people of prayer) on account of their aggressive and extensive modes of prayer that are completely different from the liturgically organized modes of historic mission Christianity. Indeed in Zimbabwe, Daneel explains that these churches refer to themselves as *maKereke oMweya*, meaning "churches of the Spirit." The nomenclature from the different contexts underscores a single point: that is, the critical role of the Holy Spirit in the rise and functioning of these churches. Thus although internal differences are important, certain religious tendencies and emphases which are mostly of a Pentecostal/ charismatic nature, are present in all of them. These tendencies and emphases include speaking in tongues, prophecy, healing, exorcism, deliverance from emotionally disturbing behaviours, testimony sharing, visions and revelations, fervent and ecstatic prayers, and an exuberant, expressive and dynamic worship, all attributed to the presence and activities of the Holy Spirit.

The older groups of churches or AICs have generally been referred to in the academic literature as "African independent churches." Recent scholarship has tended to refer to these independent churches either as "African initiated churches" or "African instituted churches." Whichever of the three designations is employed, the acronym AICs applies to them and the churches concerned have continued to function as indigenous churches that have appealed greatly to ordinary African Christians. In the study of African theology, the AICs have been studied in terms of the processes of inculturation, indigenization, and contexualization of Christianity in Africa. The bottom line in these references is the fact that the AICs were seen as representing a paradigm shift in Christian belief and practice from the brand of Christianity offered by the historic mission denominations. This is how Olupona describes the churches in question:

> The prophetic independent churches include a diverse group of churches, begun by charismatic men and women who claimed that they were called by God through visions and prophetic utterances to begin a spiritual church. The founders emphasized the efficacy and sufficiency of prayer alone as a panacea for all human needs and as a solution to life's problems. (Olupona 2002: 11)

Olupona's references to these groups as "prophetic independent churches" and their founders as "charismatic men and women" called by God "through visions and prophetic utterances," is very significant. Wherever AICs appeared, there were three major characteristics associated with their brand of Christianity. First, was their commitment to aggressive prayer which led to the organization of all-night vigils, retreats to mountain sites and forests and the creation of prayer camps which are locations of prayer rituals for supernatural intervention. Second, there was always a charismatic figure at the centre usually designated as a prophet. These persons, I noted earlier, mainly functioned as custodians of spiritual power and became the fulcra around whose charismatic personalities their movements revolved. Third, the central theological concern of the AICs was healing. The prophet was therefore first and foremost a person of prayer with the ability to provide leadership in healing rituals. He or she had the ability to diagnose sickness and prescribe the appropriate therapeutic method for dealing with it. It is on account of the emphases on prophecy and healing that Harold W. Turner (1979) referred to the AICs as "prophet-healing" churches. In the words of Olupona, "even though there are significant differences among these prophetic churches, in large part they all accept and practice faith healing, prophetic visions, fervent ecstatic prayer and glossolalia" (Olupona 2002: 12).

Transition in Religious Innovation in Africa

The AICs in their various manifestations across Africa remain the most intensely studied streams of indigenous Christianity in Africa since the turn of the twentieth century. To this end, one of the leading players in the academic field of African Christianity, the late Adrian Hastings, observed that scholars looking for interesting research topics in the field of African religion at the height of the popularity of the AICs in the 1960s, could hardly fail to be attracted by one of the almost innumerable new churches springing into vibrant existence in Africa. "African Christianity," according to Hastings, suddenly became "a popular subject indeed but almost entirely in terms of the independent churches" (Hastings 1990: 2004). The early studies included Bengt G.W. Sundkler, *Bantu Prophets in South Africa* (1948; 1961); John D.Y. Peel, *Aladura: A New Religious Movement among the Yoruba* (1968); Marie-Louise Martin, *Simon Kimbangu: An African Prophet and His Church* (1975); Harold W. Turner, *The Church of the Lord Aladura* (2 vols. 1967) and Christian G. Baëta, *Prophetism in Ghana* (1962). More recently, Afeosemime U. Adogame has published *Celestial Church of Christ: The Politics of Cultural Identity in a West Afrian Prophetic-Charismatic Movement* (1999) and Allan Anderson has written *African Reformation: African Initiated Churches in the 20th Century* (2001), in which he sustains the view that the AICs have contributed significantly to the growth of Christian presence in Africa.

The transition from this type of prophetic Christianity to the rise of new Pentecostal/charismatic movements has led to a shift in academic focus, as far as the study of African Christianity is concerned. Within the last decade, we have received from the academic stable the following publications, among several others, on the new charismatic churches: Paul Gifford, *Christianity and Politics in Doe's Liberia* (1993), *African Christianity: Its Public Role* (1998); *Ghana's New Christianity* (2004); and *Christianity, Politics and Public Life in Kenya* (2010); Birgit Meyer, *Translating the Devil* (1999); Allan Anderson, *African Reformation* (2001)—already mentioned—and *Introduction to Pentecostalism* (2004); Ogbu U. Kalu, *African Pentecostalism: An Introduction* (2008); J. Kwabena Asamoah-Gyadu, *African Charismatics* (2005); Matthews A. Ojo, *God's End-Time Army* (2006); Asonzeh Ukah, *A New Paradigm of Pentecostal Power: A Study of the Redeemed Christian Church of God in Nigeria* (2008); and Ruth Marshall, *Political Spiritualities: The Pentecostal Revolution in Nigeria* (2009).

The growing academic attention to the new brand of Pentecostalism is testimony to its current significance in African Christianity. It has become imperative then that some attention be given to the continuities and discontinuities between the spiritualities of the two streams of Christianity, that is, the older African independent churches and the new charismatic ministries. It has become impossible to understand African Pentecostalism without looking at the key theological emphases of the two movements. Andrew F. Walls has made it clear that there is a connection—in terms of theological emphasis—between the older and newer AICs:

> Until recently these prophet-healing churches could be held the most significant and the fastest-growing sector of the indigenous churches. This is no longer so certain. Nigeria and Ghana, to name but two countries, are witnessing the rise

of another type of independent church ... Like the prophet-healing churches, they proclaim the divine power of deliverance from disease and demonic affliction, but the style of proclamation is more like that of American Adventist and Pentecostal preaching. Gone are the African drums and the white uniforms of the Aladuras; the visitor is more likely to hear electronic keyboards and amplified guitars, see a preacher in elegant *agbada* or smart business suit and a choir in bow ties. Yet these radical charismatic movements are African in origin, in leadership, and in finance ... All the new movements share with the prophet-healing churches a quest for the demonstrable presence of the Holy Spirit and a direct address to the problems and frustrations of modern African urban life. (Walls 1996: 92–3)

Except in Southern Africa where they still seem to be doing well, according to current studies, the older AICs have largely been overshadowed by the neo-Pentecostals. That notwithstanding, their theological contribution continues to be felt through the sorts of pneumatic phenomena they so passionately emphasized and the constructive engagement with traditional religious worldviews. Through these two approaches to the faith, indigenous prophets and Christian movements they led from the early years of the twentieth century took African Christianity to a phenomenal level. They led an African Christian Reformation by emphasizing the importance of the ministry of the Holy Spirit and an interventionist theology that challenged the ecclesiology of historic mission Christianity. Western mission Christianity, for all its contribution towards the vernacular translation of the Scriptures enabling Africans to receive the gospel in their own mother tongues, was rarely able to deal with the African worldviews of transcendent realities and mystical causality. Belief in witchcraft, for example, was denounced as figments of folk imagination and a psychological delusion. But in Africa, religion is essentially a survival strategy and the alternative spiritual spaces offered by the new independent churches proved very attractive in dealing with the fears and insecurities of ordinary people.

The emphasis on practical salvation, the ability to work within indigenous worldviews of mystical causality, the integration of charismatic experiences into Christian worship, the use of oral theological discourses and the innovative ways in which the spiritual gifts of women were recognized and used, all through the AICs, undoubtedly saved Christianity from suffering a moribund fate in Africa. This is how Lamin Sanneh summarized the contribution of these older AICs to Christianity on the continent:

A process of internal change was thus initiated in which African Christians sought a distinctive way of life through mediation of the Spirit, a process that enhanced the importance of traditional religions for the deepening of Christian spirituality. The Charismatic Churches, therefore, combined the two fundamental elements of Christianity and African culture in a way that advertises their Christian intentions without undervaluing their African credentials. Biblical material was submitted to the regenerative capacity of African perception, and the result would be Africa's unique contribution to the story of Christianity. (Sanneh 1983: 180)

The sheer numbers of research works and publications on the AICs is testimony to their significance not only in African but even world Christianity. The AICs gave Christianity a cutting edge by emphasizing key elements that are central to African religiosity.

Reinvention of Prophetism

Divine healing and the prophetic ministry, we have noted, are two of the areas in which the presence and impact of the AICs continue to be felt within independent indigenous Pentecostalism in Africa. Healing camps and prayer places, such as the "Mercy Ground" (see Adogame 1999) of the Celestial Church of Christ, originally associated with the AICs have now sprung up all over sub-Saharan African countries, with many of them owned by modern Pentecostal movements. The contention here is that many of the new types of healing strategies and prophesying build on the religious legacy of the AICs. For instance, on the way the AICs managed to present healing as an integral element of Christian salvation building on indigenous worldviews of causality, Andrew F. Walls noted:

> In traditional Africa, healing was usually performed in a religious context; the time and manner in which medical missions developed prevented (in most areas) a smooth transition from the old religion of healing to the new. It was the independents who made the logical connection: If the Christian was to trust Christ and not entreat the old Powers, should he not trust Christ for all the things for which he once entreated the Powers? ... What the independents have done time and again is to challenge the half-Christian who goes to church respectably, but then in secret, and with guilty feelings, goes off to the diviner to seek the cause of sickness and the way of healing. The earthiness of African life demands that African salvation shall be as solidly material as biblical salvation. (Walls 1996: 117)

In the early 1960s, Baëta also predicted that "prophetism," the key element in African initiated Christianity, was a perennial phenomenon of African religious life and was likely to reappear in different forms of this type of Christianity. Towards the end of the twentieth century, the ministry of the prophet as a key religious functionary re-emerged within modern forms of indigenous Pentecostalism represented by the new charismatic churches. Gifford discusses the nature and ministry of the new prophets in his book on *Ghana's New Christianity* (Gifford 2004: 89–112, 186). This new manifestation of prophetism within modern Ghanaian Christianity is remarkable when considered in the light of predictions made by Baëta almost half a century ago:

[Prophetism] appears to me to be a perennial phenomenon of African life, and the basic operative element in it seems to be personal in character. Whether in relation to or independently of events or developments in society, the individual endowed with a striking personality and the ability to impose his own will on others, believing himself, and believed by others to be a special agent of some supernatural being or force, will emerge from time to time and secure a following. Powers traditionally credited to such persons, of healing, revealing hidden things, predicting the future, cursing and blessing effectually, etc., will be attributed to him whether he claims them or not. Some will make a more successful showing than others. Such things as the above-mentioned endowment, inward illumination, a sense of divine vocation, spontaneous enthusiasm ... are facts of life and have their effects in African society. (Baëta 1962: 6–7)

In its modern forms, prophecies are even delivered over the airwaves and in live internet broadcasts to people in their homes and Africans living abroad who may be looking for divine favors and interventions. The early twentieth century prophets did not deny the reality of the supernatural world as their mission church counterparts were wont to do. Rather they offered what local people, with their ardent belief that the world was enchanted, considered to be more effective ways of dealing with the powers and principalities of this world. Prophetism has resurfaced within African neo-Pentecostalism, leading Cephas Omenyo and Abamfo Atiemo to speak of "neo-prophetism" in contemporary African Christianity (Omenyo and Atiemo 2006). To these new prophets, members of the general public often go for what the Akan of Ghana refer to as *akwankyere*, guidance as they seek either to understand their unhappy destinies or seek protection from envious enemies and witches.

Democratization of Charisma

The ecclesiological implications of the changes that have occurred within African Christian within the last century are very profound and worth noting (Asamoah-Gyadu 2005: chapter 4). The Pentecostal insistence on personal experience of the Holy Spirit by members, that we noted at the beginning of this chapter, means that there is a certain democratization of ministry that was not too pronounced within the older independent churches. The special anointing carried by a modern Pentecostal or charismatic church leader is still very much a cherished phenomenon within African Christianity. However today, neo-Pentecostal churches refer to themselves as "charismatic ministries" because there is some encouragement for participants to function within their particular graces of the Spirit. Time and space did not permit us to look into all the reasons why the older AICs were not doing as well as they did up until the early 1970s or thereabouts. By then, the charismatic and prophetic leaders whose personal experiences and psychology moved the independent churches were ageing or dying. Many of them did not develop alternative ministries such as children's and youth ministries or even nurture other charismatic persons to take over the churches. A number of them, like the African Faith Tabernacle Church in Ghana, have fallen apart on the demise of their founders. The neo-Pentecostals, in my judgment, are unlikely to suffer the same fate. Although they also suffer secessions, the rate has not been as high and rampant as we had under the older independent churches. The open access to the Spirit effectively means that healing, prophecy and other such ministries may be practiced by any who possess those gifts and not just by the leader. Thus the changing nature of Pentecostal ecclesiology is a major area in which the charismatic churches differ from the older AIC compatriots.

Conclusion

Although statistical data is hard to come by, the older AICs seem to be declining numerically, but their diminishing physical presence has not erased their unique contribution to African Christianity and theology. In fact, their qualitative impact on African Christianity continues through an enduring religious and theological heritage that puts an emphasis on the role of the Holy Spirit in the Christian church. Perhaps their greatest contribution to Christianity in Africa is that they bridged the gap that formerly existed between primal spirituality and Christianity. In contrast to Western Christian theologies that seem on the whole to be a system of ideas, primal religions, according to Ghanaian theologian Kwame Bediako, are generally conceived "as a system of power and of living religiously as being in touch with the source and channels of power in the universe" (Bediako 1995: 106). In primal religiosity, finite human beings stand in need of the powers and blessings of benevolent transcendent powers, and draw on such sources for protection from evil forces through appropriate covenant relationships with such transcendent benevolent helpers.

The independent churches became popular in African countries because they affirmed the reality of God through the power of the Holy Spirit and other supernatural entities within the cultural context in which they worked. Destructive and malevolent powers seeking to destroy people and angels representing the Christian equivalent of transcendent benevolent powers both featured prominently in the worldview of the typical African independent church. That into the twenty-first century, some of these ideas are sustained in contemporary African Pentecostal theology and seems to have become characteristic of the African church shows how seriously African Christians consider an understanding of salvation that is based on the work of the Holy Spirit among God's people.

We owe our understanding of African initiated Christianity to scholars like Olupona and the others we have listed who drew attention to the independent churches, and affirmed them as truly indigenous Christian movements whose innovative Christianity had much to teach about what it meant to be African and Christian at the same time. That their religious ideas are sustained in the ministries of the new Pentecostals only serves to underscore what Africans consider important to their faith. The world has certainly not heard the final word on independent indigenous Pentecostal/charismatic Christianity in Africa. Within the last decade alone, several publications have emerged on various aspects of Christian religious innovation on the continent and there is reason to believe that there are others on the way. Wherever the story of religious innovation in Africa is told, the contributions of the African churches discussed here will continue to be an important part of the historical analysis. So we will continue to encounter them as we continue to explore what lies embedded in indigenous African Christianity that God wants preserved during this period when the centre of gravity of the Christian faith has so decidedly—to use the words of Barrett, Walls and Bediako—shifted from the northern to the southern continents.

Bibliography

Anderson, Allan, *African Reformation: African Initiated Christianity in the 20th Century* (Trenton, NJ: Africa World Press, 2001).

Adogame Afe, *Celestial Church of Christ: The Politics of Cultural Identity in a West African Prophetic-Charismatic Movement* (Frankfurt am Main: Peter Lang, 1999).

Asamoah-Gyadu, J. Kwabena, *African Charismatics: Current Development within Independent Indigenous Pentecostalism in Ghana* (Leiden: E.J. Brill, 2005).

Baëta, Christian G., *Prophetism in Ghana: A Study of Some Spiritual Churches* (London: SCM Press, 1962).

Bediako, Kwame, *The Renewal of a Non-Western Religion* (Edinburgh: Edinburgh University Press, 1995).

Daneel, Marthinus L., *All Things Hold Together: Holistic Theologies at the African Grassroots* (Pretoria: University of South Africa Press, 2007).

Gifford, Paul, *Ghana's New Christianity: Pentecostalism in a Globalizing African Economy* (Bloomington and Indianapolis: Indiana University Press, 2004).

Hastings, Adrian, "Christianity in Africa," in Ursula King (ed.), *Turning Points in Religious Studies: Essays in Honour of Geoffrey Parrinder* (Edinburgh: T&T Clark, 1990), pp. 201–10.

Kalu, Ogbu U., *African Pentecostalism: An Introduction* (Oxford: Oxford University Press, 2008).

Omenyo, Cephas N. and Abamfo O. Atiemo, "Claiming Religious Space: The Case of Neo-Prophetism in Ghana." *Ghana Bulletin of Theology: New Series*, 1.1, (2006): 55–68.

Olupona, Jacob, "Africa, West (Survey)," in Stanley M. Burgess and Eduard M. van der Mass (eds.), *The New International Dictionary of Pentecostal and Charismatic Movements. Revised and Expanded Edition* (Grand Rapids, MI: Zondervan, 2002), pp. 11–21.

Sanneh, Lamin O., *West African Christianity: The Religious Impact* (Maryknoll, NY: Orbis, 1983).

Turner, Harold W., *Religious Innovation in Africa: Collected Essays on New Religious Movements* (Boston, MA: G.K. Hall, 1979).

Ukah, Asonze,. *A New Paradigm of Pentecostal Power: A Study of the Redeemed Christian Church of God in Nigeria* (Trenton, NJ: Africa World Press, 2008).

Walls, Andrew F., *The Missionary Movement in Christian History: Studies in Christian Faith* (Maryknoll, NY: Orbis, 1996).

Chapter 12

Perceptions of Women's Health and Rights in Christian New Religious Movements in Kenya

Philomena N. Mwaura and Damaris S. Parsitau

Introduction

Africa is depicted by scholars of religion and history as a continent with a triple religious heritage: namely Islam, Christianity, and African Traditional Religion. Religion is central to her very existence and this is manifested in the way Christianity has been embraced throughout the continent. Besides the traditional forms of Christianity initially established by missionaries, there exist African initiated churches that are a product of the revival within Christianity all over the world. This manifestation of Christian presence in Africa has generated renewal and a proliferation of charismatic ministries that have gained significance all over Africa in the last three decades. The character of this Christianity is Pentecostal or charismatic. These newer religious formations have generated conflicts that have resulted in violence with adverse consequences for women and children.

The phenomenal growth of Christianity has arisen in the context of economic decline, rising poverty, bad governance and international indifference, emergence of an increasingly mass-mediated public sphere, increase in discourses concerning human rights and religious freedom, and new challenges of religious pluralism and the state management of this plurality (Hackett 2004: 151–2). Economic liberalization policies pushed by the World Bank and the International Monetary Fund since the 1980s have resulted in government withdrawal of subsidies in education, health, sanitation, housing, and the like. Due to this, women's welfare and particularly health have suffered adversely and even deteriorated.

While these churches are viewed as liberational and filling the vacuum created by social, political, and economic hardships, their perceptions of women and children's health and rights can sometimes be at variant with human rights as they affect women. They provide social and spiritual support to the marginalized among whom are women and youth. But what exactly is this support mediated by the charismatic churches? Have they resulted in the empowerment of women? To what extent do they promote women's rights, both human and reproductive? What is the nature of gender relations in these churches? This chapter explores the perception and practice of women's rights and women's reproductive health rights in charismatic churches in Kenya. It begins with a brief discussion of the theology of the churches and their attitude towards women and then explores their perspectives on sexuality. It concludes by arguing that Pentecostal/charismatic theology and practice has been inimical to women's well-being, especially due to its attitude to women's human rights that relate to their moral agency in matters of reproductive health, and which have consequences for their vulnerability to HIV/ AIDS.

Methodology

The methodology for this chapter combines both field and library research. Data were obtained from oral interviews with several adherents from charismatic churches in Nairobi, Kenya, namely: Mavuno church, Jubilee Christian centre (JCC), House of Grace Ministries, Triumph Ministries, Morning Star Ministries, and Victorious Faith Assembly. These are new-generation churches which are Pentecostal/charismatic in faith and practice. Though they are based in Nairobi, they hold evangelistic crusades in other parts of the country. The authors have been involved in research on charismatic Christianity in Nairobi since 2001 to the present.

Theology of Charismatic Christianity in Africa

Charismatic Christianity is the fastest growing type of Christianity in Africa. This phenomenon has marked the beginning of a vigorous Christian awakening in Africa. It has attracted millions of educated young people and is popular because of its adroit use of the media to draw attention to their presence and theology. Pentecostal/ charismatic movements all over Africa have their roots in para-church evangelical associations of the 1970s which gained much prominence in the 1990s. These associations were greatly influenced by international and inter-denominational evangelical students' organizations like the Student Christian Movement, Christian Union, and Scripture Union in the 1940s and the Campus Crusade, Life Ministry, and Navigators in the 1970s. From the 1980s to date they have been influenced by American neo-Pentecostalism or the faith movement whose greatest proponents have been Kenneth Hagin Sr., Kenneth Copeland, and John Avanzini. Many African founders of Pentecostal/charismatic churches have been trained and mentored by these personalities. The movements gradually crystallized into churches, although many associations are still non-denominational and hence attract Christians of all denominational persuasions and from all walks of life.

Charismatic/Pentecostal movements adopt a faith gospel focused on this-worldly blessings and a deliverance theology. Gifford (1998: 320) observes that this theology, "though built on African traditional conceptions is expressed strongly in terms of modern charismatic thinking." Like other Pentecostals, the new movements identify with the central act of conversion in which the individual consecrates his or her life to Christ, atones for past sins and becomes "born again" or saved (Marshall 1995: 244). Charismatics exhibit many new characteristics that make them different from other Christian churches or religious movements. They overtly display a rejection of African culture although their theology, particularly deliverance theology, is informed by the African worldview. There are also "often compromises and adjustments to certain traditional features" (Ojo 1998: 184). They attract upwardly mobile youth, have a lay oriented leadership, mostly urban congregations, an ardent desire to appear successful reflecting a modern outlook and portraying an international image, use English as the medium of communication, emphasize the manifestation of gifts of the Holy Spirit, and have prominent roles for women and youth.

Another distinguishing characteristic is the centrality of the Bible in their faith and practice. Being Pentecostal, experience is more central than doctrine, but their attitude to the Bible has led to their being labelled fundamentalist. The Bible is their source of authority and doctrine. The churches use the Bible as a law code and this leads to a legalistic theology. To them the Bible is unerring in every single detail and is to be taken literary. This attitude has implications for issues regarding the place and role of women, marriage, family, and sexuality. Their life is also an ardent quest for individual sanctity. It places the focus on one's personal holiness. As a result, some fundamentalists/charismatics are unconcerned about the complexities of sin and evil, particularly the social dimensions of injustice. Nevertheless, some more liberal charismatics have been able to develop a theology of social engagement and their focus on individual transformation is geared towards societal transformation and revitalization through individual holiness.

Charismatics have been accused of having a retreatist attitude to the world. They are depicted as unconcerned with issues affecting the world like indebtedness, materialism, poverty, conflict, war, and ethnicity. They are accused of offering simplistic and quick explanations and solutions to these situations. To them, the devil is responsible for life's insecurities. All one has to do is simply "accept Jesus" and reject the devil. The "born again" Christian will be blessed with health and wealth. The Christian duty to deprived non-believers is merely to convert them so that they, too, can be healthy and prosper. This theology makes people dependent on miracles from God and robs them of the will to change their lives. When applied to personal lives, this theology can be enslaving rather than liberating. Let us now examine charismatics' view of women.

Perception of Women in Charismatic Churches

The preponderance of women in new religious movements has been noted by several scholars (Jassy 1971; Jules Rosette 1985; Hackett 1987; 1995; Asamoah-Gyadu 1998). Not only are women there as participants, they have also assumed significant roles as founders and heads of churches. They also function as pastors, healers, and prophetesses. Just like men, they are mediators of God's grace and spirit. Due to their Pentecostal theology that provides avenues for the expression of charismatic gifting irrespective of gender, the attitude to women in these movements have been positive. For these reasons, it has been suggested that Pentecostal and charismatic movements have transformative effects on women, particularly those in search for equality. Yet and as Browning and Hollingsworth (2010) both critically point out, Pentecostalism has "the dubious and paradoxical character of being at once liberating and disempowering for women seeking equality in spiritual matters." Nevertheless, to the extent that women's roles are circumscribed by a literalist biblical interpretation of their roles and functions, a closer examination of their place in the churches reveals certain handicaps and paradoxes.

An examination of structures of authority in these movements reveals not an egalitarian structure influenced by a democratic spirit but a hierarchical structure that invests a lot of authority on the founder bishop/pastor. Such a structure nurtures problematic attitudes and practices, particularly among "ordinary" adherents. These attitudes include lack of a creative imagination or capacity for dialogue, a critical spirit and an increase in appeals to obedience, submission, renunciation, and humility. Adherents are expected unquestioningly to accept the teachings of the pastor on all issues ranging from personal matters like marriage and the upbringing of children, to investments and the work ethic. It has been observed that women, who generally form the majority of members in these churches, believe in the pastor so much that they will appeal to his or her authority, even on very private domestic matters. This has resulted in conflicts in relationships and has been a threat to family stability.

Charismatics' views about women show fundamentalist tendencies. Although they recognize the need and value of women's occupation outside the home out of economic necessity, for them the sign of true womanhood is a woman devoting her life sacrificially to the demands of her husband and children. Her primary function is as wife and mother and being subject to the authority of her husband in all spheres of her life. Though, as mentioned earlier, charismatics endorse expression of women's spirituality and even leadership in the churches, they equate women's emancipation as propagated by the feminist movement with destruction of the family. Like most fundamentalists, they believe that the family can only be saved by being returned to male control. Adherents are advised not to listen to gender activists in church and civil society, charging that they are out to wreck the family with their views on women's rights.

A husband is the head of the wife and she is expected to defer to him in all matters. Being a "help-mate" to the husband implies a helper, assistant. She has to show loyalty, respect, and love. Although most writers and pastors advocate the application of democratic principles of fairness and justice in the running of families and the need to consider the views of women in decision making, the underlying theology and ideology governing marriage is one of subordination of women to men. The theology that underpins the conceptualization of marriage and male–female relatedness in these churches is patriarchal and sexist and therefore problematic to women. Consider the case of Mavuno church in Nairobi. In a televised church message titled "the strength of a woman," the preacher asked women to use their beauty and femininity and other assets to get to the boardroom. The audience was asked to confess these words three times: "when God created you (woman), he was not hoping for a boy: I am glad to be a woman of influence, a glorious woman." The preacher then went on to enumerate five assets that women possess and which they should use to succeed in their work place. These are beauty, words, relationships, intuition and femininity. The preacher explained that women are both beautiful and mysterious creatures and they should use their beauty to rise to the boardroom. "When you combine this with your professional studies, you are sure to succeed," he said. You should also appreciate your femininity and make use of it. You should also appreciate and celebrate the girl child, he said. Women should also use their beauty for business. At the end of every sentence, women were asked to shout, "Thank you God for making me a woman of influence, a glorious woman."

In this televised service, Dr. Gladies Mwiti, a renowned psychiatrist was brought in and interviewed by the pastor. She explained to the women that while she is very successful, well travelled, and has a Ph.D. (which she called "pull your head down") she is still a submissive wife and loving mother, a role model and mentor to girls and women. She submits and honors her husband despite being hugely successful and highly educated[1]

These types of messages do not encourage women to work hard to excel but instead to use their beauty and femininity to excel in the boardroom. They are not only sexist but also portray women as objects to be admired and to gratify men who can then give them promotion not because of their brains but because of their beauty and femininity. The call for women to submit to their husband is standard phraseology in most charismatic and Pentecostal churches in Kenya. Married women are expected to submit to their husbands. Pastors' wives especially are the epitome of submission and humility. These women are expected to submit to men at home, in the church, and in the society. Pastor Lucy Muiru of Maximum Miracle Centres, Rev. Judy Mbugua of Ladies Homecare Spiritual Fellowship, and Rev. Kathy Kiuna of Jubilee Christian Centre have all alluded to the fact that despite their prominence both in their churches and in public sphere, when they go back home, they submit to their husbands who are the heads of their families. These women, while they have retained spiritual independence and have excelled as public figures, still experience tensions between the demands on women to obey and submit to their husbands and the call for believers both male and female to submit to Christ (Soothil 2007: 114).

Yet there are a lot of tensions and politics in the concept of submission, particularly for married women. In the Deliverance Church Nakuru for example, women are sometimes viewed as subordinate to men. Commenting on relationships between men and women during a church service, one pastor put it this way: "men are the heads and women are the neck." He explained that the head cannot stand without the neck neither can the neck stand on its own without the head. Both

---

[1]   Mavuno church televized message, Citizen TV(9–10 a.m.) in July 2010.

need each other and complement each other, but the man remains the head. There cannot be two heads in one house, only one head and the neck. This is how God wanted it to be so, sisters, learn your places in your marriage. At the same time, he said, if you are in this church and you still beat up your wife, shame on you! You cannot be born again and hit your wife. Men, you must love your wives as the Lord loved the church. Women must respect their husbands as the Lord decreed it.

This message is both contradictory and ambiguous. While the church's leadership teaches men to respect women and discourages gender-based violence, it at the same time places women in a subordinate place where they are the necks not the heads. This is the politics of gender empowerment espoused by the Deliverance Church and many other Pentecostal and charismatic churches in Kenya.

This theology literally prescribes and encourages women's silence and submission at home, in church, and in wider society. It is considered normative and a basis of shaping attitudes and behaviour within the churches. These churches embrace the household codes in the New Testament that prescribe the silence of women and apply them literally in their practices. Matthews Ojo, writing about perceptions of sexuality among charismatics, in Nigeria says: "The wife should be obedient and submit completely to the husband ... A sure and unmistakable mark of a woman's spirituality is her meek, humble and obedient and whole hearted submission to the husband in everything unto the Lord."[2]

Although this teaching is biblical, an uncritical acceptance of it has adverse implications for women's well-being, particularly in matters of sexuality and the current problems posed by HIV/AIDS. It is a theology that is also inimical to women's rights, both human and reproductive. In expecting obedience in everything, it presumes the moral and practical validity of the decisions made by the man in all matters and at all times. It discourages critical thinking and moral agency in women. Since it does not encourage a relationship of mutuality that would enhance the welfare of the family in all areas, such a unilateral rule of obedience disadvantages the woman and in any case may render her vulnerable to abuse. In fact, women are encouraged to address their husbands as lords and masters. Cases of misogynist attitudes and domestic abuse of women have been noted among some adherents. This abuse is also evident among single women who are also expected to be submissive to church authority. This perception is evident in much of Pentecostal literature that promotes women's subordination. A casual look at the titles of magazine articles produced by these churches says as much: "the power of a praying wife", "qualities of a good wife," "the power of submission." While many Pentecostal churches endeavour to teach women self-confidence and self-esteem, this is meant to make the married attractive to their spouses and raise confidence in those seeking spouses.

---

[2]   Ojo 1998: 198. This same observation was made by adherents of the Victorious Faith Assembly and Triumph Ministries. Oral interviews with Pastor Aigboje of Victorious Faith Assembly Nairobi, March 2003 and Evangelist Eileen Njeri of Triumph Ministries, Nairobi, May 2004.

Again, insistence that obedience and whole-hearted submission to the man is the "unmistakable mark of spirituality" may lead women to endure violent and dangerous relationships for fear that in choosing to leave such relationships they are disobeying God or sinning. "God hates divorce" (Malachi 2:16), "what God has joined together, let man not separate them" (Mathew 19:6) are verses commonly quoted by many Pentecostal clergy whenever they teach about marriage and divorce. These verses are also, surprisingly, quoted to women who seek a pastor's advice or opinion concerning their not so perfect unions, and one that has caused many women to endure abusive marriages because they cannot question or offend God. Such unqualified obedience is an abuse of women's human rights and is particularly dangerous in the context of HIV/AIDS. A theology that silences and subordinates women mutes their voices and so they cannot voice their discontent or opinion on any matter affecting their lives. When obedience is theologically presented for women, it makes it difficult for them to negotiate and navigate domestic issues, particularly on matters of sexuality and reproductive health. Given the importance of such communication, a theology that silences women becomes life threatening. This theology needs to be challenged if women's welfare is to be addressed and improved.

But not all these churches sidestep women and children rights. When it comes to children's rights, some of these churches appear keen on protecting the rights of women and children. In one of Faith Evangelist Ministries' single ladies meeting at Charter Hall, Nairobi on March 21, 2009 for example, the speaker was Justice Martha Koome, a children and women rights activists and one of the founding members of FIDA-Kenya. She took the largely female audience through the rights of children such as the right to education, love, and protection. The judge taught the women that children of single parents have rights to inheritance. She talked to women about the Ministry of Gender and Children Affairs and also FIDA-Kenya which provides legal advice to women. She explained to single parents in the meeting that a child has a right to know the father, and that children must be protected from rape, incest, child prostitution, and child labor. She also talked to women about their rights as married or divorced women and urged them to get empowered economically. She equally spoke on issues affecting single women in the church, and on wife beating, sexual violence, and spousal abuse.[3]

Charismatic Perspectives on Sexuality

All over Africa, charismatic movements have shown concern for the ways in which the marriages and sexual behaviour of their members influence spirituality within the movements. A variety of literature in print and electronic media exist detailing acceptable and unacceptable sexual conduct, preparation for marriage

---

[3] Participant observation Karen Sanctuary, Nairobi, 10 a.m.–1.00 p.m., Saturday March 21, 2009.

for the youth, and family life. They are concerned about the whole area of sexuality, marriage, and parenting. There are, however, more books on marriage than sexuality. To the charisismatic movements, sexual behaviour can influence religious commitment and therefore adherents are urged to lead holy and morally upright lives, and avoid temptation in thought and deed.

Christian marriage, to them, mirrors the relationship of Christ to the church and should therefore be guarded carefully. The institution of marriage is also seen as being threatened by the devil through popular media, family planning agencies, and professional secular marriage counsellors. Adherents are called to observe purity in sexual behaviour and marital relationships. Their views on sexuality and marriage are to some extent influenced by traditional Africa cultural norms and the Bible. Concerning sexuality, charismatics accept that males and females are created differently and the peculiarity of each influences their functions and roles in society. In their views on sexuality, they oppose premarital and extra-marital sex. In trying to regulate sexual conduct between the unmarried male and female, charismatics teach that Christians should guard against the corrupting influences of worldliness. Young people can be friends but no intimate relationships are allowed. In addition, secret love is not entertained. When two young people become close friends, they are expected to declare this to the elders of the church. The conversation and attitude between the opposite sexes must reflect purity. This should be reflected in the manner of dressing, and kissing is not allowed. As Ojo (1998: 186) comments: "Charismatics have attempted to sustain the purity of adolescence by stressing the doctrine of holiness and applying such to lifestyles among their members." In this sense, charismatics have entered into a contested moral minefield in which they are attempting to sexually and morally discipline their members (Parsitau 2009).

Because of their strict views on adolescent sexuality, charismatics are opposed to contraceptive use and abortion. Particularly salient is the fact that Pentecostal and Charismatic churches vehemently opposed some features of the new constitution that they perceive as too liberal and might impact on the family. This includes abortion, same-sex marriages/unions, and pornography. These clergy wanted the constitution to state that life begins at conception and not at birth. This has put Christian churches in collision with gender activists and pro-life advocates and the medical fraternity. But this is not only peculiar to the Kenyan context as these are issues that most Christian denominations all over the world would reject. Anthony Balcomb (2004: 8) cites the examples of post-Apartheid South Africa where many evangelicals and Pentecostals condemned the constitution's emphasis on individual rights and civil liberties when it comes to freedom of speech and choice, especially its pro-choice position on abortion, the forbidding of discrimination based on gender and sexual orientation and its intolerance of pornography. He further suggests that the threat to some of their freedom brought about by the new constitutional dispensation in South Africa may have propelled Pentecostals into active politics with a new and combative zeal.

These churches also opposed provisions in the constitution that includes emergency exceptions to the country's abortion ban. This is despite the fact that many women and girls die annually trying to procure unsafe abortions in a country whose previous constitution made abortion illegal.[4] It is telling that Bishop Margaret Wanjiru of Jesus Is Alive Ministries, for example, has vehemently opposed the inclusion of abortion legalization and same-sex unions in the new Kenyan Constitution.[5] Women's reproductive health includes the right to safe abortions and these are issues that affect many women in Africa, Kenyans in particular. Bishop Wanjiru's opposition to these issues that affect the women for whom she claims to speak is not only contradictory but also ambiguous.

Generally, charismatics differ in their attitudes to artificial family planning among the married. While some support it on the grounds that there is no theological justification against it in Scripture and marriage is complete even without children, others oppose it on the ground that God intends human beings to procreate. They do not seem to have a well-developed theology in this area. Some churches, like Deeper Life Bible Church in Nigeria and Kenya, insist on the practice of natural family planning among their members. They even warn against frequent sexual intercourse which is viewed as a sign of lust. Contraceptive use is condemned because of its link to increased promiscuity among the youth and hence poses a moral problem. Abortion on demand is condemned as murder, for to them life begins at conception.

Conclusion

We have seen that neo-Pentecostal/charismatic movements have been on the rise in Africa. They have contributed to the reshaping of society through their revolutionary codes of behaviour and a demand for purity and morality in personal and communal lives. They have encouraged the use of women's charismatic gifts which are evident in women's functions in church leadership and promotion of the welfare of the churches. However, this empowerment of women in certain ecclesiastical functions does not translate into an acceptance of women's moral agency in matters of their reproductive health and rights over their own bodies.

Women are still subject to male control in their churches and families. This has adverse implications on women's well-being if they do not have power to negotiate in matters of sexual practice or cannot voice protest against oppressive authority at home and church. It is therefore important that these churches be open to views on reproductive health rights and women's human rights. They should be

---

[4]   A recent study links the ban to the death of at least hundreds of women a year. *In Harms Way: the Impact of Kenyans' Restrictive Abortion Laws*, Centre for Reproductive Rights accessed at http://reproductiverights.org/sites/crr.civicactions.net/files/documents/ InHarmsWay_2010.pdf

[5]   Participant observation during worship service, Nairobi Miracle Centre, May 2002.

open to a more liberating reading of the Scriptures so that they can interpret them in the context of present problems and needs. There are many health problems affecting women and girls and they can only be addressed through networking with organizations that are involved in addressing them. While advocating ethical and spiritual life styles is commendable, it is not enough. Women and girls need to be exposed to the choices available to improve their lives and also the various moral imperatives that exist through a liberating interpretation of Scripture and current problems and issues.

Bibliography

Asamoah-Gyadu, Kwabena, "'Fireballs in Our Midst' West Africa's Burgeoning Charismatic Churches and the Pastoral Roles of Women," *Mission Studies*, 15.1 (1998): 15–31.

Balcomb, A.O., "From Apartheid to the New Dispensation: Evangelicals and the Democratization of South Africa," *The Journal of Religion in Africa*, 34.1–2 (2004): 5–38.

Browning, M.D. and A. Hollingsworth,, "Your Daughters Shall Prophesy (As Long as They Submit): Pentecostalism and Gender in Global Perspective," in Michael Wilkinson and Steven M. Studebaker (eds.), *The Liberating Spirit: Pentecostals and Social Action in North America* (Eugene, OR: Pickwick 2010), pp. 161–84.

French, Marylin, "Fundamentalism: Religious Wars against Women," in Sheila Ruth (ed.), *Issues in Feminism: An Introduction to Women's Studies* (Mountain View, CA: Mayfield Publishing Company, 1998), pp. 141–8.

Gifford, Paul, *African Christianity: Its Public Role* (London, Hurst and Co., 1998).

Hackett, R.I.J. (ed.), *New Religious Movements in Nigeria* (Lewiston, NY: Edwin Mellen Press, 1987).

—, "Women and New Religious Movements," in Ursula King (ed.), *Religion and Gender* (Oxford: Blackwell, 1995), pp. 257–90.

—, "Prophets, 'False Prophets,' and the African State: Emergent Issues of Religious Freedom and Conflict," in P.L. Lucas and T. Robbins (eds.), *New Religious Movements in the 21st Century: Legal, Political and Social Challenges in Global Perspective* (New York: Routledge, 2004), pp. 151–78

Jassy, Marie-Perrin, "Women in the Independent Churches," *Risk*, 7.3 (1971): 46–9.

Jules Rosette, Benneta, "Cultural Ambivalence and Ceremonial Leadership: The Role of Women in Africa's New Religious Movements," in John C.B. Webster and Ellen L. Webster (eds.), *The Church and Women in the Third World* (Philadelphia: Westminster Press, 1985), pp. 88–104.

Marshall, Ruth, "God is not a Democrat: Pentecostalism and Democratization in Nigeria," in Paul Gifford (ed.), *The Christian Churches and the Democratization of Africa* (Leiden: E.J. Brill, 1995), pp. 239–60.

Ojo, Matthews, "Marriage and Piety among Charismatics in Nigeria," in James Cox (ed.), *Rites of Passage in Contemporary Africa* (Cardiff: Cardiff Academic Press, 1998), pp.180–97.

Parsitau, D.S., "'Keep Holy Distance and Abstain till He Comes': Interrogating a Pentecostal Church Discourses and Engagements with HIV/AIDS and the Youth in Kenya," *Africa Today* (special issue on Christianity and HIV/AIDS in Eastern and Southern Africa), 56.1 (2009): 44–64.

Soothill, J.E., *Gender, Social Change and Spiritual Power: Charismatic Christianity in Ghana* (Leiden: E.J. Brill, 2007).

Chapter 13

Religion and Divine Presence: Appropriating Christianity from within African Indigenous Religions' Perspective

Victor I. Ezigbo

Introduction

The continuing influence of indigenous religious beliefs on the majority of African Christians demands revisiting of the question: "What have African Indigenous Religions to do with Christianity?" I will engage this question simultaneously with another question in mind, namely: "What has Jesus to do with both Christianity and African Indigenous Religions?" At a meeting of the African Association for the Study of Religions in Chicago in November 2008, Professor Jacob Olupona commented: "If we require the leaders of Africa who have stolen the wealth of their countries to take an oath in the shrines of the local gods they will stop stealing. Christianity's teaching on future judgment has helped to perpetuate the criminal activities of many African leaders." As a theologian with interest in the relationship between Christianity and African Indigenous Religions, his comment struck me as profound. It intensified my curiosity and desire to rethink, from a theological perspective, the relationship between Christianity and indigenous religions of Africa. I left the meeting pondering whether the Christian religion has done more harm than good to Africans. This chapter is partly the result of my reflections on Olupona's comments.

Christianity discovered and *is* discovering its unique identity in the contexts of other religions. It discovered its identity in its earliest beginning in the contexts of Judaism, the religions of Samaria, and Greco-Roman religions. In twenty-first century Africa, it is discovering its full potential in the contexts of indigenous religions, Islam, Hinduism, and other religions. As expected, Christianity has not always enjoyed a good relationship with the neighboring or resident religions it encounters when executing its witnessing mission. I will explore some of the difficulties the Christian religion faces in its attempt to discover and live out its identity in the context of African Indigenous Religions.

The second-century theologian Tertullian might have been the one who opened the door for rigorous interrogation of Christianity's relation to the "other" when he asked in *Against Heretics*: "What indeed has Athens to do with Jerusalem?" (Tertullian 1969: 246). However, since Tertullian's query, Christian theologians have had to deal with similar issues in their own *sitz im leben* (settings in life). It was in the mid-1950s that sub-Saharan African Christian theologians began to iron out the relationship between Christianity and African Indigenous Religions. But major constructive theological works on the issue only began to emerge in the 1960s (e.g., see Mulago (1965), Idowu (1965; 1973), Mbiti (1971), Pobee (1979); Kato (1975), Shorter (1975), McVeigh (1974), Dickson (1984), and Bujo (1992). While some theologians have engaged the issue constructively, others have ignored it, constructing their theologies in a way that avoids the indigenous religious issues that inform many beliefs of African Christians. Yet some others have approached the issues from a negative apologetic mindset toward indigenous religions and their attendant concerns.

In this chapter, I will explore the works of E. Bolaji Idowu and Byang H. Kato. They represent the two major opposing theological positions in Africa. While Kato championed "Conservative Evangelicalism," Idowu pioneered what can be described as "Evangelical Liberalism,"[1] The theological models of these theologians remain foundational to contemporary discussions on the relationship between Christianity and the indigenous religions of Africa.

What have African Indigenous Religions to do with Christianity? Bolaji Idowu and Byang Kato have constructed theological models that respond to this question. I will argue that although these theologians have made helpful contributions to the discussion, their proposals fail adequately to deal with crucial religious and theological issues that underlie interreligious dialogue. In contrast, I will propose a new model for engaging the blurry relationship shrouding the role of African Indigenous Religions in contextualizing and appropriating Christianity in Africa. Below is the summary of the two major arguments of the model.

First, in order for a "Christian" theology to be simultaneously "African," it must engage the indigenous religious matters that inform African Christians' experiences. This contextual way of thinking entails that (a) theologians must perceive the indigenous religions as unique interpretations, expressions, and responses to Divine presence; and (b) the theological language and content of a Christian theology designed for African contexts must embrace and interact with the indigenous religious thought forms of Africa. This may require dropping some classical Western Christian languages and expressions, however orthodox they may appear to be, and taking on uniquely African expressions.[2]

---

[1]　Kato's theological work was largely an extension of the theologies of his Dallas professors and the theologies of the SIM missionaries with whom he worked.

[2]　Okot P'Bitek's warning on the danger of using foreign languages to express African ideas is most helpful. He writes: "African writers who choose to use English or French set themselves certain problems. They wish to express African ideas, but they have chosen a non-African language to express them. There is a grave danger that with the tool of language they will borrow other foreign things. Every language has its own stock of common images expressing a certain people's way of looking at things" (P'Bitek 1966: 1).

Second, successfully to answer the question "What have African Indigenous Religions to do with Christianity?" we must simultaneously ask another question, namely: "What has Jesus Christ to do with Christianity?" The implication of the latter question is that it allows the theologian to rethink the relationship between Jesus and all religions, including Christianity. African Christian theologians need not depend solely on classical or contemporary non-African Christian interpretations of the Christ-Event to imagine and appropriate the meaning and significance of God's action in Jesus Christ in African contexts. While they certainly can learn from foreign interpretations, they must seek in-house interpretations from within the social-religious heritage and experience of Africans. In what follows, I will articulate the theological model of Idowu.

Bolaji Idowu

Bolaji Idowu (1913–93), a Nigerian Methodist minister and theologian, was undoubtedly one of the brightest minds of his time. His contribution to the study of African Indigenous Religions and African Christian theology was profound. He was close to the centre of the development of African theology in the 1950s and 1960s. As a contextual thinker, his desire to dismantle and discredit Western derogatory estimations of the indigenous religions of Africa, and also the search for a correlation between Christianity and African Indigenous Religions, reverberated in his thought. He obtained his doctorate from the University of London in 1955 under the watchful eyes of Geoffrey Parrinder, a prominent expert in African religions. *Olodumare: God in Yoruba Belief* was the product of his doctoral research (Idowu 1962).

Early Idowu: Christianity as Fulfiller of African Indigenous Religions' Aspirations

Although most of Idowu's writings were located within Nigerian contexts, he "entertained little doubt that his conclusions have relevance for the whole of tropical Africa" (Bediako 1992: 268). Several noteworthy things shaped his theology. First, his frustration with the foreignness of Christianity in Nigeria (and in the majority of Africa) and his relentless efforts to contextualize Christianity reveal his affinity with nationalism and negritude. Like many nationalists, he was suspicious of the intentions of Western missionaries and feared they helped to perpetuate both the political and mental colonization of Africans. He contended that Nigerian churches must ponder "whether Christianity is not, after all, a European institution which has no beneficial relevance for Nigerians, but which has nevertheless been imposed upon them as an engine of colonial policy by their European overlords" (Idowu 1965: 1). Second, his pastoral vocation reflected concretely on his vision for Christian ecclesia, particularly its correlation to African indigenous understanding of community. He was highly critical of African churches that retained the worship culture of Western missionaries but failed to draw insights from their own contexts (Idowu 1965: 26–40).

Third, his Western education propelled his constant conversations with Western versions of Christianity from within African contexts. In his writings, he engaged Western anthropologists, theologians, and scholars of religions. In some cases, he was highly critical of Western writers, particularly those whose interpretations of African religious realities and histories portrayed Africans as merely superstitious. Fourth, he was a contextual theologian. As he saw it, twentieth-century Nigerian Christianity lived mainly on foreign theology. He considered this state of affairs both inadequate and unwarranted. He wrote:

> Theologically, [the church in Nigeria] has been spoon-fed by Europeans all along. Her theology is book theology; that is, what she read in books written by European theologians, or what she is told by Europeans, is accepted uncritically and given out undigested in preaching or teaching. What this reveals is the sad fact that Nigerian Christians have not yet begun to do their own thinking and to grapple spiritually and intellectually with questions relating to the Christian faith. (Idowu 1965: 22–3).

The theologian who aims to construct a theology from diverse religious and cultural contexts must be prepared to enter into the arena of the theology of religions. Idowu was well aware of this theological requirement. While his constructive engagement with Christianity–African Indigenous Religions relations appeared in *Towards an Indigenous Church* (1965), his theological position on the issue was already present in *Olodumare* (1962), albeit, in skewed forms. His theology of religions underwent development. Convinced that there was continuity between African Indigenous Religions and Christianity, he adopted a "fulfillment theory" in his early work. He wrote in *Olodumare* that

> a vacuum is being created with regard to religion in Yorubaland. And there are contending forces for the filling of the vacuum. Of the forces at work, Christianity, by its unique and universal message, stands the best change of fulfilling that which is implied in the Yoruba concept of God, and that for the benefit of the people and country. (Idowu 1962: 215)

But, for Idowu, a theology of religion that is designed for Nigeria should "bear the distinctive stamp of indigenous originality" and should also inspire people to imagine "who Jesus is, what he has done and is doing for them corporately and individually, and what he means to them as the absolute Lord of life—the whole of life—within the context of the world in which they live" (Idowu 1965: 23). In this process, the theologian's task is to distinguish the Christian message from its transmission vehicles which are culturally laden. This mindset informed his arguments against Western missionaries for underestimating the weakness and inappropriateness of communicating the Christian message with Western cultural categories in Africa. The missionaries, he insisted, failed to acknowledge that they were simply "vehicles" and "transmitters" of the Christian message and not its custodians or sole possessors (Idowu 1965: 8).

Idowu's earliest theology of religion was christological. He argued that although Nigerian Christianity must draw insights from indigenous religion for its theological language, it "must preserve full allegiance to the Eternal, Cosmic, Unchanging Christ, who is her only Lord" (Idowu 1965: 7). Since, in his thinking, Christianity is the religion that encapsulates and preserves God's revelation which climaxed in Jesus Christ, he accords to Christianity a special place in human salvation history. He writes: "Christianity is a Universal Religion instituted of God through Jesus Christ the Saviour of the whole world [and] it came into being in consequence of the invincible love of God for the world which He created and in which His redemptive purpose has always been at work" (Idowu 1965: 7).

This superiority accorded to Christianity in Idowu's early work accounts for his understanding of its *fulfillment* role in its relationship with African Indigenous Religions. The anticipated consequence of the relationship was an *indigenized church*. For him, a church that is indigenous should worship God in the ways which are compatible with its spiritual temperament, prays to God, and hears his word in the local idioms (Idowu 1965: 11). It is a church whose life derives from "the Lordship of Jesus Christ, the church in which in all things He is pre-eminent" (Idowu 1965: 11). It is also a church which negotiates its identity in the light of the "presence of the One Holy, Catholic, and Apostolic Church" (Idowu 1965: 11). It is a church that must strive to be both financially and theologically independent from Western churches. While it can accept "all the legitimate help" from Western churches, it must be willing to "struggle and suffer in order to live rather than to continue to receive any kind of help which is likely to fetter, paralyze, or throttle her, and choke life out of her" (Idowu 1965: 54–5). The church must take what are foreign—Hebraic and Western deposits—and clothe them with indigenous metaphors and thought forms. To sum up, in his early theology of religions, Idowu construed Christianity as the religion—by virtue of its connection with Jesus Christ—that is superior to and fulfills the religious aspirations and gaps of the indigenous religions of Africa. And on the basis of this understanding of Christianity, he contended that the African versions of Christianity must be contextualized if they were to become meaningful and relevant to African peoples.

Later Idowu: Christianity and African Indigenous Religions as Valid Responses to Divine Revelation

Interestingly, in his later theological work, Idowu breaks with his early fulfillment theory and moves radically in the direction of religious pluralism and universalism.[3]

---

[3]   *African Traditional Religion: A Definition* (Idowu 1973) is the most constructive and detailed work of his writings that reflect his new theological position, particularly the

Many of his critics such as Kato concentrate mainly on his later work (Kato 1975: 96–104). Unlike his early theology, in the later works, Idowu no longer perceives Christianity as possessing a superior role over African Indigenous Religions. He sees all religions as human constructs and responses to divine revelation. All religions, therefore, are sufficient for their adherents and have the same status before God. He wrote:

> There are those who will argue that religion could be divided into two categories: the religion based on God's climatic revelation in Jesus Christ, and what they call man-made religion, i.e. other religions besides Christianity. This, of course, is a deliberate or unwitting flying in the face of truth. If revelation indeed means God's self-disclosure, if he has left his mark upon the created order and his witness within man—every man—then it follows that revelation cannot be limited in scope and that it is meant for all mankind, all rational beings, irrespective of race or colour. (Idowu 1973: 56)

Idowu's pluralist view of religions undoubtedly fell like a bombshell on the playground of African theologians and scholars of religions. Evangelicals, of course, were the most disturbed among his contemporaries. The writings of Kato and other Evangelical theologians demonstrate great suspicion and dissatisfaction with Idowu's views of religions. It was as if Idowu rediscovered the true nature of religions: they "result from divine activity and man's response" (Idowu 1973: 203). In his newly found voice, the language of religious negotiation or dialogue was hardly present. He became impatient with Christianity for its desire to oppress or take over other religions. He was clear in his contention that the Christian God was *Olodumare*—"God as known and experienced in Yoruba pre-Christian religious tradition" (Idowu 1973: 205).

But whether or not Christianity would eventually succeed in suppressing indigenous religions of Africa, for him, was highly debatable and perhaps impossible. What was clear in his mind was

> that in strictly personal matters relating to the passages of life and the crisis of life, African Traditional Religion is regarded as the final succor by most Africans ... . [And] in matters concerning providence, healing, and general wellbeing ... most Africans still look up to "their own religion" as "the way." (Idowu 1973: 206)

A lasting legacy of Idowu that has to a large extent preserved his pluralist view of religion is *Orita*—the University of Ibadan Journal of Religious Studies—that he helped to develop. The provocative cover page of the journal captures the agenda and philosophy of the university's religion department. *Orita*, a Yoruba word that literally means "where the ways meet" or an "intersection," is depicted on the

relationship between Christianity and African Indigenous Religions.

cover page of the journal as a circle that represents the "intersections" where three roads (figuratively, African Indigenous Religion, Islam, and Christianity) meet. This depiction conveys the idea that each of these religions is unique, valid, and capable of leading its true adherents to God. In addition, it conveyed the idea that although these religions are unique, they can be compatible.

This latter mindset informed the theological consensus of African theologians who met at a Consultation held at Ibadan in 1966 (under the auspices of the All Africa Conferences of Churches) to discuss the state of African theology.[4] Their theological confession is noteworthy:

> We believe that God, the Father of our Lord Jesus Christ, creator of heaven and earth, Lord of history, has been dealing with mankind at all times and in all parts of the world. It is with this conviction that we study the rich heritage of our African peoples, and we have evidence that they know Him and worship Him (Dickson and Ellingworth 1969: 16)

Also, they agreed that

> God's self-disclosure is, in the first instance, to the whole world and that each race has grasped something of this primarily revelation according to its native capability. To deny this, as some have been trying to do, is to approach theology with a cultural bias and be traitors to truth. (Dickson and Ellingworth 1969: 12)

Undoubtedly, Idowu was a key contributor to the development of this form of African Christian theology.

I will argue that Idowu's theology of religion, like Kato's, entrenches God in religions. This theological mindset permeates and sustains the fuzzy relationship between Christianity and African Indigenous Religions in both scholarship and the daily lives of many African Christians. I contend that entrapping God in religions is theologically inadequate. I will return to explore the implications of Idowu's theologies after articulating Kato's view.

Byang Kato

Byang Kato (1936–75), like Idowu, desired to present the Christian gospel message in the ways that befitted his African contexts. He obtained his theological undergraduate degree from London Bible College and his doctorate in theology from Dallas Theological Seminary in the United States of America. His interpreters can only guess on what his matured theological views would have looked like. After

---

[4] The All Africa Conference of Churches (AACC) was formed in Kampala on April 20, 1963.

a relatively short life, the only main work that Kato left behind was *Theological Pitfalls in Africa*, a book that consists mainly of his doctoral research.[5]

Christianity and African Indigenous Religions as Disjunctive

"Kato presents the remarkable instance of one, who though trained in theology on a Western model like his fellow African theologians of modern times," writes Kwame Bediako, "yet unlike them, retained that model for his theological reflection in his African context" (Bediako 1992: 386). Bediako goes on to describe him as one who embodied the "reaction to, and a rebuttal of, much that went to constitute the African theology of the last two decades" (Bediako 1992: 386).

Conversely, many Evangelicals (both within and outside of Africa) viewed Kato as a hero: the one who stood, against many odds, to defend *biblical Christianity*. For example, in the Foreword of *Theological Pitfalls in Africa* (Kato 1975), Billy Graham wrote:

> Paul, Peter, and Jude would all have approved of the theme of this book, for they too were on guard against the destructive effect of heretical ideas ... Dr. Kato provides us here an update in the perennial concern the Christian Church ought to have against what he calls 'unhealthy trends in theology.'.

Sophie De la Haye, in her biography of Kato, called him an "ambassador for Christ" and viewed him as one whom "God chose," prepared, and used "at a particular point in the history of the church in Africa, to give strong leadership ... to sound the alarm to the churches of Africa against possible inroads of erroneous ideologies" (De la Haye 1986: 9).

The Nigerian theologian Tokunboh Adeyemo, in the preface to De la Haye's book, called Kato a "prophet." He went on to say that Kato

> predicted that for the next ten years (i.e. from 1972) the battle for the Church of Africa would be theological. He was right. His emphasis was twofold: the trustworthiness of the Word of God against all theological liberalism and the proper contextualization of theology in African setting without adulterating the Gospel. It was his challenge that God used into the ministry. (Kato 1975: 11–12)

Adeyemo has provided a helpful summary of Kato's theological vision: to forewarn, and therefore, to forearm African Christianity against the danger of universalism and religious syncretism (Kato 1975: 16). Like Idowu, Kato was well aware that many African Christians return to the indigenous religions for their spiritual needs. But he understood this state of affairs, unlike Idowu, as the consequence of a "superficial understanding of the teaching of Christianity," and

---

[5]   A good biography of Kato is De la Haye (1986).

"lack of biblical knowledge" in African Christianity (Kato 1975: 15). He sought to address these problems in his writings.

Whether or not Kato can be regarded a contextual theologian is a matter of intense debate. One of his commentators, Keith Ferdinando, views him as a truly contextual theologian "whose understanding of contextualization reflected his time" (Ferdinando 2003: 169–74). However, it is vital to note that Kato's construal of Christianity as a "divinely revealed religion" impacted his perceptions of the relationship between Christianity and African Indigenous Religions, and consequently his "contextualization" approach. He wrote that the "uniqueness of Christian revelation knows no compromise for the sake of peaceful coexistence" with other religions (Kato 1975: 93). With this conviction, he marched fearlessly to dismantle ecumenical ideologies and African theologies that questioned the inerrancy and inspiration of the Bible (Kato 1975: 140–1).

For him, to deny the authority of Scripture was to deny God's revelation. This conviction defined his understanding of contextual theology. He wrote:

> The tendency to identify African culture and religions with political ethos seems to be arising. A rejection of non-Christian beliefs is sometimes taken to mean a rejection of one's own heritage. Adherence to biblical principles is taken for lack of patriotism. It is hoped that no African ruler or politician will think that the evangelical Christian is being unpatriotic when he rejects a religio-cultural practice that contradicts the Christian belief. Rejection of liberal ecumenism is based purely on doctrinal matters. The deviation from biblical teaching so evident in world ecumenism presents a threat to the survival of orthodox Christianity. (Kato 1975: 177)

Regarding the relationship of African Indigenous Religions and Christianity, he argued: "The evangelical also rejects veneration of African traditional religions" (Kato 1975: 177). This negative attitude towards indigenous religions, he argues, is intended to "safeguard the unique gospel of Christ, which alone provides the way of salvation" (Kato 1975: 177). He goes on to argue that cultural heritage which is "compatible to Christianity can be baptized into Christian enrichment. The gospel content, of course, needs no addition or modification. It is because of this irreducible message that Christianity has produced the third race comprising men and women from all races" (Kato 1975: 177).

In summary, Kato's theology of religion elevates Christianity to the status of a "divinely revealed religion" and as such it stands above all other religions that are man-made, such as African Indigenous Religions. He rejects the language of fulfillment and insists that Jesus "meets the thirst" and aspirations embedded in indigenous religions of Africa "not by filling up the measure of idolatry but by transformation" (Kato 1975: 114).

I will now turn to critiquing Kato's and Idowu's models and also to articulate an alternative model. I will locate the new model within the contexts of the conversations that Jesus had with a certain woman of Samaria and the conversation he had with his disciples at Caesarea Philippi.

Christianity and Indigenous Religions as Asymmetrical and Symbiotic

The major problem that Kato's and Idowu's models share is the entrapping of God's revelation and Jesus Christ in religions. They failed to acknowledge that religion arises as a response to Divine Presence and not vice versa. Consequently, they perceived religion as a closed box or system within which God resides, allowing little or no room for the divine presence and divine revelatory manifestation to critique or disassociate itself from the religious truth-claims that distort and mistrust it. While Idowu localized God's presence in all religions (including African Indigenous Religions), Kato entrenched God's revelation in Christianity.

In his 10-point proposal on how to safeguard biblical Christianity in Africa, Kato argued that it is important to "express Christianity in a truly African context", so long as it is presented in a way that allows it to "judge the African culture and never allow the culture to take precedence over Christianity" (Kato 1975:182). Evidently, he gives virtually no room to God and God's revelation embodied in the Christ-Event to judge and critique Christianity. His understanding of Christianity allows God to operate only within it and not outside of it.

Toward the Liberation of Divine Presence in Religions

In contrast to Idowu's and Kato's perceptions of religion, I argue that religion must be construed as an open system that allows God to interact with it immanently and at the same time to stand outside of it as the *Other*. Kato's and Idowu's models fail to account for the dialectics of divine immanence and transcendence. Christian religion, properly understood, emerged when some adherents to Judaism and some adherents to its neighbouring religions recognized Jesus as the Messiah and began to imagine and appropriate Divine Presence in the light of the Christ-Event. Two things are noteworthy here.

First, based on this perception of the origin of "Christianity", anyone who qualifies as a follower of Jesus Christ (one who embraces Jesus' mission, his understanding of God's purpose for humanity, and his understanding of his identity) is technically a "Christian" or a follower of Christ even though they do not publicly identify with any Christian denomination. The earliest disciples of Jesus created the precedent. They did not consider it impossible simultaneously to follow Christ and remain adherents to Judaism, albeit with the intent to modify their Judaistic religious traditions in the light of their master. Judaism was an essential factor that defined their identity. Jesus did not require them to abandon their religious tradition as a prerequisite for becoming his followers. To demand such a prerequisite is tantamount to denying the validity, uniqueness, and relevance of the pre-Christ-Event revelatory manifestations of God as articulated in Judaism. The relevant implication of this is that it is an error to require Africans to abandon all aspects of their indigenous religious traditions and embrace Western interpretations and appropriations of the Christ-Event as a prerequisite for becoming authentic Christians. The core of the gospel message of Christianity—the Christ-Event—should be a "light" to African Indigenous Religions and not the "end" to it. What African Christians need to know is that Jesus has the ability to touch every aspect of their lives.

Second, as the "Truth" (John 14:6), no religion, including Christianity, can encapsulate the mystery of Jesus Christ. As such, he continues to be the "other" even though he is "with us." One of the theological errors of the early theology of Idowu is his understanding of Christianity as that which fulfills the aspirations of African Indigenous Religions. He fails to recognize that Jesus Christ, and not the Christian religion, has such capacity. As the revealer (one who embodies, communicates, and interprets) of divinity and humanity, Jesus Christ undoes the misunderstandings of God's presences and revelatory manifestations in all religions. This perception of Jesus Christ derives from his conversation with the woman of Samaria (John 4).

The Sychar Motif and Experience: Jesus and Divine Presence

The closest we come to Jesus' theology of religions is the conversation he had with a Samaritan woman near Jacob's well in Sychar (John 4:4–26). A careful examination of the contents of the conversation reveals two different religions, namely, Judaism and a religion of Samaria, in direct confrontation. The confrontation stands out vividly in one of the comments of the woman: "Our fathers worshipped on this mountain," she reminded Jesus, "but you Jews claim that the place where we must worship is in Jerusalem" (John 4:20). The lengthy response of Jesus to the woman's comment is most revealing. It is in this response that he provides a clue to what I consider his theology of religions. He makes two important theological observations in John 4:21–4. First, he reminds the woman that God's presence is neither entrapped in Jerusalem nor in Mt. Gerizim. Second, he reveals to the woman that since God is spirit God's true worshippers can only worship God in spirit and in truth.

What are the implications of the two theological observations Jesus made? A few are noteworthy. First, he undoes the assumption that God is localized and entrenched in a given religion. He criticizes the attempts of the Jews and Samaritans to entrap God in their religions. For him, both the Jews and Samaritans are guilty of inadequate theology for perceiving God in ways that strips God of the ability to simultaneously interact with and distance God's self from human religions. Jesus was preparing the ground to reveal to the woman that God has chosen to be "with us" concretely and definitively in the Christ-Event (John 4:26). The adherents to Judaism are therefore mistaken to assume that they can control or encapsulate Divine Presence. It is God, and not any particular religion, that has the capacity to decide how and where God is to be worshipped.

Historically, Christianity is guilty of the same religious errors that Jesus criticizes. Many Christians continue to construe "Christianity" as the arbiter of Divine Presence and its interpretations in other religions. The construal of God in Christianity, in most cases, has reduced God to the status of the "colonized." Most Christians have divested God of the right to decide on *who is* and *who is not* the object of God's mercy and the recipient of God's salvific work. But Christianity impersonates God if it assumes that it encapsulates Divine Presence and therefore has the sole right to act on behalf of God in matters of religious aspirations. This mindset is evident in Idowu's and Kato's theology of religions. The corollary of this mindset is the entrenching of God in religions.

We need to recognize that all religions (including Christianity and African Indigenous Religions) arose as a result of the attempts of human beings to humanize the spiritual and to appropriate God's presence in the world. Religions are contextualized, ongoing, and mutational expressions and appropriations of God's revelatory manifestations. Since they are human projects and also since "human beings are fallen", to use a popular orthodox Christian phrase, religions are prone to human distortions. These distortions, historically, have appeared in two forms, namely, *idolatry*—encapsulating and privatizing God, and *mistrust*— construal of divinity and humanity in a way that contradicts God's expectations as demonstrated in the Christ-Event.

Another noteworthy implication of the theological observations that Jesus made in the conversation is his unveiling of himself as the one who embodies God's presence and revelation. The woman should no longer anticipate a message for she was standing with him (John 4:26). The implication is christological: Jesus reminded the woman that both Judaism and the religions of Samaria must be subjected to the same christological test. God requires that God's true worshippers relate to God in truth and in spirit. As the messiah and the truth (John 14:6), Jesus is the only one who can effectively and ultimately act on behalf of God.

Although Jesus' understanding and interpretation of Divine Presence upset its construal in Judaism and the religions of Samaria, his theology can effectively speak to and work with the theologies of these religions (John 4:13–14, 21–6). It is vital to note that Jesus' agenda in the conversation was not to create a meeting point for both Judaism and the religions of Samaria. It was rather to speak to and critique the theologies of both religions and to inspire a new imagining of God (on the basis of his identity) from within the perspectives of the two religions. This is the heart of Jesus' theology of religions. Both of these religions are in error if they see Jesus as the messiah of God who can operate only within their closed systems and enclaves.

In like manner, Christianity and African Indigenous Religions should be subjected to the same christological tests—the test of Jesus' identity and the test of his mission. The key questions here are: "Do these religions construe themselves in a way that accepts or competes with Jesus' understandings of and vision for the *kingdom of God*?" "Can these religions be developed in the ways that allow Jesus Christ to simultaneously relate and critique them?" And: "Do they construe themselves in a way that embraces or competes with Jesus' understanding of his identity as the revealer of both humanity and divinity?"[6] Jesus' questions and responses show that he views himself as the one whose message transcends all religious values and yet at the same time interacts with them. Jesus can reshape all religious values and truth-claims to conform to the intended meanings and purposes of God's manifestations of God's self in human history. I will explore this further in the following section.

The Caesarea Philippi Motif and Experience: Jesus as the Revealer of Humanity and Divinity

"Who do people say I am?" "'But what about you?' he asked, 'Who do you say I am?'" (Mark 8:27–30, cf. Matthew 16:13–19; Luke 9:18–20). Christians' interpretation of God's presence embodied in the Christ-Event should be contextual: that is, "seeing as." This is Jesus' expectation. He intentionally invites his disciples to "work out for themselves what the events they have witnessed and the teaching they have heard imply about the person they recognize" as their teacher and lord (France 2002: 326).

The answer that Peter supplies is crucial: "You are the Christ" (Mark 8:29). Matthew's account expounds Jesus' response and reaction to Peter's answer, indicating the divine revelatory origin of Peter's confession. The disciples' christological speculations and appropriations are to revolve around the mystery of the Christ-Event. But we are not to equate the Christian message about Jesus (Christians' interpretations of the Christ-Event) with the source of the message (Jesus Christ). Interestingly, Peter was guilty of this error. His Judeo-Christian theology of Divine Presence was wrong (Mark. 8:31–3). To him, the messiah wears the crown and does not go to the cross. He "exposes a fundamental misunderstanding of Jesus' mission" (Turner 2008: 410). Consequently, Jesus rebukes him for propounding a devilish theology.

It is arrogant, blasphemous, and idolatrous for Christians to assume that Christianity encapsulates, masters, and controls God and God's self-presence and self-revelation in Jesus Christ. It will be catastrophic for a Christian theologian to operate with these mindsets. They create roadblocks to a meaningful and successful conversation between Christianity and other religions. Kato was guilty of this error. Idowu was guilty of a similar error in his later work in the ways he construed the relationship between God and world religions. Our interpretations of God's presence and revelation are mediated and as such they fall short of the glory of God. They will always remain liable to divine critique and transformation.

---

[6]   For extensive discussion on the Revealer Christology Model, see Ezigbo (2010: 143–74).

Although Christianity and African Indigenous Religions anticipate similar religious results—divine experience, embrace, and relationship—they pursue these agendas from different, unique, and sometimes competing ways. Their relationship is asymmetrical in relation to God's presence and manifestations in the world. It is therefore dubious and unhelpful to seek to determine the validity and relevance of the truth-claims of any of these religions on the basis of the other's truth-claims, that is, their contextualized interpretations and appropriations of God's presence.

But Christianity and African Indigenous Religions can enjoy a symbiotic relationship. The latter provides unique cognitive and religious tools for contextualizing the former in Africa. Christianity provides the knowledge of the Christ-Event as a new outlook to imagine and appropriate God's presence from within African indigenous religious and cultural contexts. Christianity, however, can learn from African Indigenous Religions, particularly in retrieving and reliving the religious contexts in which Jesus lived and ministered. For example, the belief in the impact of the spiritual world on human daily affairs reminds us of the interconnectedness that underlies the perceptions of the relationship between the spiritual and human worlds at the time of Jesus.

It is important to note that *hospitality* (i.e. the ability to welcome, embrace, and nurture the other) is ingrained in African Indigenous Religions. This makes them, to use the words of Jacob Olupona, "receptive to change" (Olupona 1991: 31). It is this character of African Indigenous Religions that allowed Christianity and Islam to take root in Africa and to permeate the religious experience of Africans. But it will be a mistake to assume, Olupona warns, that the adaptability of African Indigenous Religions undercuts its resilient character. He writes: "African traditional religion was not just a house of cards that collapsed at the instance of change … it has the potential to adapt to change on its own, in response to changes taking place around it" (Olupona 1991: 32).

Conclusion

Christianity that is designed for the African contexts must listen to and interact with both Apostolic Christianity and African Indigenous Religions. On the one hand, since Apostolic Christianity provided us the Scripture, the primary sacred text that contains the words and actions of Jesus, and also the interpretations of his person and work by his earliest followers, the theologian who aims to construct "African Christian theology" must listen to and interpret this text. The theology that ignores what the Christian Scripture says about Jesus Christ cannot be called "Christian." The theology that hopes to qualify as "African" must be able to engage the identity and message of Jesus from the perspective of the unique ways Africans have imagined and construed God's presence and revelatory manifestations. Elsewhere I have argued that

> The Scripture is a circumference ... of contextual Christology. This
> circumference is not closed-ended but open-ended: it should be broad and
> elastic enough to allow African Christians to develop ... concepts and images
> that synchronize with their history, culture, and experience of Jesus Christ.
> Understood in this way, the biblical images of Jesus must be allowed to take on
> new forms of expressions and meanings when they encounter the indigenous ...
> socio-religious realties of Africans. (Ezigbo 2008b: 62)

It is inadequate to impose a preconceived Christianity's beliefs and aspirations on
African Indigenous Religions. The existence of what Enyi Udoh calls "religious
schizophrenia" or living with dual religious minds in African Christianity,
demonstrates that Kato's model fails on crucial grounds (Udoh 1988). Kwame
Bediako in his 2007 lecture on "The Emergence of World Christianity and the
Remaking of Theology" at Nagel Institute, Calvin College, argued that

> In the midst of other faiths, Jesus remains Lord, and gospel ... does not have to
> be imposed or surrendered, as one is so often tempted to do in Western setting.
> If Christian theologians of the South and indeed ordinary Christians too became
> more aware of what their Christian interaction with their religious and cultural
> environment has done for them, they would realize what a significant gain this
> is for Christian theology..(Bediako 2007)

It will not do for an African Christian theology simply to translate Jesus into an
indigenous religious symbol, for example, to call Jesus an ancestor. While it can
be helpful to describe Jesus with a local metaphor, theologians must allow the
identity of Jesus—his person and mission—to shake, reinterpret, restructure, and
prune the truth-claims of Christianity and African Indigenous Religions.

The problem with imposing Western Christian theologies and interpretations
of Divine Presence on African Christian communities is that this has hopelessly
failed to adequately address the perennial theological issues that ordinary African
Christians faced daily as they struggle to remain faithful with what has made them
distinctively *African* and also distinctively *Christian*. Many of them are curious to
know the relationship between Divine Presence and human knowing and role of
the ancestors in the knowing process. Some face the issue of a dual allegiance—to
Christianity and to the religions of the forebears. Others are concerned with spiritual
power-exchange among divinities—they want to know about the involvement of
God, ancestral spirits, and evil spirits in daily affairs.

If the "shower" of Christianity is not to become the "rain of curse" upon
Africans, and if the "story of Christianity" is to become the "African story,"
divine presence embodied in the Christ-Event must be appropriated in the manner
that properly accounts for the reality of African Indigenous Religions as "an
integral part of [Africans'] way of life which they cannot do away with" (Magesa
2004: 34). And it is also important for African Christians to acknowledge that
Christianity and African Indigenous Religions are subject to Jesus' critique. In the

matters of contextualizing Christianity from within the vantage point of African Indigenous Religions, the Christ-Event, and not Christianity, should be allowed to function as the arbiter of divine presence. The interpretations and appropriations of God's revelations in Christianity and African Indigenous Religions should be re–imagined in the light of the person and teaching of Jesus Christ.

Bibliography

Appiah-Kubi, K. and S. Torres (eds.), *African Theology En Route* (Maryknoll, NY: Orbis, 1979).

Bediako, K., *Theology and Identity: The Impact of Culture upon Christian Thought in the Second Century and Modern Africa* (Oxford: Regnum Books, 1992).

—, "The Emergence of World Christianity and the Remaking of Theology," unpublished (2007).

Bujo, B., *African Theology in Its Social Context* (Maryknoll, NY: Orbis, 1992).

De la Haye, S., *Byang Kato: Ambassador for Christ* (Achimota, Ghana: African Christian Press, 1986).

Dickson, K.A., *Theology in Africa* (Maryknoll, NY: Orbis, 1984).

Dickson, K.A. and P. Ellingworth (eds.), *Biblical Revelation and African Beliefs* (London: Lutterworth, 1969).

Ezigbo, V.I., "Re-thinking the Christ-Event: Interpretations and Appropriations of Jesus Christ in Nigerian Christianity," Ph.D. Dissertation, University of Edinburgh (2008a).

—, "Rethinking the Sources of African Contextual Christology," *Journal of Theology for Southern Africa*, 132 (2008b): 53–70.

—, *Re-Imagining African Christologies: Conversing with the Interpretations and Appropriations of Jesus in Contemporary African Christianity* (Eugene, OR: Wipf & Stock 2010).

Ferdinando, K. "The Legacy of Byang Kato," *International Bulletin of Missionary Research* 28.4 (2003): 169–74.

France, R.T., *The Gospel of Mark*, New International Greek Testament Commentary (Grand Rapids: Eerdmans, 2002).

Idowu, E.B., *Olodumar: God in Yoruba Belief* (London: Longman, 1962).

—, *Towards an Indigenous Church* (London: Oxford University Press, 1965).

—, *African Traditional Religion: A Definition* (London: SCM Press, 1973).

Kato, B.H., *Theological Pitfalls in Africa* (Kisumu, Kenya: Evangel, 1975).

Magesa, L. *Anatomy of Inculturation: Transforming the Church in Africa* (Maryknoll, NY: Orbis, 2004).

Mbiti, John S., *New Testament Eschatology in an African Background: A Study of the Encounter between New Testament Theology and African Traditional Concepts* (London: Oxford University Press, 1971).

McVeigh, M.J., *God in Africa: Conceptions of God in African Traditional Religion and Christianity* (Cape Cod: Claude Stark, 1974).

Mulago, V., *Un visage africain du christianisme. L' union vitale bantu face á l'unité vitale ecclésiale* (Paris: Présence Africaine, 1965).

Olupona, Jacob K., "Major Issues in the Study of African Traditional Religion," in Jacob K. Olupona (ed.), *African Traditional Religions in Contemporary Society* (New York: Paragon House, 1991), pp. 25–33.

Pobee, J.S., *Toward an African Theology* (Nashville: Abingdon, 1979).

P'Bitek, O., *Song of Lawino and Song of Ocol* (Oxford: Heinemann, 1966).

Shorter, A., *African Christian Theology* (London: Geoffrey Chapman, 1975).

Tertullian, *Against Heretics* and *Against Praxeas*, in Alexander Roberts and James Donaldson (eds.) *The Ante-Nicene Fathers*, vol. 3 (repr. Grand Rapids: Eerdmans, 1969).

Turner, D.L., *Matthew*, Baker Exegetical Commentary on the New Testament (Grand Rapids: Baker, 2008).

Udoh, E.B., *Guest Christology: An Interpretative View of Jesus Christ in Africa* (Frankfurt: Peter Lang, 1988).

Chapter 14

African Traditional Religion in the Study of the New Testament in Africa

Lovemore Togarasei

Introduction

The use of the Bible in Africa has a very long history. With Christianity being a religion of the book, the Bible was introduced as early as when the religion itself was introduced, at least in its oral form. In this long history of usage, the Bible has been studied at various levels. It is read by individuals, by families, in Bible study groups, in churches, in schools and at institutions of tertiary education. This chapter discusses the use of African Traditional Religion (ATR) in the study of the New Testament (NT) in Africa. Of course, this sounds over ambitious. It is an over ambition in a number of ways. First, the long history of the study of the New Testament in Africa makes it impossible for one to do justice to the topic. Second, Africa is a large continent divided not only along political and linguistic lines but also along colonial historical lines. Literary works produced and demonstrating the use of African Traditional Religion in the study of the New Testament are therefore in different languages. Often Africa is divided into Anglophone, Lusophone, and Francophone countries. A comprehensive and exhaustive discussion of an African subject would therefore require competence in the English, Portuguese, and French languages in which most of the literature exists. For this reason it is therefore important for me to begin by defining the boundaries of my discussion of the use of ATR in the study of the NT in Africa.

By virtue of my location in sub-Saharan Africa, my discussion of Africa will be limited to this region, especially the Southern African region. In discussing ATR in NT study I will be limited to literature produced in English. NT study in Africa has not only been conducted by those trained in biblical interpretation. As I mentioned earlier, in Africa, the Bible is read and interpreted at various levels by people trained and not trained in biblical interpretation. To a large extent, biblical interpretation in Africa has not been to fulfill intellectual curiosity. The Bible is *lived* in Africa. It is used to address the daily joys and struggles people experience. For this reason, biblical interpretation has not been limited to the use of specific scientific approaches. The use of source-, form-, redaction- criticism and other historical-critical methods promoted in Western biblical scholarship since the Enlightenment period has not been very popular with many scholars in

Africa, even among those trained in them. African scholars have been involved in what is called socially engaged biblical scholarship, "engaged hermeneutics" to quote the words of J.S. Ukpong (2002: 21). They have used the Bible to address the issues that affect African societies: colonialism, poverty, war, gender-based violence, Christianity and African culture, diseases, especially HIV and AIDS, and many other social issues. Interpretation is therefore based on the needs of the people. Those who do the interpretation are often believers who use the Bible from the point of view of believers. G. LeMarquand (2000: 93) expresses this approach better: "African exegesis is need-driven and faith oriented. African biblical studies is almost always explicitly confessional ..., in the broad sense of not bracketing the Christian faith in the academy." Thus the Bible is interpreted by both biblical and non-biblical scholars. The difference between a biblical scholar and a theologian's use of the Bible is therefore blurred. In this chapter I therefore do not distinguish between biblical scholars and theologians. I generally look at how ATR has been used to interpret specific NT texts by those who use the Bible.

In interpreting the Bible, African scholars have taken their context seriously: the African religious and cultural context. It is this use of the African religious and cultural context in the study of the NT that is the focus of this chapter. The chapter endeavours to show how African cosmologies and religious beliefs have informed those interpreting the NT for the needs of their communities. After showing this, it will end by looking at the methods that scholars have used to appropriate ATR in NT interpretation.

The Place of African Religion in Africa

Despite the early missionaries' onslaught on African traditional/indigenous religion, it has remained alive among Africans. Possibly due to its lack of sacred scriptures and elaborate worship structures like temples, the early missionaries thought Africans had no religion or that if they had any, it was so primitive that it celebrated evil. Efforts were therefore made to do away with this "primitive" form of religion in order to win Africans to Christianity. However, despite all these efforts, ATR has remained alive among Africans. Even those who have accepted Christianity have had to walk on two legs, one in Christianity and the other in ATR. One reason why ATR has remained is that it is consistent with the lives of Africans. It is actually not easy to separate ATR from the culture of Africans. For this reason, for the NT to be understood in the African context, it is better interpreted in the context of African traditional religion and culture. African biblical interpreters have taken serious note of this. In the rest of this chapter I therefore consider how ATR has been used to interpret the NT.

African Religion in NT study

The use of ATR in NT study can best be described as revolutionary. It is revolutionary because African biblical scholars have realized that the missionary interpretation of the Bible that condemned African religion was culturally influenced. Their interpretation of the Bible made Christianity the same as Western culture. As J.N. Amanze (1998: 51–3) says, in the teaching of the missionaries, for one to be a good Christian one was supposed to embrace Western culture. The use of ATR in NT study was therefore a realization that if Christianity is a universal religion, it should be understood within one's own culture. A. Shorter (1978: 7) says that this kind of interpretation was "a revolution against cultural passivity, against being a mere consumer of the products of Western civilization. It is a call to a new creativity which has its roots in the African past." The use of ATR in NT study should therefore be seen from the point of view of the African struggle against colonialism. In *Postcolonial Interpretation of the Bible*, M. Dube (2000) takes a position that has mainly led to the use of ATR in biblical interpretation. This is the position that civilization (Western), Christianity, and commerce were brought to Africa packed in the same box. Dube (2000: 7) goes further to note: "The centrality of the Bible in facilitating Western imperialism remains evident to African people and provides the cause for much reflection." One way of reflection and indeed of responding to this Western influence of the Bible has been to highlight that which is African from the Bible. E.M. Yamauchi (2004: 206–7) notes that the African response to Eurocentric interpretations of the Bible has been Afrocentric interpretations of the Bible. African scholars have sought to find Africa and Africans in the Bible (Adamo 199;, 2006). It is the purpose of this chapter to show that in this response to Eurocentric biblical interpretation, African scholars have not only sought to show the place of Africa and Africans in the Bible but have gone further to use ATR to interpret the NT and the Bible in general. But as highlighted above, African interpretation of the Bible has been contextual and confessional. The Bible is interpreted to address specific problems that Africans face. I discuss how ATR has been used to interpret NT texts in order to address specific contextual problems below. I will focus on the contexts of colonialism, poverty, disease, gender, evangelical, and missiological issues.

Colonialism

The bulk of African biblical interpretation has been on the subject of colonialism. Since almost all of Africa has experienced colonialism, with the generality of Africans believing that the Bible and especially biblical interpretation played a role in their colonization (for example, Jomo Kenyatta's words, "When the missionaries arrived, the Africans had the land and the missionaries had the Bible. They taught us to pray with our eyes closed. When we opened them, they had the land and we had the Bible" (Mbefo 1989: 16–17)), attention has been given to how the same Bible can be interpreted for African liberation. One might assume that after attaining political liberation from Western oppression Africans would do away with the Bible as it was a weapon used for colonization. But that was not what happened. Christianity had become an "African religion" (Bediako 1992). How then would the Africanness of Christianity be expressed? This is where the use of ATR in Bible study came in. The use of ATR has been handy in Africanizing Christianity. It is, however, important to note that African scholars were not the first people to use ATR to interpret the NT. The early missionaries first did so, especially through translation of the Bible from their languages to the indigenous African languages. This, however, they did in colonizing ways. For example, they often used the traditional and indigenous names of God to translate the Christian God.

D.R. Mbuwayesango (2001) notes how the missionaries among the Shona in Zimbabwe suppressed local divine powers by translating the Christian God into Mwari, the God of the Shona. This translation was colonizing as it "was aimed at replacing the Shona Mwari with the biblical God in everything else but the name. ... The adoption of the Shona name Mwari for the biblical God was in reality the religious usurpation of the Shona. The missionaries took the Shona captive by colonizing the Shona Supreme Being" (Mbuwayesango 2001: 67). G.S. Ntloidibe-Kuswani (2001) also makes the same point of colonization through using ATR in the translation of the Christian God among the Tswana in Botswana. Ntloidibe-Kuswani sees the missionary attempt to equate the Christian God with local divinities as a result of an attempt to present a general and a global theory of religion that can be suitable for all religious traditions. This attempt, however, was colonizing, as Ntloidibe-Kuswani (2001: 80) further notes: "part of the hijacking, Christianizing, westernization and gendering of African concepts of the Divine and spiritual spaces was informed by the colonial ideology that believed in the superiority of the Christian religion over the local religions."

There are many other examples of the colonizing tendency of the missionaries' use of ATR in the study of the NT. Often missionaries wanted to show that ATR was evil and that those who embraced Christianity were supposed to completely abandon traditional religion and culture. M. Dube (1999: 33–59) and L. Togarasei (2009: 51–64) discuss how translation of specific NT texts by the missionaries demonized African religion and culture. We will return to these works soon.

Although the Bible was used to colonize Africans and to demonize ATR, it is also the same Bible that has been used to fight colonialism. Thus the appropriation of the Bible is part of the problem as well as the solution. To use it as a solution African biblical scholars have, first and foremost, exposed the colonizing and demonizing tendencies of Western biblical interpretation. Walking along the same pathway with nationalists and politicians, they have condemned Western missionaries for failing to understand ATR and therefore condemning it in its entirety. They have pointed out a lot of similarities between African traditional religion and culture and Christianity. ATR has been used to fight colonialism through interpretation of the Bible. Although the Old Testament has mainly been the most influential part of the Bible, the NT has also been informative. Using ATR, the Gospels have been interpreted to present Christ as "our ancestor" (Moyo 1983; Nyamiti 1984), as master of initiation (Sanon 1991) and as chief (Kabasele 1991), attributes which are derived from African traditional religious worldviews. Through postcolonial reading of NT texts and informed by ATR, African NT scholars have exposed the negative interpretation of ATR in African interpretation of the Bible. Dube (1999) takes to task the London Missionary Society missionaries' translation of evil spirits as *badimo* (the Setswana word for ancestors). Focusing on Matthew 8:28–34, 15:22 and 10:8, she argues that the missionaries' translation of evil spirits as *badimo* was a deliberate attempt to tell the indigenous people that ancestors are evil spirits and are therefore not worthy to be venerated. Togarasei (2009) makes the same observation in relation to the Shona Bible. Describing translation as interpretation, he argues that the missionaries' translation of 'banquetings' in 1 Peter 4:3 as *mabira* "was a total blow to the Shona religion and cosmology" (2009: 58). Both Dube and Togarasei have gone further to suggest better translations and interpretations of the texts in ways that respect ATR.

Poverty

Millions of Africans live under extreme situations of poverty. African NT scholars have also addressed poverty using ATR for NT interpretation. Although not directly addressing ATR, Ugandan theologian J. Waliggo (1991: 176) advocates an African Christology which is very much influenced by ATR's teaching on living life in full in the here and now. He says Africans want a Christ who is a liberator in all dimensions of life. They want "the tangible, functional, African and dynamic Christ with whom they can fully and at all times feel at home" (Waliggo 1991: 176). In like manner, U.C. Manus (2003) uses the figure of Jesus to challenge African leaders to rise to the task of reconstruction in post-independent Africa. He notes that Africa faces poverty and all other ills due to leaders who have lost their religion in pursuit of wealth, passion, and position (Manus 2003: 153). Rereading Matthew 18:12–14 // Luke 15:1–7 in the African context, he calls for the return of such leaders to the religious fold, as Africa has no room for the non-religious according to ATR.

Among the many causes of poverty in Africa are ethnic and religious conflicts. African NT scholars have appealed to ATR in their interpretation of the NT for conflict resolution. Manus (2003: 121–38) rereads Matthew 18:15–22 for conflict resolution in Nigeria and Kenya. He uses ATR as his interpretive lens. He notes that Jesus' call for forgiveness is better understood from the perspective of traditional African belief systems and codes of conduct. For this reason, he says, the text of Matthew 18:15–22 should be reread in light of the African traditional religious and cultural practices of a communal family for conflict resolution and reconciliation.

M.W. Dube-Shomanah (2006: 193–207) finds the causes of poverty in Africa in skewed international relations. She notes that Africa has suffered under colonialism and continues to suffer from the nature of contemporary international relations that send African leaders to Western countries to beg for food for their people. Dube Shomanah uses the story of the Canaanite woman in Matthew 15:21–8 to argue her case. To interpret this NT text, she makes use of the ATR method of divination. A method used to find out the causes of ill health, both physical and social, Dube Shomanah says divination is a method to be used by Africans to read texts in the same way a diviner-healer reads divining bones.

Another cause of poverty in Africa is the individualism introduced by Western culture. Many Africans in positions of authority abuse their authority to enrich themselves at the expense of the majority of the people. African biblical scholars have appealed to ATR in interpreting the NT to address such social ills. J. Punty (2004), for example, makes use of the value of *ubuntu* to interpret the Pauline letters with a special focus on the letter to the Galatians. *Ubuntu*'s emphasis on communitarianism ("I am because we are and because we are, therefore I am") calls for cooperation between the individual, his or her society and the rest of creation. Punty therefore uses the ATR value of *ubuntu* to argue against the interpretation of Pauline letters as promoting individuals and their interests. Such an interpretation is important in fighting social ills like corruption that provide a breeding ground for poverty in Africa.

Disease

The subject of health is the one mostly addressed through NT interpretation in Africa. In addressing issues of health, ATR has become handy for NT study. It has helped in presenting Jesus as the healer, for example. This is because, as C. Kolie (1991: 132) correctly notes, Africans cherish life and eternity and so people who work to promote life and health hold a place of eminence. The value of life in traditional African thought, the healing powers of Jesus, and the reality of diseases and especially incurable HIV and AIDS, have made African New Testament scholars take notice. C. Kolie (1991: 149) has concluded: "we are surely obliged to acknowledge that the face of Christ in Africa today is more that of the ill than that of a healer." Dube (2004: 380) questions: "How then should one read the healing miracles of Jesus in a context where there is no healing?"

Interpreting the healing miracles of Jesus in the context of illnesses and diseases, African scholars have therefore gone on to use ATR. Togarasei (2008), for example, interprets the healing of the leper (Mark 1:40–5 and parallels) in light of traditional African understanding of disease and healing. He notes that Jesus' healing in this particular story is holistic just as healing is understood in African tradition. Not only is the healing of symptoms sought, but Africans in particular seek the cause of an illness (Dube 1989; Bourdillon 1993; Larby 200; and Shoko 2007). Togarasei (2008) then argues that this understanding of holistic healing helps in understanding why Jesus had to send the leper to the priest after he had cured him.

Interpreting the NT using ATR has also been employed to expose certain African traditional and cultural practices that tend to fuel diseases like HIV and AIDS. This comes out clear in Manus' (2003: 139–51) rereading of Mark 1:40–5 in the context of the HIV and AIDS pandemic. Manus (2003: 140) writes against ATR practices that tend to fuel HIV and AIDS:

The continued acceptance of the traditional role of the *jater*—"the professional female purifier" or inheritor of widows before such women are re-integrated into the kin-group after the demise of the husbands in Luoland of Kenya or the practice of *chiramu* in parts of Zimbabwe where a young girl of 12–13 years of age has to be "sexually" touched by the sister's husband; a practice that has led to the sexual abuse of many teenage girls, is quite worrisome. The continued prevalence of such customs raises valid ethical questions on the values such Africa societies attach to these practices today given the contemporary malaise contexts. The worldviews that produced and kept these customs and practices to survive to date must be confronted with the Word of God for change.

A. Boniface-Malle's (2004) interpretation of Matthew 15:21–8 in the context of HIV and AIDS in Tanzania also exposes other dangerous ATR practices. Boniface-Malle sees in the Canaanite woman four types of African women: a widow, an unwed mother, a sex worker with a child, and a woman in a polygamous marriage. She accuses the church in East Africa, especially the mainline churches, of not providing space for lamenting and groaning to God when people experience suffering. She then uses the East African traditional and cultural practice of lamenting to interpret Jesus' interaction with the Canaanite woman. Boniface-Malle (2004: 183) states:

> Matthew puts emphasis on the dialogue and delays the healing as the last step in meeting the need. Matthew portrays Jesus as one who listens to the cry before rushing into giving answers or solutions. We also learn this fact from the Canaanite woman. The woman was not afraid to bring her predicament to Jesus. … she comes from a different background where crying and expression of feelings and grief are permissible.

Boniface-Malle therefore makes use of the traditional and cultural African practice of expressing grief in interpreting Matthew 15:21–8 to challenge the church to allow lamenting and mourning.

Gender Issues

The place of women both in church and in society in general is a cause for theological reflection in Africa. Although African feminist biblical interpretation is young (Krog 2005), it has made huge strides in the development of African biblical scholarship. African feminist scholars have tended to prefer the New Testament rather than the Old Testament in their theological reflections. This is mainly because the Old Testament books, written from patriarchal contexts, tend to be androcentric, and throughout the history of the church have been used to oppress women. More feminists have therefore used the New Testament for the liberation of women (see for example Dube 2000; Amoah and Oduyoye 1994). In interpreting the New Testament, feminist scholars have, however, used ATR it in two different ways. First, they have used the New Testament to critique certain African traditional religious practices that oppress women. Second, they have appealed to some African traditional religious practices that liberate women in their interpretation of the New Testament. Let us consider some of the works.

Christianity, as defined from the New Testament, is generally regarded as having brought some liberation to women in Africa. African feminist scholars like T. Okure (1994: 47–52) have underlined the liberating role of the gospel. They note the role of women in the birth of Jesus, the founder of Christianity, by a woman and the roles that women played in his ministry. They underline especially the role of women as God's co-creators and agents of life. This way, they critique ATR for denying women certain roles in society when God has given them important responsibilities. The denial to women of such functions as leadership or ritual specialists on the basis of ATR and the Bible is then criticized. Okure (1994: 56, 57), for example, argues: "It demands that both men and women be involved in every sphere of human endeavor ... There is need to awaken and free people from centuries of sociocultural and theological conditionings based on false understanding of the teaching of the Bible concerning women." E. Amoah and M.A. Oduyoye (1994) emphasize the liberation role of Christ as well. They note that Christ transcended cultural boundaries and therefore religious and cultural practices that oppress women have been transcended.

In interpreting such texts as 1 Timothy 2:11–14 and 1 Peter 3:7, Manus (2003: 171–2) uses some African sacred narratives from Nigeria to show that both ATR and the sacred scriptures of Christians have been used to oppress women. He says both traditions have associated the fall of humanity and the presence of sin with women. He therefore calls for a struggle against these traditions in order to liberate African women and allow them fully to participate in the development of their continent and the world.

Some African scholars, however, also find ATR liberating for women and so use it to interpret NT (biblical) texts that prove oppressive to women. This is quite evident in African scholars' discussion of the gender of God. Ntloedibe-Kuswani (2001: 78–97) notes that understanding God from the traditional Botswana perspective removes the problem of the gender of God that Western feminist scholars have struggled with. N.T. Taringa (2004: 174–9) also makes the same observation among the Shona of Zimbabwe. Through an analysis of Shona metaphors for God, Taringa concludes that the traditional Shona God is both male and female. Lastly, using J. Pobee's Christology of Christ as *okyeame* (go-between), Amoah and Oduyoye (1994) highlight the African tradition's acceptance of women as go-between to argue that Jesus can be male or female when understood from the Ghanaian view of *okyeame*.

Evangelical and Missiological Issues

This is one issue that has been addressed through the use of ATR for NT interpretation. In view of the missionary onslaught on ATR, African NT scholars have endeavored to use ATR to interpret the NT for evangelical and missiological purposes. Again, this has been done in two ways: first, through affirming certain ATR practices and beliefs and, second, through dismissing certain ATR practices and beliefs. Manus (2003: 67–83) interprets the speech of Paul at the Areopagus (Acts 17:22–34) using ATR. Specifically, he compares the speech to the Igbo folk narrative and comes to a five-point conclusion that underlines the need to take ATR seriously in preaching the gospel in Africa. He writes (2003: 82–3):

> When the speech is understood in light of the African narrator's creativity and his narratological genius; then Paul will have been understood as providing a characterization of the fiendish nature of African Traditional Religion as is found especially in the un-churched regions and rural areas where all kinds of misanthropic activities associated with traditional religion still hold sway.

Affirming ATR, Manus argues that the Areopagus speech shows that Paul agreed that in proclaiming the gospel in Africa there is need to make use of culture in order to touch Africans and their world. He says the speech also shows that African Christians should adopt a positive attitude with regards to wholesome traditional religious values of Africa for, as Acts 17:23 affirms, the God whom our un-churched Africans worshipped without knowing him is now preached to us. The positive evaluation of ATR in NT interpretation is also made by Togarasei and Chitando (2005). In analyzing the practice of tombstone unveiling among the Shona in Zimbabwe, the two scholars note that NT texts like Matthew 23:28–9, Luke 22:19; 1 Corinthians 11:24, and others show that early missionaries misunderstood African death rituals and therefore wrongly vilified them. They therefore conclude that it is time such vilification should be abandoned as we respect certain traditional and religious practices that do not contradict Christianity. Togarasei (2007) affirms ATR in his interpretation of the conversion of Paul. He argues that after his conversion to Christianity, Paul did not do away with his Jewish religious background but rather used it to understand and interpret Christianity. In the same way, Togarasei further argues, African Christians should "continue to borrow from African religion and culture when practicing Christianity ... (as in doing this) ... they will be following on the heels of Paul who understood Christianity from his traditional and cultural perspective" (Togarasei 2007: 121).

As I mentioned above, certain ATR practices have been seen as hindrances to mission work in Africa and therefore the NT has been interpreted from that perspective. Manus (2003: 67–83) also sees the speech of Paul at the Areopagus "as saying that Africans should desist from idol worship and the culticisms (*sic*) associated with the African Traditional religion, the religion of fear and dread of the gods of the ancestors as it is still known and practiced in some parts of Africa" (Manus 2003: 83).

Methods Used to Engage ATR in NT Study

African scholars' attempt to read the NT in light of the ATR means they had to come up with new methods of biblical interpretation. As I show below, these methods were developed in light of the scholars' contextual reading of the NT and the Bible in general. African NT scholars have underlined the need to take seriously the context of the reader in interpreting NT texts. They have thus rejected Eurocentric and universalistic readings of the Bible, calling for diversity and plurality in interpretation. This call for diversity and plurality has allowed the use of ATR in NT interpretation. Ukpong highlighted this need in his address to African NT scholars: "We must go out on set purpose to use the lenses of our cultural and existential life contexts, our African biases and interests to read biblical texts against the grain of the traditional understanding and so uncover something new of their inexhaustible dimensions" (Ukpong 2004: 40–1). Some of the methods that have been used are the comparative method, inculturation hermeneutics and liberation hermeneutics. We briefly explain how they have allowed the use of ATR for NT interpretation below.

Comparative Method

The comparative method is the oldest method by which African scholars have used ATR to interpret biblical texts. Ukpong (2000: 12) sees this as the method that marked the first phase of African biblical hermeneutics. He says the method was reactive and apologetic in its attempt to legitimize African religion and culture. As I have demonstrated above, African scholars were reacting against the unjust condemnation of African religion and culture by early missionaries. They then reacted by comparing African religion and culture with the culture and religion of the Bible. Although similarities and therefore justification of African religion and culture was found mainly in the Old Testament, the fact that the NT shares the same cultural background with the OT was also used to draw similarities between African culture and religion and Christian culture and religion as reflected in the NT (Ukpong 2000: 12). The comparative method has therefore been foundational in allowing the use of ATR for biblical interpretation.

Inculturation

One method through which African scholars have incorporated Africans religions in NT interpretation is inculturation. Ukpong (2002: 12), one of its proponents, defines it as "a hermeneutic methodology that seeks to make any community of ordinary people and their social-cultural context the subject of interpretation of the Bible through the use of the conceptual frame of reference of the people and the involvement of the ordinary people in the interpretation process." In this method, the African context and traditions including traditional religion provide the necessary resources for biblical interpretation. Thus inculturation is an attempt to rehabilitate and appropriate the religious and cultural traditions of Africa into the Christian traditions. It respects the interpretation of ordinary readers of the Bible. As a postcolonial method of biblical interpretation, it argues for the respect of African culture by Christianity. For African Christianity to be fully African, and for Africans to feel at home in the Christian religion, indigenous belief patterns as enshrined in ATR should be taken serious in African biblical interpretation.

Liberation

Contextual reading of the NT in Africa has made the use of liberation methods of interpretation indispensable. As G. Cloete (2004) correctly puts it: "The most existential experience of Africa is that of disadvantagement (*sic*) through poverty, oppression and racism." Anyone interpreting the NT or the whole of the Bible in Africa cannot afford to ignore this reality. Interpretation of the NT has to liberate the people from these forms of disadvantage. Liberation hermeneutics, especially that based on traditional and cultural beliefs and practices of the African people, have been used in NT study. This is because, as Cloete (2004: 165) goes on to say, "liberation in African is not understood to be a secularized concept, … but that it is interwoven with cultural traditions and religious images." Thus, in interpreting the NT for liberation, African scholars have used cultural traditions and religious images. Liberation hermeneutics has been used for liberation from colonial oppression, for the liberation of women from patriarchal oppression, and for liberation from all other forms of oppression that the African people experience. With its call for justice and living life holistically, ATR has become an important tool for interpreting biblical texts for African liberation.

Conclusion

The goal of NT interpretation in Africa should be justice-seeking, life-giving, and life-affirming. It should also be community-building and problem-solving (Mouton 2006: 50–82). All this flows from African biblical scholars' engagement with the needs and struggles of their people. African people, as J.S. Mbiti (1969) long ago noted, seek life here and now. Their religious beliefs and activities seek the same and therefore there is no distinction between that which is physical and that which is spiritual. Aware of this, African scholars have interpreted the NT for justice-seeking, life-giving, life affirming, community-building, and problem-solving. The NT is interpreted to address the needs of the people. It is this contextual reading of the NT that has made use of ATR for NT interpretation.

This chapter has looked at how African scholars have done this by looking at issues such as colonialism, poverty, diseases, gender, and evangelism and mission. It is clear from the discussion above that scholars have used ATR in two different ways. First, they have used it to reject Western-oriented interpretations that vilified ATR and, second, by using the NT to counter certain ATR practices and beliefs that are not life-affirming. The chapter ended by spelling out specific methods that have allowed the use of ATR in NT interpretation.

Bibliography

Adamo, D.T., *Africa and Africans in the Old Testament* (Benin City: Justice Jeco Press & Publishers Ltd, 1998).

—, *Africa and Africans in the New Testament* (Lanham, MD: University Press of America, 2006).

Amanze, J.N., *African Christianity in Botswana* (Gweru: Mambo Press, 1998).

Amoah, E. and M. Oduyoye, "The Christ for African Women," in V. Fabella and M.A. Oduyoye (eds.), *With Passion and Compassion: Third World Women Doing Theology* (Maryknoll, NY: Orbis, 1994), pp. 35–46.

Bediako, K., *Theology and Identity: The Impact of Culture upon Christian Thought in the Second Century and Modern Africa* (Oxford: Regnum Books, 1992).

Boniface-Malle, A., "Allow Me to Cry Out: Reading Matthew 15:21–28 in the Context of HIV/AIDS in Tanzania," in M.W. Dube and M. Kanyoro (eds.), *Grant Me Justice! HIV/AIDS & Gender Readings of the Bible* (Maryknoll, NY: Orbis, 2004), pp. 169–85.

Bourdillon, M.F.C., *Where Are the Ancestors?: Changing Culture in Zimbabwe* (Harare: University of Zimbabwe Publications, 1993).

Cloete, G., "'Rainbow Hermeneutics' on the African Horizon: Relevance of the Epistle to the Galatians," in J.N.K. Mugambi and J.A. Smit (eds.), *Text and Context in New Testament Hermeneutics* (Nairobi: Acton, 2004), pp. 157–82.

Dube, D., "A Search for Abundant Life: Health, Healing and Wholeness in Zionist Churches," in G.C. Oosthuizen, S.D. Edwards, W.H. Wessels, and I. Hexham (eds.), *Afro-Christian Religion and Healing in Southern Africa* (Lewiston: Edwin Mellen Press, 1989), pp. 109–36.

Dube, M.W., "Consuming a Colonial Cultural Bomb: Translating *Badimo* into 'Demons' in the Setswana Bible (Matthew 8:28–34; 15:22, 10:8)," *Journal for the Study of the New Testament*, 73 (1999): 33–59.

—, *Postcolonial Feminist Interpretation of the Bible* (St. Louis, MO: Chalice Press, 2000).

—, "Mark's Healing Stories in an AIDS Context," in D. Patte and N. Duran (eds.), *Global Bible Commentary* (Nashville: Abingdon Press, 2004), pp. 379–84.

Dube-Shomanah, M.W., "Divining Texts for International Relations: Matthew 15:21–28," in E.P. Antonio (ed.), *Inculturation and Postcolonial Discourse in African Theology* (New York: Peter Lang, 2006), pp. 193–208.

Kabasele, F., "Christ as Ancestor and Elder Brother," in R.J. Schreiter (ed.), *Faces of Jesus in Africa* (Maryknoll, NY: Orbis, 1991), pp. 103–15.

Kolie, C., "Jesus as Healer?" in R.J. Schreiter (ed.), *Faces of Jesus in Africa* (Maryknoll, NY: Orbis, 1991), pp. 128–50.

Krog, L., "African Hermeneutics: The Current State," Thesis submitted to South Africa Theological Seminary, 2005.

Larby, K, "Healing," in T. Adeyemo (Gen. Ed.), *African Bible Commentary* (Grand Rapids: Zondervan, 2006), p. 447.

LeMarquand, G., "New Testament Exegesis in (Modern) Africa," in G.O. West and M.W. Dube (eds.), *The Bible in Africa: Transactions, Trajectories and Trends* (Leiden: E.J. Brill, 2000), pp. 72–102.

Manus, U.C., *Intercultural Hermeneutics in Africa: Methods and Approaches* (Nairobi: Acton, 2003).

Mbefo, L.N., *Towards a Mature African Christianity* (Enugu: Spiritan Publications, 1989).

Mbiti, J.S., *African Religions and Philosophy* (London: Heinemann, 1969).

Mbuwayesango, D.R., "How Local Divine Oowers Were Suppressed: A case of Mwari of the Shona," in M.W. Dube (ed.), *Other Ways of Reading the Bible: African Women and the Bible* (Atlanta: Society of Biblical Literature, 2001), pp. 63–77.

Moyo, A.M., "The Quest for an African Christian Theology and the Problem of the Relationship between Faith and Culture: The Hermeneutical Perspective," *Africa Theological Journal*, 12/2 (1983): 94–102.

Mouton, A.E.J., "The Pathos of New Testament Studies," *Journal of Theology and Religion in Africa*, 30/1 (2006): 50–86.

Ntoidibe-Kuswani, G.S., "Translating the Divine: The Case of Modimo in the Setswana Bible," in M.W. Dube (ed.), *Other Ways of Reading the Bible: African Women and the Bible* (Atlanta: Society of Biblical Literature, 2001), pp. 78–100.

Nyamiti, C., *Christ as Our Ancestor: Christology from an African Perspective* (Gweru: Mambo Press, 1984).

Okure, T. "Women in the Bible," in V. Fabella and M.A. Oduyoye (eds.), *With Passion and Compassion: Third World Women Doing Theology* (Maryknoll, NY: Orbis, 1994), pp. 47–59.

Punty, J., "Value of Ubuntu for Reading the Bible," in J.N.K. Mugambi and J.A. Smit (eds.), *Text and Context in New Testament Hermeneutics* (Nairobi: Acton, 2004), pp. 83–111.

Sanon, A.T. "Jesus, Master of Initiation," in R.J. Schreiter (ed.), *Faces of Jesus in Africa* (Maryknoll, NY: Orbis, 1991), pp. 85–102.

Shoko, T., *Karanga Indigenous Religion: Health and Well-Being* (Aldershot: Ashgate, 2007).

Shorter, A., *African Christian Spirituality* (London: Geoffrey Chapman, 1978).

Taringa, N., "African Metaphors for God: Male or female," *Scriptura: International Journal of Bible, Religion and Theology in Southern Africa*, 86 (2004): 174–9.

Togarasei, L., "The Conversion of Paul as a Prototype for Conversion in African Christianity," *Swedish Missiological Themes*, 95.2 (2007): 111–22.

—, "Jesus' Healing of the Leper as a Model for Healing in African Christianity: Reflections in the Context of HIV and AIDS," *Journal of Religion and Theology in Africa*, 32.1 (2008): 114–28.

—, 'The Shona Bible and the Politics of Bible Translation', *Studies in World Christianity*, 15/1 (2009): 51–64.

— and E. Chitando, "Tombstone Unveiling among the Shona Christians: Phenomenological and Biblical Reflections," *Missionalia*, 33/1 (2005): 166–78.

Ukpong, J.S., "Developments in Biblical Interpretation in Africa: Historical and Hermeneutical Directions," in G.O. West and M.W. Dube (eds.), *The Bible in Africa: Transactions, Trajectories and Trends* (Leiden: E.J. Brill, 2000), pp. 11–28.

—, "Reading the Bible in a Global Village: Issues and Challenges from African Readings," in J.S. Ukpong, M.W. Dube, *et. al.*, *Reading the Bible in the Global Village: Issues and Challenges from African Readings* (Atlanta: Society of Biblical Literature, 2002) pp. 9–40.

—, "Contextual Hermeneutics: Challenges and Possibilities," in J.N.K. Mugambi and J.A. Smit (eds.), *Text and Context in New Testament Hermeneutics* (Nairobi: Acton, 2004), pp. 22–55.

Waliggo, J.M., "African Christology in a Situation of Suffering," in R.J. Schreiter (ed.), *Faces of Jesus in Africa* (Maryknoll, NY: Orbis, 1991), pp. 164–80.

Yamauchi, E.M., *Africa and the Bible* (Grand Rapids: Baker Academic, 2004).

Chapter 15

Southern African Islamic Studies Scholarship: A Survey of the "State of the Art"

Muhammed Haron

Introduction

Azevedo (1998), Martin (2001), Ludwig and Adogame (2004), Zeleza (2006), and a host of others acknowledged the fact that African Studies and its allied disciplines such as Religious Studies and Islamic Studies have been constructed and developed by scholars in the West (i.e. Europe and the USA). As Western constructs, these disciplines have been rooted in and dominated by a range of Eurocentric theories that have influenced and changed the attitudes of Africans (and African Muslims) towards their respective communities. Although African scholars have been searching for alternative theoretical models, quite a number have succumbed to the European models that they found somewhat impossible to shake off.

African Studies scholars (and African scholars who specialized in Islamic Studies) have engaged one another in heated debates regarding the continuous use of these Western-invented theories in their research and at their institutions. In their debates African scholars have debated—as bona fide insiders—against the idea of being solely dependent upon them, and they have argued in favor of searching for and devising appropriate theories that would serve the interest of the communities that they are concentrating upon and aiming to reach a balanced understanding about the issues that are being investigated. Despite the engaging scholarly debates that have taken place at African/Islamic Studies fora and symposia in and outside the African continent over the past two decades, African/Islamic studies scholarship recorded these theories' shortcomings and acknowledged the need to continue the search for alternative models and paradigms. In the process of their search, both African Studies and Islamic Studies scholarship have managed to come up with and proffer viable models.

In this chapter we undertake an evaluation of "Islamic Studies" as a social science discipline within the broader area of African Studies (and as a sub-discipline of Religious Studies in Africa). We consciously pursue this approach since Jacob Olupona did not restrict himself to African Traditional Religions and Christianity but has also shown a keen interest in "Islamic Studies" as a discipline in the Western academic setting. He conducted a lively series of seminars on "Islam in Africa" during 2008 and offered an exciting course on "Islam in Sub-Saharan Africa" during 2010 at Harvard University. Before we assess the outputs of "Islamic Studies" scholarship within the confines of Southern Africa's tertiary institutions, we first clarify what is meant by "Islamic Studies" and we thereafter locate it within the broader disciplines of African Studies and Religious Studies, respectively. We restrict ourselves, however, to a small sampling in this chapter. The purpose is to demonstrate to what extent changes have taken place in the discipline and to what degree (African) Islamic Studies scholarship has assisted in bringing about a better understanding of Africa's Muslim communities in Southern Africa. Among the questions that we intend to respond to in this chapter are: whether Religious Studies (or more specifically Islamic Studies) is an objective or subjective science, and whether "Islamic Studies" as a discipline has been Africanized as a result of its African context.

Islamic Studies: Towards a Definition

In the opening paragraphs we alluded to the fact that Islamic Studies, as a discipline within the African context, straddles and relates to both Religious Studies and African Studies. However, regardless of its intimate connection to these two vast disciplines, Islamic Studies have occasionally evolved independently of these two on the continent. One reason may be attributed to the fact that Islamic Studies, like Religious Studies and African Studies, cover a broad terrain. As a result of the extent of Islamic Studies' coverage, social scientists have had difficulties in defining the term and there have been disagreements as to what it contains or rather it should contain. From within a Muslim context there are those who argue that the term is an all-embracing one and from within a non-Muslim context there are those who opine that it only encapsulates certain aspects of Islam and Muslims.

During the nineteenth and early twentieth centuries, Western scholars who had specialized in the field of Oriental Studies (that subsequently branched out into Islamic Studies) investigated the discipline by adopting a historicist-linguistic approach and thus studied it within a purely historical frame and employing philological tools. This was unlike the classical/medieval Muslim scholars who adopted a holistic approach. In the earlier centuries, when Muslims were at the forefront and advancing research the field, the field of "Islamic Studies" was not referred to or known by this term; this is a new expression to say the least. The term that the early Muslim (and non-Muslim) scholars readily used was *'ulum islamiyyah* (i.e. Islamic sciences); a term that was regarded as comprehensive and all-encompassing. Under this rubric they studied, among others, theology and jurisprudence as concomitant subjects of astronomy, mathematics, and medicine. This, as a matter of fact, is how the fifteenth- and sixteenth-century Timbuktu scholars understood and applied the term when they produced their illuminating and understudied (African) manuscripts; many of which have lamentably been neglected and have not been properly preserved (cf. Jeppie and Diagne 2008).

Since Muslim scholarship was in general decline throughout the Enlightenment era (c. 1700–1900), European scholarship was gradually on the rise and subsequently influenced the expansive production of (secular) scientific knowledge in and beyond Europe. In the process of colonial expansion, European scholars established the Oriental Studies project to study the subjugated and colonized communities (Said 1978; Hussain et al. 1984); an issue that we shall return to shortly. At this juncture, let us address the main task of this section and that is to define the discipline of Islamic Studies. And let us take heed of Jacques Waardenburg's statement: "there is no generally accepted definition of the discipline of Islamic Studies, that its boundaries are not clearly fixed, and that there are no uniform and generally accepted programmes ... It constitutes a field of studies employing various disciplines" (quoted by Khir 2007: 260). Being aware of these observations as well as the differences of opinion, Izzi Dien (2007) suggested that the phrase "Study of Islam" be considered rather than the term "Islamic Studies." Notwithstanding this significant observation, in both the USA and the UK, where Islamic Studies have flourished as either independent academic disciplines or as subjects offered within Institutes of African Studies or Departments of Religious Studies, specialists in the field have offered definitions. Space constraints prevent us from surveying all of these institutions in order to assess definitions that they suggested and applied, but we will look at one UK report that was prepared in 2007.

Siddiqui (2007) was commissioned by the UK's Ministry of State for Life Long Learning, Further and Higher Education to undertake a special study of Islam at England's tertiary institutions. Siddiqui underlined that there were marked disagreements about what Islamic Studies include and exclude and he observed that some argued that the Arabic language was a core subject when embarking on the study of Islamic Studies. He noted that there were others who proffered the opinion that anthropological and ethnographic studies that focus on Muslim societies should not be regarded as essential ingredients of an Islamic Studies syllabus. He pointed out that "some consensus amongst the interviewees (was) that while the knowledge of Arabic could form the basis for the understanding of the Qur'an and *sunnah* (the two primary sources of Islam), some knowledge of other sciences has to be part of Islamic Studies." An interesting comment that Siddiqui concluded with was that the interviewees disagreed whether Islamic Studies should be referred to as a "discipline". This disagreement, he stated, was based upon the fact that some stressed that it "emerged from a melange of several disciplines into one well-defined discipline" (Siddiqui 2007: 28), and he added that another group differed because Islamic Studies do not possess the required features to be called a discipline.

Despite all of these differing responses, Siddiqui catalogued a list of definitions of which the following two—that we have radically altered—may be considered appropriate for our chapter and focus: (a) Islamic Studies should be viewed as a discipline that is academically rigorous and one that critically analyzes Muslim communities in their respective regional settings and evaluates Islam as a complete civilization (Siddiqui 2007: 29) and (b) Islamic Studies cover every aspect of Islam (i.e. it deals with, among other matters, the cultural and religious, economic and political, social and philosophical, past and present, regional and universal dimensions). In the light of these working definitions, we turn to another aspect of Islamic Studies that briefly reflects upon this discipline's roots and development.

The Discipline's Roots and Development

Now that we have a workable definition of the discipline, we should back track and in brief trace the roots and development of the discipline of Islamic Studies. As already noted in the previous section, this discipline had its roots in Oriental Studies, a discipline that was initiated and constructed by European scholars when they accompanied the colonial powers to Africa and Asia. Nanji (1997), who examined how the discipline of Islamic Studies flowed out of Oriental Studies, demonstrated when, why and how this discipline and the term came into popular use. In his appraisal he opined that the academic study of Islam by European scholars was primarily "associated with the general discipline of thought and expertise known as Oriental Studies or Orientalism." Hussain et al. (1984); Martin (1985); and Nanji (1997) highlighted that Oriental Studies adopted the historical-philological approach: an approach that concentrated on the variety of languages (i.e. Arabic, Persian, Turkish, and Urdu) that were employed in the Muslim heartlands in order critically to study the historical and cultural texts of the Muslim communities that straddled the regions (cf. Khir 2007).

When we reflect upon the status of Islamic Studies we observe that—like African Studies and Religious Studies—it was deeply affected and scarred by Orientalist (European) scholarship for more than a century. This fact was brought to the fore by Edward Said's celebrated work *Orientalism* (1978); a work that has been challenged by dedicated Orientalists such as Bernard Lewis (Nyang and Abed-Rabbo 1984; Hughes 2007). Said graphically demonstrated how European scholarship accompanied European colonial political powers to non-European regions such as Asia and Africa; whilst the colonial powers secured the regions' resources, their scholars took an interest in the cultures, literatures, and religions. During the decades when these scholars stationed themselves in these regions, they recorded and wrote on almost every aspect of the Muslim community's life, using the historical-philological approach mentioned earlier. The purpose of their intellectual invasion was "to understand, in some cases to control, manipulate, even incorporate, what is a manifestly different world" (Said 1978: 12); their contribution as scholars basically assisted the colonialists to legitimate their forays and conquests (Hussain et al. 1984). For Said, Orientalism, according to McCuthcheon (1999: 19), essentially denoted "a complex series of associations, assumptions, texts, political policies, representations etcetera, that maintain and legitimize the superiority of the European world."

Notwithstanding these socio-political and scholarly developments and as a result of Said and a few others' intellectual interventions at a key period in history (about 10 years before the end of the Cold War), the writings of European scholars were not just closely scrutinized but critically assessed. This was the case when the theories and methods of well-known scholars such as Duncan Black Macdonald, Hamilton Gibb, Gustave von Grunebaum, Kenneth Cragg, and Bernard Lewis, who—ironically—transformed Islamic Studies into an exciting discipline in and outside Europe and the USA, were seriously questioned. Besides the coterie of Asian and African scholars who decidedly queried their intentions and outputs, these scholars' works were also subjected to analysis by emerging scholars within their own ranks (cf. Hussain et al. 1984). Coincidently, the scholarly inputs of the mentioned Orientalists—or Islamisists as they were also referred to—happened at the time when the scientific study of the history of religion was being consolidated and during the time when the study of Islam within the discipline of Religious Studies was being accommodated (Martin 2001; Khir 2007). From the beginning of the 1980s there was a gradual shift in the nature of the outputs. Scholars who were reinforcing theoretical models of their predecessors broke away from these models, and some adopted more challenging approaches such as Marxist, post-structural, and critical theories that provided a different insight into issues that were being studied and evaluated; one text that comes to mind is Hamid Enayat (1988), that critically assessed Muslim political thought.

Looking back at how the field developed throughout the twentieth century (c. 1900s– 1980s) and comparing it to how developments unfolded in the late twentieth and early twenty-first centuries (c. 1990–2010) when fresh theories and models gained ascendancy in the social sciences, we observe a qualitative difference in the output. This observation is based upon a variety of factors. Among these were the new Islamic Studies programs that were mounted at universities around the world including Africa and an increasing number of researchers who entered the field and participated in interdisciplinary conferences and symposia (cf. Platvoet et al. 1996; Zeleza 2006). Many of these scholars who began to make their presence felt in academia rebutted the works of European/American scholars who had undermined African scholarship, and produced texts that opened new opportunities for other scholars to pursue.

To conclude this section, it may be stated that though scholars such as Hughes (2007) and others have had major epistemological problems with Said's *Orientalism*, they cannot deny the fact that as a text it stimulated rethinking of the fields of Islamic Studies, Religious Studies, and African Studies, since they were dominated and influenced by outsiders. On this very last note, the issue of who has a license to teach and research has also come under the scholarly microscope and it is an issue that relates to what Cabeson and Davaney addressed in their edited text titled *Identity and the Politics of Scholarship in the Study of Religion* (2004).

We shall, of course, touch upon these issues in passing whilst we examine Islamic studies scholarship in Southern Africa.

Southern African Islamic Studies Scholarship

Before going any further we need to once again state that it is beyond the scope of this chapter to cover the whole of Southern Africa: a region that stretches from Angola to South Africa. For the purpose of this chapter, we shall confine the focus to four countries: namely, South Africa, Zimbabwe, Mozambique, and Botswana, where research on Muslims and Islam has taken place over the past two decades. Perhaps it is appropriate to mention in passing that even though a few scholars provided an overview of "Islam in Southern Africa", none of them succeeded in offering a satisfactory overview; here the book chapters of Mandivenga (1991), Tayob (1999), Shell (2000), and Amra (2006) come to the fore. A similar criticism applies to those lengthy chapters and articles that tried to cover "Islam in Sub-Saharan Africa" or "Religion in Africa". The contributions of Mazrui (1995), Robinson (1995), Levtzion (1997), and Haron (2010) reveal how problematic it is to offer overviews. Azevedo (1998b) offered a cursory view of the expansion of Islam and did not say much about the miniscule numbers of Muslims in Southern Africa; only Mozambique was mentioned. Bongmba (2006), who looked more at the scholarly contributions, only referred to the South African research produced by Abdulkader Tayob and Ebrahim Moosa and failed to refer to the respective booklets of Ephrahim Mandivenga and James Amanze. The same argument applies to Moyo (2007). Notwithstanding these critical remarks, we start this section by providing a survey of the study of Islam in South Africa and then weave the scholarship of those from the neighboring states into the body of the chapter.

In Context: From Oriental Studies to Islamic Studies

When reflecting upon the teaching of "Islam" in Southern Africa academia, we can trace two historical phases: the first phase, which criss-crosses the whole region, was a period that was initiated by Christian theological seminaries and the faculties of theology at different Southern African universities, and the second phase, which corresponds to the globalization phase that Bongmba (2006) mentioned, began when Muslim organizations—that came under the spell of the process of Islamization—convinced specific universities to appoint qualified Muslim staff to teach courses on "Islam," and to either set up independent "Islamic Studies" programs in Departments of Religious Studies or offer the program in separate departments. A careful inspection of both phases brings to the fore the insider/ outsider debate that was briefly mentioned at end of the previous section. Since aspects of the first phase have previously been covered, we shall only reflect upon the second (c. 1990–2010).

Islamic Studies: A New Directions, A Fresh Discipline

Before giving specific attention to "Islamic Studies" in South Africa where major changes took place from the beginning of the 1990s, we should note that developments were also under way at the Department of Religious Studies, Classics, and Philosophy at the University of Zimbabwe, and the Department of Theology and Religious Studies at the University of Botswana. In both departments scholars such as Ephraim Mandivenga and James Amanze taught courses on Islam and pursued research on Muslims in these two Southern African states. And at both institutions concerted attempts were made to appoint Muslims in the lectureship positions; this move was unthinkable between the 1960s and the 1970s when these departments were staffed by theologians and missionaries. These signs indicated that the institutions realized that they needed to open up opportunities to those best qualified and trained in the field, even if the individual is an outsider and not an insider (Westerlund 1991). And notwithstanding some of our critical comments on these Christian theological institutions, it cannot be denied that they, like the Oriental Studies project, have initiated the teaching and dissemination of "Islam" within the academic arena and opened up an opportunity for critical reflection.

The missiological programmes that included the "study of Islam" courses caused a stir among members of the respective Muslim communities in the region. They opined that a Muslim should be appointed to an "Islamic Studies" post and the only method to succeed in this was to muster the communities and lobby the universities, where they wielded some form of influence, in appointing well-qualified and trained Muslim scholars who could teach undergraduate and postgraduate courses in "Islamic Studies" in the existing Departments of Religious Studies. Whilst this was a problem in some instances, it was not so in others. There were occasions when Muslim theologians, who did not have the necessary academic training, applied for the posts and failed to be appointed. Conservatives in the Muslim community considered this an affront since, in their subjective opinion, these individuals possessed the relevant knowledge of Islam and were in the best position to teach the courses on offer.

However, appointees who were Muslims and trained in local Southern African and European/American universities were expectedly not favored by these conservative groups since they are said to have been trained in a purely secular system and operate in a secular environment. The most recent appointment of Professor Faried Esack in the Study of Islam program at the University of Johannesburg is a case in point. His appointment was not openly welcomed by the Gauteng-based Jami'at ul-Ulama (Association of Muslim theologians). Even though he was trained in a Pakistani Muslim theological seminary and completed his doctorate at the University of Birmingham in the UK, he, along with Associate Professor Ebrahim Moosa (another Muslim seminary-trained scholar)—who is presently attached to Duke University after spending a few years at the University of Cape Town, adopted an undeniably critical approach towards Islam and Muslims: a stance that has been rejected by the mentioned theological body.

In spite of these intra-Muslim squabbles as to who qualifies and who does not, those who hold these positions have been exposed to postgraduate studies programs offered at Southern African and European/American universities where they have pursued the social scientific approach; an approach that has yielded very useful research results in all disciplines that have adopted one of the many social approaches. The issue of approach or method has also been raised by those in the field of Islamic Studies because they are expected to adopt a dispassionate approach to the topic or subject that they teach (cf. Izzi Dien 2007). This has been quite problematic for those who cannot make that transition, arguing that as a Muslim academic one should not be allowed to, for example, critically question the contents of the Qur'an. Two secular oriented (Muslim) scholars who have been among those who advocated the social scientific approach as a viable alternative approach in understanding Islam and its variety of sources were the Algerian Paris-based Mohamed Arkoun (1995) and the late Pakistani Chicago-based Fazlur Rahman (2001).

Even though these scholars advocated the social science approach as a better alternative to the Eurocentric approaches prevalent in Oriental Studies as well as the traditional approach preferred by conservative Muslim academics, the latter group seems to hold back in adopting the social science approach as a viable technique. As a consequence, these conservative Muslim academics do not in the main open themselves to any form of critical thinking, which is an essential part of the social science approach. They, as a matter of fact, merrily apply social science approaches selectively and subjectively without realizing the negative impact this selective/subjective method has on research outcomes. The scholarly outputs of Dr. Mohamed Ashraf Docrat (University of Johannesburg) and Dr. Ismail Jaffer (University of South Africa), who were trained in Muslim theological seminaries, are commendable; in spite of their limited research outputs, both demonstrated that they need more exposure to social scientific approaches to the study of Islam and Muslims in order to make a more incisive contribution to the field. What we gather and conclude from this discriminating approach—and one that is in support of Olupona's (2007) response to Simeon Ilesanmi—is that the discipline of Islamic Studies (as well as Religious Studies) is an "innately subjective" and not an objective science.

Academic Platforms: From Conferences to Journals

Scholarship on Islam and Muslims in Southern Africa has not so much been influenced and affected by academic outputs in the Muslim heartlands but by the scholarly work of academics in Europe and North America where research has been rigorous and vibrant. So whenever theoretical and empirical issues pertaining to Islam and Muslims have been and are discussed in American and European academic circles, then Southern African scholars automatically take them up and explore them further. This has been the trend during the past two decades and one that has been concretized through the hosting of interdisciplinary conferences and symposia. Many academic (and popular) conferences, symposia, and workshops have taken place in the region during the past two decades and it would be well-nigh impossible to record each and every one that took place. We shall therefore only refer to a few that specifically focused on Islam but will refer to others in passing where necessary.

Public Presentations: Forming Networks

One of the first important academic ventures in this regard was the "Approaches to the Study of Islam" conference that was jointly organized by Abdulkader Tayob and Ebrahim Moosa, who were members of the Department of Religious Studies at the University of Cape Town (UCT), in 1991. Whilst this conference was a critical endeavor to deal with social science approaches instead of conforming to the traditional normative historical approach, it regrettably did not capture the proceedings in a publication to reflect the type of issues that were discussed and debated. Fortunately, the papers that were presented at the regional conference of the International Association for the History of Religions in Zimbabwe held during September 1992 were published. The proceedings' title was *The Study of Religions in Africa: Past, Present and Prospects* (1996) and it was co-edited by Jan Platvoet, James Cox, and Jacob Olupona. The anthology of papers ranged from critical pieces rooted in theory to descriptive essays that underline normative historical approaches. Though the regional conference was hosted by the University of Zimbabwe where Dr. Ephrahim Mandivenga did some significant descriptive research on Islam/Muslims in Zimbabwe (1983), it was observed that there was no contribution on the status of Islam or religion or religious studies in parts of Southern Africa (other than South Africa). Whilst this demonstrated the absence of scholarly texts on the social scientific study of religion in this region, it also reflected that those who wrote on religion in the 1990s in countries such as Zimbabwe, Botswana, Lesotho, Mozambique, and Swaziland lacked the necessary scholarly rigor that Olupona (1996a; 1996b) observed when he surveyed the scholarly outputs in Nigeria specifically and West Africa in general during 1992. Nonetheless, the situation has since changed in the Southern African region.

The third significant conference was an academic meeting between South African and Malaysian scholars. The focus of this conference was on "Cape Muslim/ Malay Identity" and was held at the University of the Western Cape. Muhammed Haron was the main coordinator along with Tan Sri Drs. Ismail Hussein, the then director of the Institute of Malay Studies at the National University of Malaysia and the life president of the National Writers Association of Malaysia, of this two-day conference. This was indeed a historical meeting that opened up opportunities for further relations between academics on the one hand, and peoples' relations on the other. Sadly, as with the Cape Town 1991 academic meeting, the papers presented at this conference were not published.

The fourth important conference that took place in Southern Africa was the "Islam and Civil Society in South Africa" conference that was co-organized by Mr. Iqbal Jhazbhai, a lecturer at the University of South Africa (UNISA), and Professor Tamara Sonn, who was then attached to the University of Florida. The conference was co-sponsored by UNISA, where the conference was held, and the Washington-based Institute of Peace Studies. Even though the focus was on Islam and civil society in South Africa, the conference was joined by prominent American academics such as Professor John Esposito (University of Georgetown) and Professor Richard Martin (Emory University). This was, in a sense, a historical meeting between South African and American academics. As with the Cape Town 1991 conference the proceedings were never published, despite the fact that a number of interesting papers were presented and discussed. Another interesting observation was that even though the debate was at times intense, scholars such as John Esposito remained aloof and basically adopted the status of observer rather than participant.

Paper Publications: Inscribing Ideas in Ink

After the UNISA—Institute of Peace Studies academic conference, a variety of other semi-academic and popular conferences and workshops that concentrated on Islam and Muslims were held (Haron 2004). In Southern Africa there are at least three other important annual academic meetings that take place; these, however, give attention to religion in general and do not devote their gatherings to specific religious traditions. The first organization that organized annual conferences was the Association for the Study of Religion in Southern Africa, the second was the African Association for the Study of Religion, and the third is the BOLESWA group. The last mentioned is a joint venture between the Universities of Botswana, Lesotho, and Swaziland. At these annual meetings papers on Islam and Muslims have occasionally been presented; some of these were published in the *Journal for the Study of Religion* (*JSR*) and the *BOLESWA Journal of Theology, Religion and Philosophy* (*JTRP*). The latter is under the editorship of Associate Professor James Amanze, who is attached to the Department of Theology and Religious Studies at the University of Botswana, and the former under the editorship of Professor David Chidester, who is located in the Department of Religious Studies at the University of Cape Town. Amanze, though a theologian, wrote an informative and useful monograph on *Islam in Botswana* (1999). Amanze's booklet was further complemented by Muhammed Haron's 2006 article on 'Gaborone's Muslim Community: A Vignette into their Lives', which appeared in *Scriptura*; an earlier issue of *Scriptura*, as a matter of information, contained an anthology of Peter Clarke's writings on West African Islam.

When we compare the journal edited by Amanze, which appears twice a year, to the one Chidester edits, which is also published bi-annually, they are qualitatively different in terms of their presentation, format, and contents. The *JSR* has been in circulation for more than 20 years (volume 23 was issued in 2010) and has transformed itself into a highly accredited journal in the field of Religious Studies, and *BOLESWA JTRP*, which is relatively young, has a long road ahead to reach the standard set by JSR. We hastily add that *BOLESWA JTRP* has managed to maintain fair academic standards despite its recent appearance and has much time to improve in the years to come. Another journal that we consider to be at par with the BOLESWA journal in terms of its content and presentation is *Theologia Viatorum: Journal of Theology and Religion in Africa* that is issued bi-annually from the University of the Limpopo (formerly the University of the North). So far this journal, unlike *JSR*, has not had many articles on Islam and Muslims. Perhaps the first part of the title, namely *Theologia Viatorum*, has been off-putting to anyone who wanted to present a paper on Islam or Muslims from a social science angle. The two articles that we read in earlier issues were written with a Christian audience in mind. This missionary perspective seems to be dominant among quite a few Southern African scholars of theology and religion. The reason could be that they have not been trained in Religious Studies as such and that much of their training was in Theology with minor courses in religion. In any case, a scan of one of the 2009 issues showed signs of change: it included two articles that were penned by Muslim scholars who covered different aspects of South African xenophobia. During 2010 the journal issued its 30th volume, which is indeed a feat in itself.

Up to this point, we have avoided discussing other journals that focus specifically on Islam. We wish to provide some brief comments about these before mentioning three other very important conferences that were held in South Africa. When (the former) Professor Sayed Salman Nadvi headed the Department of Islamic Studies at the University of Durban-Westville (now merged with the University of Natal to form the University of KwaZulu Natal), he edited *Al-'Ilm: Journal for Islamic Studies*: a journal, now defunct, that was quite educational and enlightening. On the whole, it filled an important gap in the compilation of knowledge about Islam and Muslims in the region. And, though not a highly scholarly product, it contained contributions that made some interesting interventions. During the time that this journal was in circulation it had to compete with the *Journal for Islamic Studies* (*JIS*) that was edited by Professor Jacobus Naude, who was then professor of Islamic Studies at the Rand Afrikaans University (now the University of Johannesburg). If we compare the two during the 1980s when they were both in circulation, the *JIS* was in some respects superior to *Al-'Ilm* in terms of the articles that appeared; however, they were generally at par. It was when the journal shifted to the University of Cape Town's Centre for Contemporary Islam in the mid-1990s that it had a face lift. After it was transformed, it attained accredited status in the eyes of the South African Ministry of Education as a noted annual publication. This happened more or less at the same time that *Theologia Viatorum* was also accredited.

Since Abdulkader Tayob's return from the Netherlands where he was the ISIM Professor at Nijmegen University for about three years, he took charge of the editorship of the *JIS* and brought it back on track when it lagged behind. During the past three years it is difficult not to notice to what extent he has made a considerable effort to change things around in the department and more specifically in the journal. As a result of his role in the management of the journal, we may argue that it now compares favorably with other similar international journals around the world. We think, for example, of the *Journal of Islamic Studies* (Oxford Institute of Islamic Studies) and the *American Journal of Islamic Social Sciences* (International Institute of Islamic Thought [Washington]). In 2007 Tayob produced a thematic issue on "Islam and African Muslim Publics". This issue's theme coincided with his appointment as the Professorial National Research Foundation Chair in African Muslim Publics; a chair that is fully funded by the NRF for five years (2008–13). Tayob, we should add, has been a full professor at the University of Cape Town for quite a while and currently directs the Centre for Contemporary Islam that issues a non-peer-reviewed annual titled *Annual Review of Islam in Africa*. Tayob has been noted for his theoretical excursions in Islamic studies. Whilst he has been commended for this, it has also been used as an argument against him for being too engrossed in theory at the expense of the available empirical data.

Nonetheless, the books that he wrote in the 1990s demonstrate his familiarity with the theoretical tools in the social sciences. The first was *Islamic Resurgence in South Africa: The Muslim Youth Movement* (Tayob 1995) and *Islam in South Africa: Mosques, Imams, and Sermons* (Tayob 1999a). Tayob, who began his earlier undergraduate studies in medicine and along the way switched to Islamic Studies, had much of his training in Religious Studies at Temple University in the USA. It is there that he was exposed to the social science theoretical tools and these were the ones that he brought along with him to the University of Cape Town (UCT) at the beginning of the 1990s. Apart from having written the books mentioned, Tayob had also published other monographs for the London-based Hurst & Co. and the Oxford-based Oneworld, a publishing company that also published Faried Esack's works, namely *On Being A Muslim: Finding a Religious Path in the World Today* (1999) and *The Quran: A Guide* (2000) as well as one of his co-edited works on *Islam and Aids: Between Scorn, Pity, and Justice* (2009). In addition to these book-length contributions, Tayob was co-opted by Professor Richard Martin as one of three Associate Editors of the prestigious two-volume *Encyclopedia of Islam and the Muslim World* (Martin 2004).

As an associate editor on this project, he brought on board some of his colleagues, namely Sa'diyyah Shaikh and Shamil Jeppie. The latter, as a matter of information, runs the significant "South African-Mali Timbuktu" project in the School of Historical Studies at UCT; being in this important position he co-edited an aesthetically pleasing work called *The Meanings of Timbuktu* (Jeppie and Diagne 2009) and co-edited another academic text with Ebrahim Moosa and Richard Roberts on *Muslim Family Law in Sub-Saharan Africa* (2010). The former (i.e. Shaikh) has been identified—along with Ebrahim Moosa and Faried Esack— as one of the prominent progressive Muslim scholars by Omid Safi (2003); Omid Safi, who is the editor of the fifth volume of the *Voices of Islam* (2004) series under the general editorship of Vincent Cornell, included an informative, critical essay by Moosa on the issue of progressive Islam. That aside, almost a decade prior to the earlier-mentioned encyclopedia project, Tayob along with Moosa and Haron also contributed entries to Professor John Esposito's *Oxford Encyclopedia of the Modern Islamic World* (1995) that appeared in four volumes.

Let us leave Tayob and move to one of the neighboring universities, namely the University of the Western Cape (UWC) where Yasien Allie Mohamed is Professor of Arabic Studies in the Department of Foreign Languages. Mohamed, unlike Tayob who works alongside two colleagues on Islam in UCT's Department of Religious Studies, operates as the only known scholar who has contributed towards Islamic studies at UWC. It is in Islamic Philosophy that he has made an indelible mark. This was after he pursued his doctorate on a little-known classical Central Asian Muslim scholar, namely Raghib Al-Isfahani. As a result of giving life to Al-Isfahani's *The Path to Virtue* (Mohamed 2006), he received an international award for it in Iran during 2009. An outcome of this was an invitation by the editors of the *American Journal of Islamic Social Sciences* to co-edit a special thematic issue on Islamic ethics during 2010. Besides his extensive research, Mohamed also serves as co-editor the Malaysian-based *Afkar: Journal of Islamic Theology* and on the advisory board of the *Journal for Islamic Studies* at UCT.

Public Networks: Cooperative Projects and Interdisciplinary Approaches

Before we bring this chapter to a close, we wish to make critical observations on three other conferences that took place in South Africa. The first was organized by the University of Pretoria's Centre for International Political Science (CIPS) that was under the directorship of Associate Professor Hussein Solomon. The theme of this conference was "Islam in the 21st century" and it took place during November 2004. This low-profile conference brought together South African and East African scholars who investigated to some extent the relations between Religion and Politics. The presentations of these papers were published by CIPS and co-edited by Solomon and Butler; and they titled it *Islam in the 21ˢᵗ Century: Perspectives and Challenges* (Solomon and Butler 2005). And subsequent to this work they also co-edited (with AkeemFadare) *Political Islam and the State in Africa* (Solomon et al. 2008). Although both volumes contained some interesting studies, it was noted that some of them did not appropriate any suitable theoretical frame within which to locate their studies. For example, a browse through the earlier edited text reveals that Karima Brown's slim chapter on "Muslims in South Africa" (Solomon and Butler 2005: 26–9) and Hagar Islambouly's "The Challenges Facing Muslims in Egypt" (Solomon and Butler 2005: 85–8) did not employ useful theoretical models for their assessments.

The second significant international symposium that took place was a joint affair between the IRCICA (an international Istanbul-based NGO affiliated to the Organization of Islamic Conference), AwqafSA (a Johannesburg-based NGO), and University of Johannesburg. The theme was "Islamic Civilization in Southern Africa" and the conference took place at the University of Johannesburg during

September 2006. The conference attracted more than a hundred participants and among the presenters were Nisbert Taringa (Zimbabwe) and Liazzat Bonate (Mozambique). Bonate, who may be described as a prolific researcher on Mozambique Islam, completed her doctorate on Mozambique's Muslims under Associate Professor Shamil Jeppie, who has produced some exciting work on the Timbuktu manuscripts and on other aspects of Islamic Studies, in 2008. Bonate and Taringa's papers on Mozambique and Zimbabwe Islam appear in Muhammed Haron and Suleiman Dangor's (University of KwaZulu Natal) co-edited work titled *Proceedings of the International Symposium of Islamic Civilization in Southern Africa* (2009). Dangor has authored numerous articles on Islam in South Africa and is known for his booklet on *Shaykh Yusuf of Makasar* (1989).

The final international academic meeting that we want to comment upon a little more extensively took place during September 2007 at the University of Witwatersrand. This international seminar was a joint venture between the School of Social Sciences and Humanities at the University of Witwatersrand and the Institut d'Études de l'Islam et des Sociétés du Monde Musulman that is attached to the École des Hautes Études en Sciences Sociales in France. The whole academic affair was generously funded and facilitated by the French Institute of South Africa (IFAS). In our view, this was a unique scholarly exercise that was markedly different from the one that took place at UNISA during 1995 between American and South African scholars. Notwithstanding this, whilst the focus of the seminar was on "Muslim Cultures in South Africa and France," its main theme was "Islam, Democracy and Public Life in South Africa and in France." The seminar identified three basic objectives: the first was to re-imagine Islam as an object of academic enquiry, the second was to explore the epistemological dimensions of the study of Islam, and the last was to foster scientific networks. Bearing in mind the three objectives, the organizers chose further to identify three focus areas, which were: (a) the status of minority religions: the case of Islam, (b) religious identity— political identity, and (c) trans-nationalism/regionalism (cf. Haron 2008). Since a number of papers were presented, the conference organizers, Professors Eric Worby and Rehana Vally, edited and published them in two separate issues of the respected *South African Historical Journal*. The first set appeared in the fourth issue of 2008 and the second set in the first issue of 2009.

The survey that we have sketched between 1990 and 2010 is still somewhat unfinished and deficient since we did not manage to discuss the outcomes of the proceedings of the African Association for the Study of Religion Conference that was held during July 2007 at the University of Botswana, the International Muslim Personal Law conferences and workshops that were held between 2000 and 2002 in the cities of Cape Town, Dakar, and Dar es Salam, and a number of other relevant academic meetings that took place during the past two decades. We also acknowledge that we did not touch upon other non-peer reviewed journals such as the *IPSA Journal of Islamic Studies* and the *Annual Review of Islam in (South) Africa* that have been in circulation for more than five years. And we are also conscious of the fact that we have left out the names of an extensive list of scholars who have made substantial contributions to the field even though they are not located in the Study of Islam or Islamic Studies units at the respective universities. Be that as it may, there is a need to reflect upon and address their contributions in a follow-up article or chapter at a later date. At this point we should wind up and make a brief evaluation.

Evaluation

This concluding section will evaluate some of the developments that have taken place in national, regional, and international circles and comment on some of the pertinent issues that we have neglected to elaborate upon in this chapter. The question that was left unanswered and that cropped up on more than one occasion in this chapter and something that Olupona would be quite interested in is: who qualifies to teach Islamic Studies? Or to allow us to slightly alter Donald Wiebe's words (1999: 271): does understanding Islam require Islamic understanding? In our chapter we mentioned that conservative Muslims hold the view that "Islamic understanding" is a prerequisite for anyone who teaches Islam; as far as they are concerned their answer would be an emphatic "yes". This is in contrast to Wiebe's response, which was a resounding "no". What Wiebe's response implied was that a non-Muslim trained in the field of Islamic Studies should be in the position to teach the discipline. The argument also applies to a Muslim who has specialized in African Christianity or, for that matter, in African Religious Traditions. A few of us—having been influenced by social science—in the field of Religious Studies would happily concur with Wiebe and oppose the argument put forward by the conservatives; both Martin (1985) and Westerlund (1991) articulated this position in their respective works.

The adoption of a social science approach to Islamic Studies or the Study of Islam has enriched the teaching and research outputs of many who have been exposed to it. The social science approach, in fact, has not rejected the normative, historical approach as is understood by conservative Muslim academics; for all intents and purposes, this approach not only complements the traditional approach but adds more value to it in terms of the findings and outcomes. In fact, when we browse the works of Liazzet Bonate, Nisbert Taringa, Gabeba Baderoon, Inga Niehaus, Eric Germain, Goolam Vahed, Sindre Bangstad, Lubna Nadvi, and many others, we observe how they have brought to their field work and research agendas various theoretical tools that were and are found in, among other disciplines, history, anthropology, psychology, and political science to enhance and develop Islamic Studies. One important conclusion that has been reached was that Islamic Studies scholarship has enormously benefitted from the social sciences and provided a good insight into and understanding of the Southern African Muslim communities. As a consequence of these valuable spin-offs, social scientists such as Zeleza (2006) have supported the idea of scholars (in

Islamic Studies) participating in interdisciplinary projects further to augment their research programmes and contributions.

This brings us to the next point, and that is intensifying academic networks and collaborating in large and small cooperative academic projects. When we reported on the conferences and symposia that took place in Southern Africa in the above-mentioned paragraphs, we noted how joint projects succeeded in bringing academics from different backgrounds together and how these individuals fruitfully networked to participate in research projects. We made reference, for example, to Professor Richard Martins *Encyclopedia of Islam and the Muslim World* that brought on board Abdulkader Tayob as an associate editor and he, in turn, identified some other South African scholars who have contributed many entries on an array of topics. The spin-off of these academic meetings led to intense and elaborate co-operation in research between academic institutions (UCT and the University of Hamburg [Germany] on Islamic education). All of these developments gained because of social science networking and cooperation.

We have witnessed that another outcome of these academic networks over the past two decades has been a gradual increase in the number of American/European/ Asian researchers who have opted to research aspects of Southern African Islam. This development has, in fact, further sharpened the binary between insiders and outsiders, which we commented upon earlier, in terms of scholarly outputs. The insider/outsider binary, we should categorically state, has not negatively affected relationships between scholars researching Southern African Islam; it hasinjected and enhanced the nature of the scholarly output and this has therefore been extremely positive in the field of "Islamic Studies" in particular and for social science scholarship in general.

It is indeed these types of developments that have caused emerging academics such as Tahir Sitoto (University of KwaZulu Natal) and Simphiwe Sesanti (University of Stellenbosch), who are indigenous African Muslims, fully to endorse the social scientific methods in understanding the Muslim communities in their respective regions. Even though Sesanti is in Media Studies and Sitoto is in Religious Studies, they have found common research tools to unpack issues that the traditional approach would never have succeeded in uncovering. We therefore look forward to their future outputs in their respective fields and to Islamic Studies more specifically. In fact, there is a desperate need—a call that was also made by Olupona way back at the 1992 Harare conference—to train more African (not only Muslim) scholars in the discipline; as a discipline the understanding at school and university still seems to be that Islamic Studies is only meant for Muslims and only taught by Muslims. This incorrect notion was, of course, and to some extent still is, perpetuated by the system of education in Southern Africa.

Though "Islamic Studies" as an area of specialization has basically been dominated by scholars and researchers who were specifically trained in it, they have, of late, been joined by a growing number of scholars who come from outside this field of specialization. A close assessment of the research papers and publications on Southern African Islam demonstrate that as social scientists or as "outsiders" to "Islamic Studies" as such they have given the field—for a lack of a more appropriate phrase—a theoretical and practical "face-lift". This point has been amply underscored by the survey in this chapter. The final question that we deliberately left for last and wish to respond to is whether "Islamic Studies," like "Christian Studies" in this region, have been Africanized.

Whilst the simple answer is a categorical "no," we can say that there is room for this process to take place. The reason why this did not happen may be attributed to the fact that most of those who were trained in the field are Southern Africans who hail from non-African ethnic/racial backgrounds. Many of these scholars were, at one stage, heavily influenced by the process of Islamization; a process that was spearheaded by the late Professor Ismail Raji al-Faruqi, the Palestinian/American, and Professor Naquib al-Attas, the retired Malaysian scholar, during the 1970s and 1980s. This process was partly instrumental in supporting the idea that Islamic Studies must be and should be taught by qualified Muslim scholars; hence the appointment of South Asian Muslim scholars at the University of Durban-Westville in the mid 1970s and the appointment of young emerging scholars at UWC and UCT in the 1980s and 1990s.

We suppose that now that we have entered the twenty-first century many new challenges are being and will be encountered as the years roll by. And the questions that come to mind are numerous; among these are: What role will the Islamic Studies specialists play in combating or dealing with new challenges? How have they responded to issues such as religious pluralism and same-sex marriages in their courses? Have they charted out an agenda for the future in which they cooperate closely with individuals who come from other disciplines? What type of research do they have in mind for the next five to ten years? How best do they see themselves serving Southern African communities and nation-states? These questions we shall leave answered and leave for another occasion. However, these are some of the questions that, we are sure, must have also crossed Olupona's mind when he surveyed religion in West Africa and when he teaches courses on Islam at American and African institutions.

Bibliography

Abdul-Rauf, Muhammad, "Approaches to Islam in Religious Studies: Review Essay," in Richard Martin (ed.) *Approaches to Islam in Religious Studies* (Oxford: Oneworld, 2001), pp. 179–88.

Amanze, James, *Islam in Botswana* (Uppsala: Alqmvist & Wiksell, 1999).

Amra, Muhammad, "Islam in Southern Africa: A Historical Survey," in Abdu Kasozi and Sadik Unay (eds.), *Proceedings of the International Symposium on Islamic Civilization in Eastern Africa* (Istanbul: IRCICA, 2006), pp. 99–118.

Arkoun, Mohamed, "Islamic Studies: Its Methodology," in John Esposito (ed.), *The Oxford Encyclopedia of the Modern Islamic World* (New York: Oxford University Press, 1995), vol. 2, pp. 332–40.

Azevedo, Mario (ed.), *African Studies: A Survey of Africa and the African Diaspora* (Durham, NC: Carolina Academic Press, 1998).

—, "African Studies and the State of the Art," in Mario Azevedo (ed.), *African Studies: A Survey of Africa and the African Diaspora* (Durham, NC: Carolina Academic Press, 1998), pp. 5–29.

Bongmba, Elias, "The Study of African Religions: A Sketch of the Past and Prospects for the Future," in Anon (ed.), *The Study of Africa: Disciplinary and Interdisciplinary Encounters* (Dakar: CODESRIA, 2006), pp. 338–74.

Cabezon, Jose I. and Sheila G. Davaney (eds.), *Identity and the Politics of Scholarship in the Study of Religion* (London: Routledge, 2004).

Dangor, Suleiman, *Shaykh Yusuf of Makasar* (Durban: Iqra, 1989).

Enayat, Hamid, *Modern Islamic Political Thought* (Austin: University of Texas Press, 1982).

Esack, Faried, *On Being A Muslim: Finding a Religious Path in the World Today* (Oxford: Oneworld, 1999).

—, *The Quran: A Guide* (Oxford: Oneworld, 2000).

— and Sarah Chitty (eds.), *Islam and Aids: Between Scorn, Pity, and Justice* (Oxford: Oneworld, 2009).

Esposito, John (ed.), *Oxford Encyclopedia of the Modern Islamic World* (New York: Oxford University Press, 1995).

Frieder, Ludwig and Afe Adogame (eds.), *European Traditions in the Study of Religion in Africa* (Wiesbaden: Harrassowitz Verlag, 2004).

Haron, Muhammed, "Academic Research on Islam and Muslims in South Africa within a Democratic Environment," *Annual Review of Islam in South Africa*, no. 7 (2004): 71–5.

—, "Gaborone's Muslim Community: A Vignette into their Lives," *Scriptura: International Journal of Bible, Religion and Theology in Southern Africa*, 92.2 (2006): 200–17.

—, "Islam, Democracy and the Public Life in South Africa and France: A Report," *American Journal of Islamic Social Sciences*, 25.1 (2008): 151–4.

—, "Africa's Muslims: Expressing their Identity," in James Amanze (ed.) *Biblical Studies, Religious Studies, and Philosophy: An Introduction for African Universities* (Nairobi: Zapf Chancery, 2010), pp. 363–79.

— and Suleiman Dangor (eds.), *Proceedings of the International Symposium on Islamic Civilization in Southern Africa* (Istanbul: IRCICA, 2009).

Hughes, Aaron, *The Past and Future of an Academic Discipline* (London: Equinox Publishing, 2007).

Hussain, Asaf, "The Ideology of Orientalism," in Asaf Hussein, Robert Olsen, and Jamil Qureishi (eds.) *Orientalism, Islam and Islamicists* (Brattleboro, VT: Amana Books, 1984), pp. 1–21.

—, Robert Olsen, and Jamil Qureshi (eds.) *Orientalism, Islam and Islamicists* (Brattleboro, VT: Amana Books, 1984).

Izzi Dien, Mawil, "Islamic Studies or the Study of Islam? From Parker to Rammell," *Journal of Beliefs & Values*, 28.3 (2007): 243–55.

Jeppie, Shamil, and Soulemane Diagne (eds.), *The Meanings of Timbuktu* (Pretoria: HSRC Press, 2008).

— , Ebrahim Moosa and Richard Roberts (eds.), *Muslim Family Law in Sub-Saharan Africa: Colonial Legacies and Post-Colonial Challenges* (Amsterdam: Amsterdam University Press, 2010).

Khir, Bustami, "Islamic Studies within Islam: Definition, Approaches and Challenges of Modernity," *Journal of Beliefs & Values*, 28.3 (2007): 257–66.

Levtzion, Nehemia, "Islam in Sub-Saharan Africa," in Mircea Eliade (ed.), *The Encyclopedia of Religion* (New York: Macmillan, 1997), vol. 8, pp. 344–57.

— and Randall L. Pouwels (eds.), *The History of Islam in Africa* (Cape Town: David Philips; London: James Currey, 2000).

Ludwig, Frieder and Afe Adogame (eds.), *European Traditions in the Study of Religion in Africa* (Wiesbaden: Harrassowitz, 2004).

Mandivenga, Ephraim, *Islam in Zimbabwe* (Gweru: Mambo Press, 1983).

—, " The Role of Islam in Southern Africa," in C. Hallencreutz and M. Palmberg (eds.), *Religion and Politics in Southern Africa* (Uppsala: Scandinavian Institute of African Studies, 1991), pp. 74–84.

Martin, Richard (ed.), *Approaches to Islam in Religious Studies* (Oxford: Oneworld, 1985, 2001).

— (ed. in chief), *Encyclopedia of Islam and the Muslim World* (New York: Thomson Gale, 2004).

Mazrui, Ali, "African Islam and Islam in Africa: Between Exceptionalism and Marginality," *American Journal of Islamic Social Sciences*, 26.3 (2009): i–xi.

—, "Islam in Sub-Saharan Africa," in John Esposito (ed.), *The Oxford Encyclopedia of the Modern Islamic World* (New York: Oxford University Press, 1995), vol. 2, pp. 261–71.

McCutcheon, Russell T., (ed.), *The Insider/Outsider Problem in the Study of Religion: A Reader* (London and New York: Cassell, 1999).

Mohamed, Yasien, *The Path to Virtue* (Kuala Lumpur: ISTAC, 2006).

Moyo, Ambrose, "Religion in Africa," in April A. Gordon and Donald L. Gordon (eds.), *Understanding Contemporary Africa* (Boulder, CO and London: Lynne Rienner, 2007), pp. 317–50.

Nanji, Azim, *Mapping Islamic Studies: Genealogy, Continuity and Change* (Den Haag: Walter de Gruyter, 1997).

Nyang, Sulayman and Samir Abed-Rabbo, "Bernard Lewis and Islamic Studies: An Assessment," in Asaf Hussain, Robert Olsen, and Jamil Qureshi (eds.), *Orientalism, Islam and Islamicists* (Brattleboro, VT: Amana Books, 1984), pp. 259–84.

Olupona, Jacob (ed.), *African Traditional Religions in Contemporary Society* (St. Paul, MN: Paragon House, 1991).

—, "The Study of Religions in Nigeria: Past, Present and Future," in Jan Platvoet, James Cox, and Jacob Olupona (eds.), *The Study of Religions in Africa* (Cambridge: Roots and Branches, 1996a), pp. 185–210.

—, "The Study of Religions in West Africa: A Brief Survey," in Jan Platvoet, James Cox, and Jacob Olupona (eds.), *The Study of Religions in Africa* (Cambridge: Roots and Branches, 1996b), pp. 211–28.

—, "On Africa, a need for nuance," *Harvard Divinity Bulletin*, 35.4 (2007).

Platvoet, Jan, James Cox, and Jacob Olupona (eds.), *The Study of Religions in Africa: Past, Present and Prospects* (Cambridge: Roots and Branches, 1996).

Pruett, Gordon, "Duncan Black Macdonald: A Christian Islamist," in Asaf Hussain Robert Olsen and Jamil Qureshi (eds.) *Orientalism, Islam and Islamicists* (Brattleboro, VT: Amana Books, 1984), pp. 125–67.

Rahman, Fazlur, "Approaches to Islam in Religious Studies: Review Essay," in Richard Martin (ed.), *Approaches to Islam in Religious Studies* (Oxford: Oneworld, 2001), pp. 189–202.

Robinson, David, "Islam in Africa, in Richard Martin (ed.), *Encyclopedia of Islam and the Modern World* (New York: Thompson Gale, 1995), vol. 1, pp. 13–19.

Safi, Omid, *Progressive Muslims* (Oxford: Oneworld, 2003).

— (ed.), *Voices of Islam*, vol. 4 (Westport, CN: Praeger, 2004).

Said, Edward, *Orientalism* (London, Verso, 1978).

Shell, Robert, "Islam in Southern Africa," in Nehemia Levtzion and Randall L. Pouwels (eds.), *The History of Islam in Africa* (Cape Town: David Phillips, 2000), pp. 327–48.

Siddiqui, Ataullah, *Islam at Universities in England, Meeting the Needs and Investing in the Future* (Leicester: Markfield Institute for Higher Education, 2007).

Solomon, Hussein, and Firoza Butler (eds.), *Islam in the 21st Century: Perspectives and Challenges* (Pretoria: CIPS – University of Pretoria, 2005).

—, Akeem Fadare and Firoza Butler (eds.), *Political Islam and the State in Africa* (Pretoria: CIPS – University of Pretoria, 2008).

Tayob, Abdulkader, *Islamic Resurgence in South Africa: The Muslim Youth Movement* (Cape Town: University of Cape Town Press, 1995).

—, *Islam in South Africa: Mosques, Imams, and Sermons* (Gainesville, FL: University Press of Florida, 1999a).

—, "Southern Africa," in David Westerlund and Ingvar Svanberg (eds.), Islam outside the Arab World (Richmond: Curzon Press, 1999b), pp. 111–24.

—, "The Past and the Present of African Islam," *Religion Compass* 2.3 (2008), pp. 261–72.

Westerlund, David, "Insiders and Outsiders in the Study of African Religions: Notes on Some Problems of Theory and Method," in Jacob Olupona (ed.) *African Traditional Religions in Contemporary Society* (St. Paul, MN: Paragon House, 1991), pp. 15–24.

Wiebe, Donald, "Does Understanding Religion Require Religious Understanding?", in Russell T. McCutcheon (ed.), *The Insider/Outsider Problem in the Study of Religion: A Reader* (London and New York: Cassell, 1999), pp. 260–73.

Zeleza, Paul T. (ed.), *The Study of Africa: Disciplinary and Interdisciplinary Encounters* (Dakar: CODESRIA, 2006).

Chapter 16
Folk Beliefs about Spiritual Power and Hinduism in Ghana

Albert Kafui Wuaku

Introduction

Shiva and Krishna, icons of Hindu spirituality currently involved in a global circulation of ideas, images, and people, are establishing homes in the religious fields of Ghana and her neighbors in West Africa. They are also garnering appeal among local worshippers. In Ghana, the general socio-economic and political context of the growing attention being given these two Hindu gods is a thorough globalizing process. This is characterized by the drying up of sources of wealth and certainty, high unemployment, and impoverishment. Because Ghanaians mostly experience mishaps as manifestations of demons, witches, and other purveyors of spiritual harm at work, a common recourse is to the supernatural for answers and empowerment. Arguably, in no period in Ghana's religious history has the services of purveyors of magico-religious power been so much sought after than presently. As people are more willing nowadays than ever before to experiment with unfamiliar sources of supernatural power, individuals claiming access to powers deriving from Hindu gods are attracting considerable attention. This development, however, represents a culminating point of a process that began during the British colonial empire when images of Hindu spirits filtered into Ghanaian communities, through a variety of local oral narratives and Hindu films. In the chaos that characterized Ghana's struggle for independence and the early post-independence years, Hinduism began to attract attention as people sought supernatural power sources to cope with life challenges.

From the late 1970s and early 1980s, some purveyors of Hindu spiritual power started to capitalize on the situation to organize their growing clientele into Hindu worshipping communities. Today, groups such as the Radha Govinda temple community, the Arya Samaj of Ghana, the Sri Satya Sai Baba group, the Akkanum Nama Shivaya Healing Church, the Hindu Monastery of Africa, the Christ Yoga church, and the Shiva Linga Healing center, provide their growing worshipping populations with ritual spaces for meeting their spiritual and moral needs. Thus, originating its African trajectory as an ethnic religion in the East and the South where a settler English colonial regime had brought in indentured labour from what became India and Pakistan, Hinduism has over the years been slowly but steadily carving a niche as an African religion with local appropriations in West Africa.

In this chapter I reconstruct the early history of one of Ghana's Hindu Temple communities, the Radha Govinda Temple, also called the Hare Krishna movement, drawing on Ghanaian folk theories about outside spiritual power as an important analytical frame in explaining the appeal it held for worshippers when it emerged on the scene in the 1970s. The chapter demonstrates the possibility of explaining a local religious experience using an indigenous frame of reference or conceptual scheme. I propose that the indigenous religious landscapes of African communities are replete with paradigms from which local people draw in engaging and evaluating new religious experiences. Yet, in seeking analytical frames to locate our explorations of local religious experiences, the tendency has been for us, both local African scholars as well as Western Africanists, to overlook local understandings and to look to Western-originated intellectual paradigms for leads. Theory, or the process of theorizing, I argue in this chapter, is neither the preserve of the West nor exclusive to the academy, dominated by the West. Even though we tend to be dismissive of them as superstitions, unscientific, or untested, even parochial, folk theories are "theories" too, in so far as they function as analytical tools for their authors, unveiling insights into the nature of their experiences, and furnishing them with ideas that guide how they shape themselves to their circumstances. Without denying the relevance of Western-originated and/ or formal academic models, I suggest that making intellectual sense of African religious experiences calls for a more respectful attention to folk beliefs or local understandings. These local conceptual schemes must be the first building blocks upon which to base future analysis (Yanka 1999: 145).

It would be proper for me to begin by locating the roots of the reliance on non-African epistemological terrains for analytical frames in exploring African religious experiences, in the politics of the global academy; "the domination of the academic discourse, the subsuming of local intellectual paradigms under received Western hegemonies, the monopolistic control of the centre of academic authority by the West, and the subsequent marginalization of other intellectuals and their local agenda" (Yanka 1999: 144). The heart of the matter is the handicapped geopolitical locus of African scholarship within the scheme of academic knowledge production and dissemination. The perception that civilization or "eye opening" must come from the West (introduced by Western missionaries and colonial agents), pervaded modern African states at the dawn of independence. As a consequence the educated African perceived his or her task as helping fellow Africans to find a way out of "darkest" Africa (Yanka 1999: 144). In the context of a discourse casting modernity as Westernization, African communities felt their mission was to emerge from the "savage" backwoods and come into the limelight where modern states and scholars were made (Yanke 1999: 144). If independence was to be beneficial, it was argued, Africa needed to modernize, that is, to Westernize or look to the West for leadership, which includes leadership in the academy.

Furthermore, the hegemony of scholarship and the production of literature are controlled by three languages, none of which is African. These are German, English, and French. When the cultures of these languages in which the discourse of universal science and scholarship is produced generate a meta-language or meta-discourse, the rest of the world, including Africa, has no choice but to struggle to cope with it. Even in the area of publishing, African manuscripts are often marginalized by Western publishing outlets, who complain of intrusive African vocabularies, titles, and texts because they are not mainstream language—such intrusions they argue, "could pose problems for marketing and smooth reading in the Western world" (Yanka 1999: 144). Manuscripts may be rejected because they are not in tune with global jargon and meta-discourse (Yanka 1999: 144).

In sum, there does not seem to be much room then for uniquely African contributions. As scholars working on data from Africa, we must for the most part fit our work somewhat into an overarching Western academic agenda—and negotiate for a space to be heard. The fault has been partly Africans' own too. It is due to the neglect on the part of African scholars to investigate and consider paradigms founded in indigenous academies as primary frames of reference. As Yanka has noted, "having agreed to dispense with our traditional sources of knowledge and imbibed wholesale the culture of the western academy, we have voluntarily provided a recipe for intellectual servitude and cultural alienation" (Yanka 1999: 145).

Spiritual Power

As this chapter is about how local notions of spiritual power mediate local engagements with incoming religions, let me also make a few notes on the place of spiritual power in African religious experiences. There is considerable literature devoted to the analysis and application of the concept of power or spiritual power, to be more specific. Yet, as Dahrendorf (1959: 166) has remarked, there is no consensus on the definition of power yet. Each discussion on power must therefore begin with a preliminary clarification of the intended usage. Following Hackett, I use the concept of spiritual power in this chapter to mean:

> The ability to transcend the normal course of events, to possess knowledge beyond human ken, to be able to effect the miraculous, to possess spiritual gifts which may be beneficial to the individual or the community, to ward off the harmful forces or adversaries, and the ability to realize the objectives of life, that is, to raise a family, enjoy economic self-sufficiency and good health. (Hackett 1993: 385)

In indigenous African religious universes, where religion is viewed as a technique for the production of welfare, discourse is not given as much importance as praxis or ritual. Ritual praxis furnishes the context in which spiritual power, the most important raw material in producing welfare, is harnessed. As an effect of God, who is considered to be the epitome of spiritual power, the universe is suffused with spiritual power, which human agents equipped with the secrets of its workings can tap into, to effect good or harm. Spiritual power, then, is a crucial concept and element in the African religious universe.

There is useful work done on African appropriations of alien religions, Islam and Christianity, to be more specific, and the nature of the conversation between them and indigenous religious notions. This literature has demonstrated how pragmatic consideration of these outside religions as reservoirs of superior spiritual power motivated local communities to enlist the help of their agents and symbols in efforts to cure disease and misfortune, and provide insurance for prosperity. For instance when Islam came into sub-Saharan Africa, its reputation for superior spiritual power motivated local African chiefs and kings to enlist the help of "Marabouts" or "Mallams" as ritual specialists in their palaces. These men provided supernatural cover against illnesses, sorcerers, competitors, and enemy states (Handloff 1982:186; Fisher 1973; Lewis 1957: 452–3; Sanneh 1976: 49–72). The kings of the Ashanti Empire, for instance, would never launch a military campaign without consulting a "Mallam" (Akyeampong and Obeng 1995: 500). Even in areas where "Mallams" or "Ulemas" were absent, Islam still participated in local efforts to probe the occult through its magic, modes of divination, and the use of ritual paraphernalia such as amulets (Masquelier 2001: 43).

Also, students of the history of Christianity in Africa such as Richard Gray (1990), Ogbu Kalu (1980), John Peel (1977; 1990), Robin Horton (1971; 1975a; 1975b), and Emefie Ikenga-Metuh (1987), describe how local communities were drawn to Christianity because of the belief that it was associated with superior spiritual power. Peel suggests that in their reception of Islam and Christianity one source of motivation for the Yoruba was their belief in the power of the religions. He summarizes a Yoruba perception of spiritual power in the following words: "Sources of spiritual power [i.e. ability to perform feats as a result of supernatural intervention or celestial knowledge] were mysterious and manifold and widely spread; illumination might come from remote quarters and a dogmatic reliance on one source was foolish" (Peel 1968: 125). Horton links the turning of local African communities to the world religions with the attribution of less power to local gods as local worlds became integrated into wider contexts. As the local gods could no longer provide sufficient knowledge, people turned to the world religions which postulated the idea of a high God considered to be more powerful and in charge of the macrocosm as a whole (Horton 1971; 1975a; 1975b). The Prosperity gospel discourse, arguably an alien import into popular African Christian theology, and a force behind the phenomenal growth of African Pentecostalism, draws appeal from its emphasis on the instrumental and magical use of the power inherent in the blood of Christ to change unfavorable destinies and paves the way for material success in the here and now (Asamoah-Gyadu 2005: 96). Drawing from the above, this chapter explores the role considerations of spiritual power-play in mediating Ghanaian encounters with Hinduism. But I take a cue from the Ghanaian sociologist of religion Max Assimeng, whose view is that: "Every logical course of human action should be seen as dependent upon a unique configuration of a particular cultural, symbolic and experiential background ... No appropriate conceptualization of behavior deriving from belief can ignore the culturally patterned cognitive map of the people concerned" (Assimeng 1977: 73).

In keeping with Assimeng's suggestion, this chapter seeks to make local concepts of outside spiritual power an important focus of the analysis. I will engage local Ghanaian notions about supernatural power that originates from far-flung sources, in an attempt to demonstrate how folk ideas mediate local encounters with incoming religious traditions, in this particular instance, Hinduism. I suggest that the wonder-working magico-religious power image of Hinduism in Ghana, which is an important source of its attraction, is a by-product of the encounter between indigenous beliefs about the power of far-flung spirits and imaginaries of Hindu spirits that filtered into Ghana through local agents of the British empire, Hindu films, and were (are still being) circulated by itinerant performers of magic. I shall demonstrate through a careful reconstructing of the early history of the Radha Govinda temple, that such notions about the magicality of Hinduism were crucial in providing it with the momentum it required to lift off in Ghana as a religion. The awe-inspiring religious power image of India rooted in local imagination and creative religiosity was the main paradigm underlying the public's evaluation of this community when it originated in the mid 1970s, and whatever appeal it had for people stemmed largely from its Indian connection. It is not my intention to argue that this Indian spiritual power connection is the explanation for all conversions to the Hare Krishna group in Ghana. As Ghanaian people became more familiar with Krishna worship in the later years, other aspects of the religion apart from its association with Indian power would begin to appeal, sometimes even more, to some people.

"Myths" and Myth Models: Conceptualizing the Influence of Folk Theories in Local African Communities

At the time Western academics began to study African societies in significant numbers (around the middle of the last century) it was suggested that oral traditions or oral cultures were becoming extinct, and that they were known only to a dying generation of old people who had access to the pre-colonial heritage. The idea was that with the strong influence of Western modernity over African cultures the significance attached to orality was becoming something of the past (Ellis 1989: 321–30). With the passage of time, however, it has been demonstrated that African cultures are still essentially oral and that oral discourses continue to thrive in African communities (Bettison 1968; Ellis 1989; Kastfelt 1989; Musambachime 1988). In fact, in southern Ghana, in spite of the development and overwhelming influence of literacy, people still give much weight to the spoken word. Popular beliefs and other forms of information transmitted by word of mouth continue to have widespread influence on people in Ghana, unlike in many Western societies, which believe little that is not written or broadcast on radio and television. One of the forms in which the influence of the "spoken word" is manifested in Ghana is "myths." In the discussion to follow I will demonstrate how a Ghanaian "myth" contributes to the aura surrounding Hindu religious symbols. But first, let us describe this phenomenon of "myths" in Ghana, and conceptualize its role as a medium for filtering local experience.

"Myths"

In the narrower and more standard, maybe anthropological sense, myths are sacred stories about God, the gods and ancestors, the origin and organization of the cosmos, the origins of human beings and human society as a whole. Myths reflect how communities make sense of their world, their origins, the nature and origins of their social institutions, their values, and their norms. Going by this understanding of myths, it would sound reasonable to suggest that they are no longer prevalent or fashionable in contemporary African societies. Even though some African communities may still have watered-down versions of ancient myths, which may be recited or performed in the context of ritual, myths in general are normally associated with "earlier societies" and are therefore considered to be something of the African past. There is, however, another sense in which myths may be said to be not only prevalent but also prolific in Africa, or at least in southern Ghanaian communities. I use the term "myth" in this chapter to describe this somewhat different but related form in which myths still exist and operate in African societies. I will use the terms "myth" and "folk theories" or "folk beliefs" interchangeably.

I borrow the idea of the "myth" from the Sri Lankan anthropologist Gananath Obeyesekere. I am inspired by his concept of "myth models" found in two of his works: *Medusa's Hair: An Essay on Personal Symbols and Religious Experience* (1981) and *The Apotheosis of Captain Cook: European Mythmaking in the Pacific* (1992). In the first book, *Medusa's Hair*, Obeyesekere writes about a category of popular cultural beliefs or notions more prevalent in non-Western than Western societies (Obeyesekere 1981: 100). Human experience, he argues, however idiosyncratic it might seem, is filtered through these cultural notions (Obeyesekere 1981: 101). Thus one function of these cultural beliefs is that they make human experience personally and publicly meaningful (Obeyesekere 1981: 100). Drawing on the belief in demons in his native Sri Lanka, Obeyesekere illustrates his idea. He says that a Sri Lankan patient afflicted by *pretas* or demons can behave in seemingly bizarre ways. But such behaviour is hardly considered bizarre in Sri Lanka. It is recognizable and readily understood as the work of demons, not only by others living within the culture but also by the patient (Obeyesekere 1981: 99), because there are beliefs in the Sri Lankan culture regarding the activity of demons and how afflicted people behave when they are possessed by these demons, and through these beliefs the meaning of the experience (which is a personal one) is filtered to the public. Also, the beliefs contain models for the culturally appropriate response to such a predicament, and these models inform people about how to handle the situation (Obeyesekere 1981: 99). Obeyesekere describes these cultural beliefs or "symbolic systems" as "myth models" (Obeyesekere 1981: 100–2). They are models in two senses; "of" and "for" reality (Obeyesekere 1981: 101; Geertz 1973: 73). They reflect Sri Lankan people's perceptions of demonic possession and so are "models of" a certain Sri Lankan reality. On the other hand, these same cultural beliefs are "models for" the way Sri Lankan people respond to such experiences.

In *The Apotheosis of Captain Cook* (1992), Obeyesekere argues that, because "myth models" shape the way people interpret, construct, and represent their experiences, fictional forms such as the novel, theatre, art, historical, and anthropological writings sometimes reflect the popular beliefs circulating in the societies in which these genres originated (Obeyesekere 1992: 10–11). Western narratives in particular, but also, other Western forms of fiction about non-Western people may simply reflect Western "myth models" (beliefs) about non-Western people and not reality (Obeyesekere 1992: 11).

The Apotheosis of Captain Cook provides a good example of the influence of "myth models" in the reconstruction and representation of history and anthropology. Obeyesekere shows how the European narratives of the adventures of Captain Cook, the English sailor and explorer, and his encounters with Pacific islanders, especially Hawaiians, reflect European "myths" about non-European "others." Obeyesekere argues that, a perennial and pervasive European "myth" underlies the narratives of Captain Cook: the "myth" of "the redoubtable person coming from Europe to a savage land, a harbinger of civilization to non-European savages" (Obeyesekere 1992: 11). This "myth" simply reflected what Europeans thought of non-European people. But its influence in shaping actual encounters between European and non-European people was profound. For instance the "myth" was later transformed in European thought to the evangelical idea of "the non-European heathens" and was used to justify missionary activity among "savages" (Obeyesekere 1992: 177).

The situations described in his two books and the focus of this chapter are quite dissimilar. But in that Obeyesekere's idea of "myth models" demonstrates the role of popular cultural beliefs in mediating meanings of human behaviour, it strikes me as a relevant conceptual tool for the discussion in this chapter. My understanding of Obeyesekere's argument is that, though they may simply be figments of people's imaginations, popular cultural beliefs function as "lenses" through which people come to understand, evaluate, express, and also respond to their experiences. They reflect the cultural perception of things, people, places, and events, and determine how people respond to these. Turning my attention to Ghana, I will use this idea to demonstrate the influence of a Ghanaian popular belief—a "myth"—associated with "outside" places and "outside" religious symbols, in shaping popular response to the Hindu religious presence. Such indigenous notions, I argue, are primary analytical categories or frames of reference we can use as first building blocks upon which to base future local scholarly analysis.

I will retain Obeyesekere's understanding of "myth models," but to distinguish my usage from his, I will employ the term "myth" to describe the Ghanaian phenomenon. I define "myths" as popularly held beliefs that circulate in a variety of narrative forms in southern Ghanaian communities. Themes in Ghanaian fictional narratives such as novels, drama, local movies, folk tales, rumours, gossip, proverbs, everyday common sayings, and forms of art, may reflect "myths." But "myths," as Obeyesekere himself has noted, are "structures of the long run" (Obeyesekere 1992: 10) in that they could be attached to non-fictional narrative forms too: biographies, autobiographies, historical, and anthropological narratives. "Myths" reflect southern Ghanaian people's deeply held beliefs about the reality of the world around them, humanity, the outside world, phenomena such as evil, spiritual power, its sources and its access. They also reflect people's real feelings, their deepest fears and beliefs, and they have a profound influence on people's behaviour. "Myths" resemble rumor and gossip. But they are more deeply rooted in the belief systems of African societies. Rumor and gossip are only outlets for the expression of "myths." An example of a southern Ghanaian "myth" might make things clearer. The belief that spiritual harm inflicted on a person is always caused by a person who knows the victim well is an enduring "myth" in Ghana. When misfortune befalls a person the tendency is for people to suspect "the people around," that is, the victim's closest friends and relatives, of causing the mishap. Even when a natural cause of the mishap is clear, for example death caused by a vehicle accident, the immediate and usual reaction is to seek the underlying spiritual cause—someone who caused it supernaturally—among the victim's circle of friends, relatives, and acquaintances. The Akan proverb, "the insect that would sting you on your thighs must have hidden in your own loin cloth," is an expression of this belief. So is the Akan concept of *effie nipa*, the "myth" that, in all families there are family members with malicious intentions who use supernatural powers to inflict harm or even kill successful relatives. Medicine men and priests or priestesses draw on this "myth" to effect cures of afflicted people. They demand to know the state of their patients" relationship with "the people around." If it is determined that this relationship went sour somewhere, the medicine man recommends making of peace with the person or people as the first remedy. But, as influential and as widespread as this belief is, it is only a popular belief, a "myth." Though anecdotes and rumours often circulate about the use of divination to confirm such suspicions, these narratives for the most part cannot be (or have not been) empirically proven to be true or false. Having described the phenomenon of "myths" I will proceed to show how a southern Ghanaian "myth" about "outside powers" helped to prepare the foundation for the success of Hinduism in Ghana.

"Outside Supernatural Power" in Southern Ghanaian Popular Imagination

Generally speaking, "outside power" (spiritual power sources from far-flung places) has a privileged place in the indigenous Ghanaian religious imagination. As spiritual causes of harm, such as witchcraft, sorcery, and the curse, are commonly located in close relatives and friends, the belief is that curative powers and protective symbols must be sought from "outside" or sources that a possible perpetrator or agent is unfamiliar with, lest he or she might render it ineffective. A strand of this local belief holds that "outside powers" generally, but especially, those that cross "seas" before they reach Ghana, are more efficacious compared with local powers. The sea, a vast and impenetrable medium, is said to house a host of spirits, some strong, others weak. Spirits and their purveyors crossing the seas either pick up extra strength from these spiritual powers or are drained of their potencies by them. A strong spirit will "suck up" power from weaker spirits in the oceans, augmenting its potency as a result. The potency of a weak spirit crossing the seas will be drained by stronger spirits in the seas. It is said of members of Ghanaian communities living overseas that they do not feel vulnerable to attacks from witches, for a witch cannot fly over the seas and still have its powers intact. A popular Fon folksong about a powerful ritual specialist captured in Abomey and sold into slavery in the new world echoes this motif. It goes, "if Abomey Atigbli indeed still has his powers intact after crossing the seas, let him escape and come back home for us to see." Not only are far-flung spirits believed to be strong, it is said that those that cross the seas pick up extra strength on their way to Ghana.

I suggest in this chapter that, underlying the appeal of religious traditions, religious personalities, and magico-religious objects, flowing in from overseas communities in southern Ghana are these indigenous notions of power from far-flung places. So deeply ingrained in the minds of many Ghanaians is this sense of confidence in "outside powers," that even when it has been acknowledged that there is an efficient ritual specialist in the immediate vicinity, it is still normal for some individuals or groups to travel far and wide (beyond the boundaries of their localities) in search of outside medicine or charms from powerful fetishes and healers to cure themselves or sick relatives. This folk theory about spiritual power is often attached to folktales that circulate in southern Ghana. A very common theme in these stories is the falling ill of the protagonist of the story—a chief, a warlord, Kweku Ananse, the tortoise, or the Hare—and the sending of emissaries to far-flung places to seek powerful medicine or powerful medicine men with effective cures.

Observing the Yoruba of Nigeria, Sandra Barnes notes a similar tendency in relation to what she describes as "outside knowledge":

> Outside knowledge enjoyed a privileged place in this kind of religious-political environment. The use and control of ritual forms ... is a special strategy for asserting leadership. Enjoying a monopoly over the communication of these forms, particularly when knowledge of how to treat and activate them comes

from outside and therefore inaccessible to the ordinary public heightens a leader's position. Outside knowledge helps to distance authorities so that they may conduct their duties at a greater remove from their followers. Distance can validate, enhance, legitimate, and buttress high positions ... The goal is greater understanding, greater power, greater control over the fateful mysteries of the universe attained with a display of wisdom and sanctity that is associated with those who are familiar with the unfamiliar. (Barnes 1990: 265)

Similarly, it could be suggested that in the spiritual worlds of some Ghanaian communities, familiarity with the unfamiliar and untested knowledge or power is considered to be a strategic advantage.

The imputing of superior magico-spiritual power to Hindu religious symbols in Ghana, then, can in part be explained by the fact that India, its birthplace, is an "outside" world from which one has to cross the seas before getting to Ghana. However, local notions about the powerful magicality of the Hindu religion can also be traced to the meanings some local people, informed by the "myth" of the superior potency of "outside powers," come to attach to three local genres of narratives on India. These are the stories featuring alleged real experiences with the powers of Hindu spirits, gods, and esoteric truths in India of Ghanaian Second World War veterans, Indian films, and depictions of India in stories told by "Professor Hindus." "Professor Hindus" are purveyors of "Magik," a category of Ghanaian popular entertainment. Because of the association of India with magic in Ghana and because the magicians themselves claimed they acquired their techniques from India, they became known as "Professors of Hindu power" or simply as "Professor Hindus."

"India" in Popular Southern Ghanaian Imagination

There are probably two images of India in popular Ghanaian opinion: a "real" image and a "mythic" image. In terms of its real image, India is considered to be a geographical and cultural space where ordinary people live, have norms and values, and go about their normal daily activities as people do anywhere else in the world. The more dominant popular view about India in Ghana, however, is a mythic view in which India is perceived as a spiritual space or a sacred land—a land full of magical, occult, and esoteric forces. It is reputed to be a place where techniques of making people spiritually potent have been developed, where knowledge beyond the human ken—the kind that would enable the bearer to unravel earthly and spiritual mysteries of our world—can be acquired.

The words "India" and "Hindu" conjure up images of magical and awesome happenings such as yogis suspending in space in meditative trance, snake charmers and multiple-headed cobras emerging from pots, people floating in space, and people vanishing and reappearing. In the contemporary Ghanaian Pentecostal religious culture, India is the epitome of evil. It is the abode of dark satanic forces—some kind of "Mecca" where witches go to revamp their evil and magical powers. Meyer features a popular story circulating in the Pentecostal community in Ghana, in which Alice, a witch, spiritually initiates her spouse, Eni, into "the Occult Society in India" (Meyer 1995: 242). A woman believed to possess effective witchcraft powers is sometimes said to "glow like a witch from India."

The notion of cultivating spiritual potency and ability is well known in indigenous Ghanaian tradition and there are traditional aspirations towards spiritual potency. India is reputed to be a place [sometimes "the" place] where spiritual potency can be cultivated. Stories about local medicine men and women travelling to India to "re-charge" their healing powers float around in almost every village in Ghana. These views about India existed and circulated in different narrative forms long before the presence of Hindu worshipping groups in Ghana. Though Hindu religious groups in Ghana often try to portray a different image of the religion, the influence of these earlier views remains to be a strong factor in shaping people's responses to them. In other words, the mythic images of India are superimposed on Hinduism in Ghana. This local image of India originated in the fusion of notions about outside spiritual power and inflowing imaginaries of Hindu spirits.

Colonial soldiers of the Gold Coast, who served in the West African Frontier Force in India, Sri Lanka and Burma during the Second World War returned home with stories of their encounters with powerful Hindu deities such as Shiva and Krishna whose supernatural covers enabled them to survive the war. Indian films, which became popular in Ghana from the mid 1940s, reinforced the images about Indian spirits portrayed in the stories. One strong source of appeal or fascination with Indian films was (and is) their awesome magical scenes making use of special effects. These include scenes of miraculous encounters with devas, of characters vanishing and re-appearing, of cobras issuing forth from *black* pots in response to flute music, of yogis floating in space, and of hydra-headed or hydra-handed or -legged creatures or people. These scenes in particular drove home the rapidly growing impression that India was indeed a land of magico-religious and awesome happenings, contributing in the process to the wonderworking magico-religious power image of the Hindu religion.

Drawing inspiration from stories about Hindu spirits and depictions of their activities in films, itinerant performers of magic on Ghana's local entertainment scene built (and still build) their careers around the claim that they derived their magical powers from these Hindu spirits when they visited India either physically or mystically. By making claims that they had been to India and actually acquired magical powers from there, and going on to demonstrate these claims further through their magical performances, "Professor Hindus" became living proofs that India was indeed one of the outside sources of powerful spirits. The phrase "powers of India" gained so much currency in Ghanaian popular culture from this time that it almost became an euphemism for describing phenomena people perceived to be spectacular manifestations of supernatural power and ability. People would boast that they were immune to any kind of spiritual attack because "Indian powers," protected them. India became synonymous with awe-inspiring magic, wonders, and supernatural ability. Popular imagination extended these attributes to persons or things associated with India.

General Kutu Acheampong, a former head of state of Ghana, at one time sent a delegation to Sai Baba, the Hindu sage in India, for "Hindu powers" so that he could, with Hindu supernatural backing, rule the nation forever (Asamoah-Gyadu 1994: 106). The point here thus far is the idea that local Ghanaian imaginations of superior powers from outside received a boost from what people heard about Indian spirits and saw in Hindu films and the feats of local performers of magic. This is the social cultural context that occasioned the emergence of the Hare Krishnas in Ghana in the mid 1970s. In the narrative that follows I describe how the community's association with India and the sense in Ghana that Indian spirits have superior power, mediated the public interpretation of some events linked with it, resulting in its appeal. In keeping with my objective of placing local notions at the centre of my analysis in this chapter, I tell the story in the words of Krishna devotees for the most part.

The Story of the Hare Krishna Community in Ghana

It was the morning of August 17, 1999. I was sitting on a mat facing Prabhu Srivas, and waiting for him to begin the story of how the Hare Krishna community came to be established in Ghana. From where I was sitting, I could hear the "gong gong" sound of *midrangas* (drums) and the clanging of bells, summoning devotees to the early morning devotional service to Krishna, which began the day. Before this day my knowledge about the Hare Krishnas in Ghana was scanty and gleaned mainly from rumor, hearsay, and "myths" about them. Because there is not much documented information on the Hare Krishna group in Ghana, I could not corroborate these stories. I concluded that the only way to reconstruct their history in Ghana was to rely on narratives of its leaders and followers. At first I was not sure whose voice to consider the most authoritative in the telling of this story. Eventually I settled on Prabhu Srivas, the national president of the community. In deciding on Prabhu Srivas, I considered the fact that he was one of the earliest converts in Ghana and so was in a position to provide me with a firsthand account of how the events unfolded. I also considered his status as the leader of the community. But I talked to other people too, devotees and some non-devotees who had witnessed the community's origins.

Prabhu Srivas is a 52-year-old, dark-skinned man. He is a Dagomba from Northern Ghana and was a Catholic before he joined the Hare Krishna movement. Before he was initiated into "Krishna Consciousness" as Srivas Das, Prabhu Srivas's name was Sylvester Bezenger. His followers call him Prabhu Srivas for short and I will refer to him in the same way in this reconstruction. Prabhu Srivas is strikingly tall, lanky, and frail looking. His followers make much of his height and some even say it has spiritual connotations, but the villagers of Medie openly joked about his thinness. They attribute this to his vegetarian diet and often made unfavourable remarks about the vegetarian lifestyle:

> *Shoaa!* [an expression of contempt] how can a person be there and say he won't eat meat. Where then does he expect to get the juice [vital food nutrients] that would make him grow fat and look strong and healthy? As for me I won't give myself to a church that would say I should not eat meat… Never! Not me!

commented Auntie Adzoa, a plump lady who owns a store where I often bought my lunch on my way to the Hare Krishna temple. She had just seen Prabhu Srivas pass by.

Like the Swamiji of the Hindu Monastery of Africa, another worshipping group, Prabhu Srivas is bald. He is married to mother Ekwe, the leader of the female devotees at Medie, where the Hare Krishna headquarters is based. They have no children. Prabhu Srivas ushered me into a nicely decorated room that Friday morning. This was his living quarters, but Prabhu Srivas also hosted important visitors here. He lit incense and sat in the lotus posture in one corner of the room. "Tell me about how this whole thing started in Ghana," I began. After a brief detour—a lecture on the importance of incense in the Hare Krishna tradition—he began the story. "Actually a Swami, a guru called Bhakti Tirtha Swami and another man brought this religion to Ghana in 1979. They came with some other devotees. In all they were about five men, all of them black American people." "You remember their names?" I cut in. "No, only Bhakti Tirtha Swami. They did not even stay for long. They went to all the university campuses first." "You know why they went there first?" I inquired. "Well … Not really. But I believe they wanted to attract young and well-educated people … People receptive to new ideas. And you know that the Krishna movement was in America first?" He stared me in the face questioningly. "Yes, I read about it," I answered. "In America they attracted young people so I am sure they believed it would work the same way here too," he explained. "Did it?" I inquired further. "Well, some people may have been convinced. But on the whole, it did not work. But they distributed books to the university libraries. But wait, this was not the first time Hindu missionaries had come from this mission. Yes, I remember now." "You mean some Krishna people came before these five men?" I was excited.

> Yes, in the mid-1970s, that would be about 1977, or 1978, a Swami called Jalaka Das came from India. He was travelling all over the world, recruiting people for what we call "international membership." He would go back to India and register them as members. First he was in Nigeria. Then he went to Sierra Leone, and then he visited Ghana. He did not preach. All he did was to register individuals. So he did not make much impact. Then, the following year these five swamis came …Yes, yes I remember now.

Prabhu Srivas was back on track.

> I remember that in 1980 a temple, the first one in West Africa, was established
> at Lagos in Nigeria. Then in 1981 they rented a house at a place called Alajo to
> begin the group here. In 1982 the second temple was established here in Ghana,
> at Odorkor and we were there for some time.

"So tell me what Odorkor was like," I urged, wanting him to say a bit more. "It
was good. That was the beginning. In fact, that was the point when the religion
really took off." "You mean that was when people began to know you?" I sought
further explanation.

> Yes, the place was bigger and Odorkor was more accessible, so more people
> joined us there ... But in 1990 we moved from Odorkor too. We had some
> farmland at Akrade so we moved there. But from Akrade we came back to Accra
> and settled at Newtown and then from there we came here,

Prabhu Srivas concluded his account.

When I went to interview Prabhu Srivas the first time, I had a set of questions
with me that I was seeking answers to. But Srivas seems to have a pattern already
worked out for telling the story of the Hare Krishna in Ghana, and though he
would answer my questions he would treat them as sidelines before returning to
his own course. In the end I only had to listen and throw in questions every now
and then seeking clarifications and wanting him to elaborate on some issues. In
any case, Prabhu Srivas's account was clear and consistent. I was particularly
impressed by his ability to recollect event after event, names and dates. But his
narrative was brief and it seemed to me that he had given me an official version of
the group's history in Ghana. Much as I found his version insightful, I still wanted
to hear the perspectives of others, especially lay followers.

Simon Wedey's version of the temple's origin story stood out among the
many accounts that I heard. Simon is a little over forty and is from the Anlo-Ewe
ethnic group. A temple devotee, Simon has been a member of the Hare Krishna
group since 1980. He joined after he returned from Spain. Simon and I became
friends because we both spoke Ewe. When he was not busy we would sit under a
tree and Simon would tell me stories about his sojourn in Spain, his struggles to
settle down when he returned to Ghana, and his eventual conversion to the Hare
Krishna community. One late afternoon our conversation veered in a direction
that resulted in Simon telling me his version of the Hare Krishna story. Simon's
version contained all the highlights of Prabhu Srivas's. But he added a new twist.
He went beyond Prabhu to explain why the new Krishna "church" experienced
growth at Odorkor, and in doing so, he revealed how local beliefs—"myths"—
about Indian spiritual powers played out in people's responses to incidents that
marked the presence of the Hare Krishna religion in their midst in its early days.
"People will tell you all kinds of stories but as far as I know, Odorkor was the place
that this mission really began," Simon began, reiterating Prabhu Srivas's earlier
point. He continued:

People really got to know us and joined us there and that was because of the incidents that happened there. We were not well known before then. Our few followers were not so sure about us ... Some were not even really serious. They knew Hare Krishna was from India but they were still waiting to see something. Other people said we were an occult group ... They said we had *juju* [sorcery].

I found this revelation insightful as it shed some light on the negative publicity the Hare Krishna community encountered, and the uncertainty of its followers in its beginnings in Ghana.

Simon described two miracles associated with the Hare Krishna group's emergence that he said, "made people see that it was really from India and they respected us for our powers." One miracle had to do with the exorcizing of a haunted house, the community's first rented premise. According to the story, people in the neighborhood believed that the ghosts of its builders who died mysteriously before its completion haunted the house. The new Hare Krishna community and observers considered the fact that they (the Hare Krishna community) lived in the house for five years without seeing signs of ghosts to be miraculous and attributed this to their Hindu powers. Simon noted accordingly:

We stayed there for f-i-v-e years [he spread the digits of his fingers to emphasize this] and we felt nothing! We saw nothing. No evil spirits. No noises. No ghosts. *Foko!* [emphasis on nothing]. In fact after our first six months of staying there, when nothing had happened to us, the people around were amazed. They said "*Shieee!* [expression of surprise] You people must have something [powerful magic]." That was when they began to warm towards us. They wanted to join us because they knew we had some powers! Prabhu, I can't even describe the situation well enough, it was miraculous! And the news spread, just like that [fast and widely].

Another version of this story said the owners of the building themselves invited the Hare Krishna community to come in to exorcise the haunted house, having learned that they originated from India. Simon told another miracle story of a second haunted premise, this time a clinic that the new Hare Krishna "church" exorcised. According to this story, for many years the doctors and nurses on night call saw a tall, lanky and headless figure roaming the wards of the clinic at night. Afraid that they might start losing customers and inspired by the community's first miracle, the owners of the clinic approached the Hare Krishnas for help. Simon described how they accomplished that feat:

So we went there too at twelve mid-night. We chanted, sang *kirtans* and played *mridangas* [drums] all night. That night nothing came. And nobody saw anything ever again ... And that was it. Just one night of mantra chanting and *mridanga* playing and that bad spirit too was gone! I will be honest with you and tell it plainly. As for me, the moment I learned that this church was from India, that was it, I knew I had to join it. But some people were waiting to see things [miracles]. And we showed it to them. So, for me, this church really began when we started to show that, yes, we really had powers from India.

Versions of these stories from other narrators added new dimensions. A *pujari* (priest) said, because the rented house and the hospital stood on an old graveyard, the residents were constantly haunted by ghosts and other evil powers angry for being displaced from their permanent homes. Another devotee told a tale of a river god whose dwelling place was a stream that flowed nearby. He said the appropriate rites were not performed to request permission from the river god to develop the area. So, feeling disrespected and angry, the god relentlessly haunted the residents at night. These two narrators, devotees at that time, both agreed that the haunting stopped when the evil forces confronted the Hare Krishn's Hindu powers and were overthrown. A female devotee from Dodowa, a village near Accra, said she had a relative living in Odorkor who also witnessed to the powers of the Hare Krishna community when they first arrived. She narrated her relative's story:

> She said she would hear noises coming from her kitchen at night as if someone was opening and closing her cooking pots and pans. She would rush in there but would see no one! She would scream *"Hei! Hei! Hei!* Thief! Thief!" But still she would see no one. The noise would stop suddenly. She would go back to her bed. The moment her head would touch her pillow, *heei*, the noise would start again! The priests from churches, the fetish priests ... They could all not stop these. Yet when the Krishna church started with their *mridanga* playing, singing and chanting ... All these stopped at once.

At the Krishna temple in Takoradi, another coastal city, I learned about another miracle involving a man called Shastra Das. This event occurred during the 1983 drought at Cynide where the Hare Krishna community is presently located. Devi, a female devotee narrated it:

> That time, the rains failed. All the river beds were dry. That was when this God brother, Shastra had a dream. He saw Krishna and Krishna took him to a place and said "Dig here. You would find water." When he told the Cynide villagers, they only laughed at him because he was a Hare Krishna man. But he insisted until a group of men followed him. He showed them a spot, a rocky spot and said "dig there." They resisted "Aah how could water be in this rocky place." He said "You just dig." So they dug and dug the entire day, but nothing came up ... So they left to continue the next day. When they came the next day the hole they dug was full of water. Clean water! They made it a well and it is there right now ... And it has water all year round, even at Harmattan [the dry season].

It seemed that versions of such incidents spread beyond the early Krishna community and circulated in the larger Ghanaian community. It became a part of the public discourse that there was a Hindu "church" "around" and it was "working," that is, performing miracles. A devotee described how she learned of the community from a "Professor Hindu" performing at a market in Asamankese, a village far away from Odorkor, the main venue of most of the happenings:

> It was in a market that I learned about Hare Krishna for the first time. That was in 1982. A Professor Hindu had finished performing when he started into stories about India. But people were making faces, so he felt we did not believe him. Then he told us "If you think I am telling lies, go to Odorkor, a new Indian Church has come. Go and see powers for yourselves. Go and see how they are working." That was the first time I heard of Hare Krishna but soon I would realize the name was all over the place.

There is a tradition of connecting the beginnings of religious communities in southern Ghana to miraculous happenings, establishing the churches as "miracle-working churches." What normally follows is an influx of people there. As a result, people seeking to legitimate the powers of their leaders or their communities would try to make miracles out of the least extraordinary happening in their communities by embellishing accounts of the events. The Hare Krishna stories did not seem to be a part of this tradition. The accounts were quite consistent, and the narrators exuded such deep sense of conviction so as to make one believe that the incidents really happened. It also seemed that when ripples of the excitement that the incidents generated reached beyond the Hare Krishna communities to the larger public, people attributed the miracles to the extraordinary powers of India. Thus, much as I accepted Srivas's explanation that their location at Odorkor and the size of their temple accounted for their growth there, I felt Simon, too, had a point in stressing the role of these miracles. The tradition was said to originate in India, and it was important for the Ghanaian public to see some signs that the "church" could successfully address worshippers' indigenous spiritual aspirations, fears, and anxieties, especially during such a tumultuous period in Ghana's history. The miracles were living testimonies that indeed, this was a "Hindu church."

Conclusion

We can explain the initial appeal of the Hare Krishna temple in the context of a variety of conversion theories whose understandings local people may not necessarily share. On the contrary, we can also locate our understandings of this appeal in the context of local popular beliefs or folk theories. My argument in this chapter is that whatever theories we adopt in explaining the initial appeal Krishna held for Ghanaian devotees must be built on the conceptual schemes of the actors involved, that is, the local notions that motivated their actions. What I have attempted to do in this chapter is to draw on Ghanaian Hindu worshippers' own understandings of the link between a spiritual power's efficiency and the remoteness of its origins to explain the initial appeal of the Hindu god Krishna. In the local imagination, far-flung spirits are more effective in neutralizing spiritual harm because they possess unfamiliar and untested power. Possible detractors are unfamiliar with how these spirits work, and cannot counteract their effects. Stories about Hindu spirits told by Second World War soldiers, scenes from Hindu films depicting the activities of Hindu spirits, and local magicians' claim that the source of their magical powers was Hindu spirits, not only reinforced local beliefs about the efficacy of far-away spirits, but also led to a particular focus on India as a locus of strong spirits. Explanations of the success of the Hare Krishna in establishing its roots in Ghana must pay respectful attention to the local notion that as a Hindu spirit, Krishna has unfamiliar and untested spiritual power that can be harnessed in mitigating supernatural harm and producing welfare for devotees.

Bibliography

Akyeampong, E. and P. Obeng, "Spirituality, Gender, and Power in Asante History," *The International Journal of African Historical Studies*, 28 (1995): 481–507.

Asamoah-Gyadu, K. "Traditional Missionary Christianity and New Religious Movements in Ghana: A Comparative Study of Attitudes towards Each Other's Faiths and Practices," unpublished M.Phil. Thesis, University of Ghana (Legon, 1994).

—, *African Charismatics: Current Developments within Independent Indigenous Pentecostalism in Ghana* (Leiden: E.J. Brill, 2005).

Assimeng, M., "The Witchcraft Scene in Ghana: A Sociological Comment," *Ghana Social Science Journal*, 4 (1977): 54–78.

—, *Religion and Social Change in West Africa* (Accra: Ghana University Press, 1989).

Barnes, S.T., "Ritual, Power, and Outside Knowledge," *Journal of Religion in Africa*, 20 (1990): 248–67.

Bettison, D.G., "Rumour under Conditions of Charismatic Leadership and Racial Political Tension," *African Social Research*, 6 (1968): 413–61.

Dahrendorf, Ralf, *Class and Class Conflict in Industrial Society*, (London: Routledge and Kegan Paul, 1959).

Ellis, Stephen, "Tuning to Pavement Radio," *African Affairs*, 88 (1989): 321–30.

Fisher, Humphrey, "Conversion Reconsidered: Some Historical Aspects of Religious Conversion in Black Africa," *Africa*, 43 (1973): 27–39.

—, "Dreams and Conversion in Black Africa," in N. Levtzion (ed.), *Conversion to Islam* (New York: Holmes and Meir, 1979), pp. 217–350.

—, "The Juggernaut's Apologia: Conversion to Islam in Black Africa," *Africa*, 55 (1985): 153–72.

Geertz, Clifford, *The Interpretation of Cultures* (New York: Basic Books, 1973).

Gray, Richard, "Christianity and Religious Change in Africa," *The Church in a Changing Society*, CIHEC Conference Reports (Uppsala, 1977), pp. 349–50.
—, "Christianity and Religious Change in Africa," *African Affairs*, 77 (1978): 89–100.
—, *Black Christians and White Missionaries* (Newhaven: Yale University Press, 1990).
Hackett, Rosalind, "The Symbolics of Power Discourse among Contemporary Religious Groups in West Africa," in J.K. Olupona and S. Nyang (eds.), *Religious Plurality in Africa: Essays in Honour of J.S. Mbiti* (Berlin: Mouton De Gruyter, 1993), pp. 382–407.
Handloff, Robert, "Prayers, Amulets, and Charms: Health and Social Control," *African Studies Review*, 2.3 (1982): 185–94.
Horton, Robin, "African Conversion," *Africa*, 41 (1971): 85–108.
—, "On the Rationality of Conversion," *Africa*, 45 (1975a): 219–35.
—, "On the Rationality of Conversion," *Africa*, 45 (1975b): 373–99.
Ikenga-Metuh, Emefie, "The Shattered Microcosm: A Critical Survey of Explanations of Conversion in Africa," in K. Holst Petersen (ed.), *Religion, Development and African Identity* (Uppsala: Scandinavian Institute of African Studies, 1987), pp. 11–27.
Kalu, Ogbu "The Shattered Cross: The Church Union Movement in Nigeria 1905–1966," in Ogbu Kalu (ed.), *The History of Christianity in West Africa* (London: Longman, 1980), pp. 340–64.
—, "The Dilemma of Grassroots Inculturation of the Gospel: A Case Study of a Modern Controversy in Igboland, 1983–1998," *Journal of Religion in Africa*, 25 (1995): 49–79.
Kastfelt, N., "Rumours of Maitatsine: A Note on Political Culture in Northern Nigeria," *African Affairs*, 88 (1989): 83–90.
Lewis, William, "Islam: A Rising Tide in Tropical Africa," *Review of Politics*, 19.4 (1957): 446–61.
Masquelier, Adeline, *Prayer Has Spoiled Everything: Possession, Power and Identity in an Islamic Town of Niger* (Durham, NC and London, Duke University Press, 2001).
Meyer, Birgit, "Delivered from the Powers of Darkness: Confessions of Satanic Riches in Christian Ghana," *Africa*, 65 (1995): 236–55.
Musambachime, C.M., "The Impact of Rumour: The Case of the Banyama (Vampire Men) Scare in Northern Rhodesia, 1930–1964," *International Journal of African Historical Studies*, 15 (1988): 201–15.
Obeyesekere, Gananath, *Medusa's Hair: An Essay on Personal Symbols and Religious Experience* (Chicago: University of Chicago Press, 1981).
—, *The Apotheosis of Captain Cook: European Mythmaking in the Pacific* (Princeton: Princeton University Press, 1992).
Peel, John David, "Syncretism and Religious Change," *Comparative Studies in Society and History*, 10 (1968): 121–41.

—, "Conversion and Tradition in Two African Societies: Ijebu and Buganda," *Past and Present*, 77 (1977): 108–41.

—, "The Pastor and the Babalawo: The Interaction of Religions in Nineteenth-Century Yorubaland," *Africa*, 60 (1990): 338–69.

Ray, Benjamin, "Aladura Christianity: A Yoruba Religion," *Journal of Religion in Africa*, 23 (1993): 267–91.

Sanneh, Lamin, "The Origins of Clericalism in West African Islam," *Journal of African History*, 17.1 (1976): 49–72.

—, "The Horizontal and the Vertical in Mission: An African Perspective," *Journal of Missionary Research*, 7.4 (1983): 165–71.

Yankah, Kwesi, "African Folk and Challenges of a Global Lore: 1998 American Folklore Society Preliminary Address," *Journal of American Folklore*, 112/444 (1999): 140–57.

Index